THE BEL CANTO VIOLIN
THE LIFE AND TIMES OF ALFREDO CAMPOLI
1906–1991

To the memory of Arthur Jacobs (1922–96)

To the memory of Arthur Jacobs (1922–96)

The Bel Canto Violin

The Life and Times of Alfredo Campoli 1906–1991

David Tunley

Routledge
Taylor & Francis Group
LONDON AND NEW YORK

First published 1999 by Ashgate Publishing

Reissued 2018 by Routledge
2 Park Square, Milton Park, Abingdon, Oxon, OX14 4RN
52 Vanderbilt Avenue, New York, NY 10017

Routledge is an imprint of the Taylor & Francis Group, an informa business

A Library of Congress record exists under LC control number: 99065846

Typeset by Pat FitzGerald

ISBN 13: 978-1-138-38819-2 (hbk)
ISBN 13: 978-1-138-38822-2 (pbk)
ISBN 13: 978-0-429-42570-7 (ebk)

Contents

List of Illustrations

The illustrations will be found between pages 64 and 65.

Foreword by Sir Charles Mackerras

I was fortunate enough to know Campoli and work with him during a two-year period in the 1950s when I was conductor of the BBC Concert Orchestra. My first encounter with 'Camp', as we used to call him, was when we did the musical illustrations for a radio programme about Paganini and he played Kreisler's arrangement of the Paganini First Concerto with amazing virtuosity. Members of the Concert Orchestra, particularly or course the string players, were immensely impressed with his technique and musicianship.

Another happy memory is Camp's playing of the Mendelssohn Concerto in a different town every night when we toured southern Britain. Everywhere he received a tumultuous reception.

Campoli was renowned in many countries as a great violinist and it has always been a source of amazement to me that the BBC never allowed him to fulfil his potential in the serious music field, just because he had been so successful before the War as the soloist and director of a light, Palm Court style, orchestra.

Professor Tunley's book evokes a musical life which no longer exists and is a fascinating historical document. Excellent reading for the music lover and especially, of course, violinists.

Introduction

Perhaps nothing points up the essentially ephemeral nature of musical performance more than does the writing of a biography of an artist no longer with us. Before the Second World War Alfredo Campoli was a household name in the field of English light music; after it the name Campoli was that of a celebrated concert artist known widely on the international scene. Nowadays it is virtually unknown to the present generation of young performers and music-lovers. It might be thought that recordings – less destructible than memories – would keep alive the reputation of performing artists, but recordings are quickly deleted from the catalogue in a commercial business in which 'stardom' is too often the result of the PR machine. In the case of Campoli there has in recent years been a gratifying release of CDs in which the artistry of his performances on earlier recordings (including light music from the 1930s) can be enjoyed again. Yet even these will eventually become collectors' items and his name known only to an inevitably shrinking number of admirers. Moreover, tastes change over a period of time. Nowadays, many people prefer historically-informed performances of baroque and classical music, an approach that Campoli had little understanding of, or sympathy towards. His was the response of an instinctive and romantic violinist – one of the last of his kind.

If the name of Campoli (Alfredo or otherwise) has been out of wide circulation for a number of years, how many more of his contemporaries – particularly those brilliant light musicians in the 1920s and 1930s – are now forgotten? Some of them, like Campoli, forced into playing light music because of the economic catastrophe of the 1930 Wall Street Crash, moved decisively into concert work after the war and established fine reputations as performers and conductors. Those who remained in light music found the post-war scene very different, as 'piped music' gradually took over from palm-court orchestras in restaurants and hotels, and as electronics transformed popular taste. The various revolutions – technical, cultural and social – have so transformed the second half of the twentieth century that the world of the palm-court orchestra is now 'history'. Yet, strange to say, it would seem that no in-depth historical study of this golden period of light music – that of the 'palm-court orchestras', as distinct from jazz and dance-bands in the London restaurants and hotels – has been written. The present book makes no claim to be such a study, but it does attempt to give a glimpse into the period, using as much documentary evidence as appropriate for the ten years in which Alfredo Campoli made his mark in the field. Unfortunately, many of the gifted light music performers have been neglected in the major biographical sources (such as the various editions of *Grove's Dictionary*), and so reliable information about them is not always easy to find. The brilliant pianist and arranger Fred Hartley (Campoli's favourite arranger) is a case in point. Another is the violinist de Groot, elegant aristocrat of the Piccadilly Hotel's luncheon, dinner and supper music, admired in his own way as much as an operatic prima donna (whose temperament he shared). Fortunately, we can learn something about de Groot from that doyen of accompanists Ivor Newton, whose first professional engagements were with him. Thus, for this period in Campoli's life considerable basic research into the period needed to be done in order to try and reconstruct a scene that has now 'gone with the wind'.

Even at the height of his success in light music Campoli, however, was also giving performances as a concert artist. He had begun his career that way, first as a child prodigy then, following his début at Wigmore Hall in 1923, as a young travelling virtuoso. In the 1930s he gave broadcast recitals over the BBC, played at the Proms under Sir Henry Wood, and performed concertos with different orchestras around the country. After the war, however, he shed his 'double life' and turned exclusively to the concert platform. Yet, such had been his phenomenal success as a light musician that the ghost of that earlier career was not easily exorcised. Part of the Campoli story is his struggle for recognition as a serious concert artist after the war, and there are many musicians who worked with him who believed that he would have risen much further if he had not had to 'live down' his years as a salon violinist. Nevertheless, there can be no doubt that he enjoyed that period of his life and made the most of it, even if it was forced upon him by the circumstances of those times.

At one end, his long career embraced playing in his father's orchestra for the silent movies, touring with Melba and Butt, establishing the Dorchester Restaurant's salon orchestra, recording with Decca in its earliest years, and broadcasting frequently for the BBC with his light music ensembles. At the other, it saw him as a celebrity artist, known and admired as much in many concert halls around the world as he was in Britain, where he was regularly heard at the Proms, at the Royal Festival Hall, over the BBC and in recitals throughout the length and breadth of the country. In the middle of that career lay the Second World War, and, as for so many others, it was a watershed in his life. With the entry of Italy on the side of Germany Alfredo and his parents (and, on the day of his marriage, his English wife) found themselves declared 'enemy aliens', the Campoli family never having taken out British citizenship. Fortunately, the embargo on his playing was temporary and he was eventually able to work again, including playing for factory workers and the forces through CEMA and ENSA. It was during this period that he reconsidered his career and moved decisively back to the kind of music that he had always wanted to play. Campoli's career was thus touched and moulded by all the great social forces at work from the early years of the century. To fully appreciate his career we must therefore know something about them. In attempting to recreate the backdrop against which his career was played out, this book is certainly as much the story of his times as of his life.

In 1950 Campoli embarked on his first major international tour – to Australia and New Zealand where he gave recitals and concertos over a period of six months. As that tour marked a significant stage in his career it has been dealt with in some detail in Chapter 6. It was a part of the world which he liked enormously and which he was to visit subsequently on a number of occasions. Yet the 'Antipodes Connection' goes further. Few people know that in the 1970s Campoli toyed with the idea of settling either in New Zealand or Australia. He felt that a warmer, drier climate might help overcome some of the increasing problems he was having with arthritis and, although he eventually decided against the move, the idea led to a three-month appointment in 1973 as Musician-in-residence at the University of Western Australia in Perth. It was there that my wife and I began the long friendship with Alfredo and Joy Campoli, which led many years later and after Alfredo's death, to the idea of writing his biography. Some preliminary research was carried out in 1993 when I was a Fowler Hamilton Visiting Research Fellow at Christ Church, Oxford, but the major research was done in 1996 when I was a Visiting Scholar at Wolfson College, Oxford, and the following year as an Honorary Senior Research Fellow at The University of Western Australia. This institutional support has been invaluable.

Nevertheless the book could not have been written without the support of Campoli's widow Joy, who placed at my disposal all the materials and memorabilia that she kept over the long period of their marriage. From the beginning of that marriage Alfredo virtually gave up writing letters, gratefully handing over all correspondence both personal and professional to Joy, who also kept all the programmes, press cuttings, and so on in meticulous order. Her extraordinary memory, clear mind and eye have been a boon to this biographer, anxious to present as definitive a study as possible of the man once described by Szigeti as 'one of the last great individualists among violinists'.

I am also deeply indebted to many other people who have helped me in gathering and interpreting the materials for such a biography. Emeritus Professor Cyril Ehrlich, now at Oxford, has given me the inestimable benefit of his detailed knowledge of the sociology of British music, alerting me to valuable sources and offering welcome advice at every stage of the writing. John Morris, ex-BBC, pointed me in the direction of many people whom I then contacted, and he and his wife Cheryl have both given me most generous help in more ways than I can record. John Allt, friend of the Campolis and to whom many of Alfredo's records and tapes were eventually given, has provided me with rare copies of performances and interviews, including one that he recorded with Campoli in 1985. Amongst the treasures I acquired during my research was a recorded interview I made in London in 1993 with Morris Taylor, who as a very young man had played in Alfredo's Dorchester Hotel Salon Orchestra in 1931 and whose vivid and clear memories of the light music scene in that decade have given me a precious personal glimpse into those bygone days. Doris Faulkner of Swadlincote near Derby shared her rich collection of musical memorabilia with me. Like everyone who researches material relating to the BBC, I am one of countless people who are deeply indebted to Jacqueline Kavanagh and her staff at the BBC Written Archives at Caversham, particularly Jeff Walden, and a similar debt is owed to Geoff Harris at the ABC Archives in Sydney. In London, John Parry of the Decca Record Company and Ruth Edge of EMI provided me with copies of those companies' archival log-books which enabled me to trace dates and details of Campoli's recording sessions reaching back to 1931. My deep thanks go to five pianists who worked with Campoli: Peter Katin, Daphne Ibbott, Valerie Tryon, who performed with him on a regular basis, Margaret Schofield, and Maurice Till who toured with him in Australia and New Zealand. From them all I gained insights into Campoli both as man and musician, as I did also from Belinda Bunt, Rebecca Shorrock and Ruth and Daniel Hudson who had studied with him. As with all my research I am once again indebted to Jennifer Wildy, Librarian of the Wigmore Music Library at the University of Western Australia for her help in so many ways. I was encouraged by Sir Frank Callaway, Foundation Professor of Music at the same institution, who invited Campoli to be the university's first musician-in-residence in 1973, unwittingly laying the path that led many years later to this book.

Space forbids full acknowledgement of the help given me by so many people in preparing this biography and the list of their names must constitute my inadequate, but heartfelt thanks for their contribution. Archivists and librarians (in addition to those already mentioned): Richard Andrewes (Music Librarian at Cambridge University Library where Campoli's music library and the printed programmes of many of his recitals and concerts are now housed); Francesca Franchi (Covent Garden); Dr J. Fowler (Theatre Museum, London); Andrew Mealey (City of Coventry Library); Tom Miles (BBC Sound Archives); Dr G. Bayliss (Imperial Museum Library); Helen Armstrong (Public Library of the Royal Borough of Kensington and Chelsea); Stephen Chappell (Arts Council of England). Others who provided information or help in some way were: Lady Barbirolli, Margaret Barton-Stefanato, Alan Billings, Lionel Bowman, Philip Bracanin, Geoffrey Brand, Kenneth Bridgewater, Margaret Campbell, Paula Clarkstone, Derek Collier, the late David Cox, Greg Dally, John Drysdale, David Ellis, Lea Foli, Elizabeth Forbes, Ken Gassmeir, Martine de Geus (The Dorchester Hotel), Sir William Glock, Desmond Gurrie, John Harper-Nelson, Lady Hayter, Tom Hoddinot, Peter Howard, Merryn Howell, Ray Irving, Leonard Isaacs, Lyndon Jenkins, Michael Jones, Robert Lewin, Ronald McDonald, Father McKenna, Addie Meher-Homji, John Meyer, Lionel Monte, Kerry Murphy, Jeremy Neville, Geoffrey Newson, Mary Norman-Thomas, Derek Pocock, Robert Ponsonby, Charles Rattray, Cormac Rigby, Lionel Salter, John Spooner, Jan Stockigt, Christine Storey, Vilem Tausky, Anthony van Toll, John Winstanley. Thanks are also due to the authorities of the Nightingale Square School (now called The Holy Ghost School) who provided me with a copy of their Register of Admission, Progress and Withdrawal for the time that the young Afredo Campoli was a pupil there.

To my wife Paula is not only owed my usual debt of gratitude for her never-failing support throughout my periods of research and writing, but on this occasion also for acting as a research assistant, sorting an enormous amount of material and entering it into a computer database. Without her help the research quite simply could not have been undertaken. She has also provided a sensitive and critical ear to the interpretation of this material.

The late Arthur Jacobs, music critic and writer, and a great admirer of Campoli's playing, was an inspiration to me at Oxford in 1996, even though it was during the last and difficult months of his life. To his memory this book is warmly dedicated.

David Tunley
The University of Western Australia

Chapter 1

'The Wonderful Boy Violinist'

It was perhaps to be expected that Alfredo Campoli would play the violin as if he were singing, for his mother used to say that he had taken part in several performances of *Aida* before he was even born. His personal appearance, so to speak, was on 20 October 1906 when Elvira Celi-Campoli, a rising opera-star, gave birth to her only child in Rome where she and her husband Romeo, a professional violinist, were then living at 14 Via Garibaldi. From infancy Alfredo was thus surrounded by music, particularly from opera, the style of which so influenced his playing that in later years he would say that the bow to a violinist was like the breath to a singer. For an example of the latter he had only to listen to his mother.

Elvira Celi's career, though short, was by no means undistinguished, and reviews of her performances suggested that it would be a brilliant one. Born in Rome on 20 July 1877, she had studied singing under the Roman teacher Giuseppe Gianoli, making her début in 1903 in Verdi's *Il Trovatore* at the Manzoni Opera House there, followed by appearances in the same composer's *Ernani*, *Attila* and Gomez's *Guarany*.[1] She was then 26 and already in the ample mould of the classical prima donna in the days when a large body was considered essential for a large voice. That it was powerful, vibrant, incisive and put to fine dramatic account is confirmed by press reviews of her début and all her subsequent appearances. Yet it could also be sweet and clear, with a technique that so scorned (as one reviewer put it) the technical difficulties of the roles she played that the following year she was engaged to sing leading roles in Bellini's *Norma*, Mascagni's *Cavalleria Rusticana* and Donizetti's *Poliuto* at the Quirino Theatre. She gained glowing reviews for them all, leading to engagements in 1905 at the Adriano Theatre in the same city, singing some of the same operas. From Rome she went to Orvieto and Terni, and by 1908 was working in Milan.[2] The height of her career was reached at the end of that year with an invitation to join the Lambardi Grand Opera Company for a tour of the United States.

Mario Lambardi, a well-known Italian opera impresario whose company, first called the Milan Touring Opera, was active from the last years of the nineteenth century up to the First World War, mainly touring the USA and South America. For his 1908/9 tour, which included Buenos Aires, San Francisco, San José, Los Angeles, Salt Lake City, St Louis, Seattle, Tacoma, Denver, Memphis and

---

[1] Some information about her career was published in the Milanese arts review *Cosmorana*, August 1909. A number of reviews of her performances in USA and elsewhere were found in a scrapbook (now in the possession of the author), many of them, however, missing dates and names of the newspapers in which they appeared.

[2] Alfredo's vaccination certificate that year gives Milan as his parents' address.

Stockton, Lambardi surpassed all his previous tours in the quality and range of his productions that he had offered to his American audiences. The repertoire consisted of *Tosca*, *Lucia di Lammermoor*, *Il Trovatore*, *Cavalleria Rusticana*, *Pagliacci*, *Carmen*, *La Traviata*, *Rigoletto*, *Faust*, *La Bohème*, *Aida*, *Il Barbiere di Siviglia* and *Un Ballo in Maschera*. For this immense season Lambardi engaged sixteen leading singers of whom Elvira was prima donna. There were three conductors: Agide Jacchia, Edoardo Lebegott and Giovanni Baravelli. Baravelli, who had at one time been Chorus Master and Assistant Director to Toscanini at La Scala (by now at the Metropolitan in New York) was also in charge of training the chorus, while production was under the direction of Ricardo Petrovich and Lambardi. American audiences had good reason to look forward to what the publicity brochure described as the 'largest and most elaborated arranged [*sic*] circuit ever undertaken by any Grand Opera Company in America'.

> The newly organised Lambardi Grand Opera Company this year is larger, better and stronger in celebrities than ever and the principals of the organisation are among the foremost singers of the present day and all have enviable records of European successes,
>
> Impresario Lambardi has engaged many artists of high reputation especially for the minor roles, which will ensure a perfect cast for all Operas presented during the coming season.
>
> This Magnificent Company of European Celebrities will be supported by a complete and thoroughly disciplined orchestra, and by forty young fresh-voiced Choristers selected from the leading Italian Opera Houses.
>
> Realising the importance of improving the chorus, Impresario Lambardi spent the Summer in thoroughly reconstructing and disciplining his chorus and promises that this year you will see in that body, fine harmonisation and splendid technique and precision.
>
> . . . In scenery and costumes the production will be new and up to date, as a revision and rebuilding of scenery has been made, with several complete new productions. New costumes have been imported for this tour and the presentations will be complete in every detail.

Despite the publicity, not all cities rose to the occasion and the company was sometimes greeted by small audiences. Yet the reviews were consistently enthusiastic and laudatory, not least about the company's prima donna. As there is no recording of her voice we must depend upon the critics' comments. In Buenos Aires she was extravagantly described as 'the equal of any dramatic soprano in the world'. In more detail one critic described her as having 'a brilliant soprano voice of great volume and flexibility, with admired pianissimo effects and artistic phrasing'. Yet, according to another, her voice also displayed some weaknesses, considering that it to be 'better in its upper and lower registers and in the former is beautifully sweet and clear. In common with a great many singers, she makes too much use of the tremolo for the best effect.' So, too, was there guarded comment on her physical appearance, as when she sang the role of Leonora in *Il Trovatore* to which she was not suited because of what one critic tactfully described as her 'physical over-development'. Nevertheless, the overall impression from the reviews is that Elvira Campoli was an exceptionally fine singer, and that her career seemed assured.

During her absence of some six months, Romeo and little 'Alfredino' had kept in touch through letters, postcards and photographs, some of which have survived, as have some from Elvira, as well as souvenirs of the tour, including a vase from San Francisco – a relic of the great earthquake which had devastated the city only three years earlier. While Elvira was creating something of a sensation in many of the places where the Lambardi Company played, Romeo's career back in Italy was far less exciting, for if hers was on the operatic stage Romeo's was in the orchestral pit beneath it.

Romeo's career in Italy was centred largely at the Costanzi Theatre in Rome (now the Royal Opera House) and at La Scala. There is a photograph of the orchestra of the Costanzi Theatre taken about 1896 in which Romeo can be seen playing the violin and Arturo Toscanini the cello. Unfortunately, very little is known about his early life beyond that he was born in 1867 and studied with the great violinist and teacher Ettore Pinelli (1843–1915). Himself a student of Joachim, Pinelli passed that master's methods on to his own students. Together with the pianist Giovanni Sgambati he founded the Chamber Music Society of Rome, both men also alternating as Directors of the Royal Court Concerts. Some years later Pinelli founded and directed the Orchestral Society of Rome. The city was also indebted to Pinelli and Sgambati for founding a school in 1871 where children of poor families could learn violin and piano. It was eventually to become the Conservatorio of the Accademia Nazionale di S. Cecilia. It seems reasonable to assume that this was how Romeo may have got to study with one of the finest violin teachers in Rome at that time, and fortunate for his son that he could pass Pinelli's methods on to him. Indeed, Romeo was to be Alfredo's only teacher. As with Elvira, we know nothing of Romeo's family background and – unusually for Italians – what family bonds there may once have been seem to have been lost sometime after the Campolis settled in England.

On her return from the United States, Elvira resumed her career in Italy gaining further success and critical acclaim. By the end of 1911 we find her singing the title-role in *Aida* at the Manzoni Theatre in Pistoia, near Florence, for which she received 'an indescribably enthusiastic ovation', as much for her robust voice as her dramatic characterisation. It seems to have been her last operatic triumph. According to family history, Elvira visited England, sending a message back to Romeo saying that she wanted to live there. By 1912 the Campoli family was settled in London.

There must have been good reasons for the move, but if Elvira had ambitions at Covent Garden these never materialised, for there is no record of her ever having sung there in any production – nor with any other English company. Possibly she may have appeared at some small event there, this in turn giving rise to Alfredo's belief that his mother had 'sung at Covent Garden'. But the true reason for the Campolis leaving Italy and living in England will probably never be known. If fact is stranger than fiction, one possibility is strange enough to be true – the weather. Elvira found the summer months in Rome unbearable, and, presumably, on a trip to England found the milder climate there much more to her liking.[3] Whatever the reason, the reality was that they arrived in a country that two years later was to be dislocated by the outbreak of the First World War. It was not the best of times for newcomers who spoke no English to find musical employment there.

Elvira's first engagement in London that can be definitely dated was at a Dinner Concert at the Hotel Cecil on 30 June 1912. Like many of the leading hotels in those days, its restaurant featured light orchestral music at lunch and tea and a more substantial programme at dinner. It was a tradition that Alfredo was to take full advantage of in the 1930s. For her contribution to the programme that evening Signora Elvira Campoli (as she was billed) sang Santazza's song from *Cavalleria Rusticana*, Tosti's *La Serenata* and Gianelli's *Sulla Laguna* accompanied at the piano by Mr P. Mavon-Ibbs. Her associate artists were Mr George Baker (baritone), and the conductor of the salon orchestra, Professor Candia.[4]

As an opera singer her career thus seems to have faded in England and her name features in none of the scholarly biographical sources, wiped from the records save those of the contemporary press. It would seem that her activities in the country where she chose to live became largely devoted to the careers of her husband and gifted son.

Romeo's first engagement in England that can be accurately dated was as a conductor of a Ladies' Orchestra at a silent movie theatre in Coventry in 1916. The Campolis had, in fact, arrived in Britain at a time when the silent movies were offering employment to the ever-growing ranks of musicians there on a scale unimagined before the advent of this revolutionary form of entertainment. For two decades up until the appearance of the 'talkies', silent movie theatres offered employment to more musicians than did any other industry, and to a total

---

3 This is a view firmly held by her daughter-in-law, Mrs Joy Campoli.

4 There are few records of later performances. Nevertheless, some fascinating mementos come from the mid-1930s when she was preparing to sing some sentimental songs popular at the time – no unusual thing, of course, even for the most renowned prima donnas. Because she had never learned to speak English except at a most rudimentary level, in order to pronounce the words correctly she transformed the texts into the closest-sounding Italian equivalents: 'Duiju ricol stette naite in giun uven feste uvi mette …' (Do you recall that night in June when first we met …), and 'Ap in the garet, e wei fron the din, sam uan is pleing en olde vaolin …' (Up in the garret, away from the din, someone is playing an old violin …).

audience larger than had ever been imagined by those whose only appearances were on the concert or opera stage. Writing at the end of that period the well-known music-critic and writer Edwin Evans was to claim in *Music & Letters*

> It is estimated, on the basis of union statistics, that picture theatres, great and small, are now providing between three-quarters and four-fifths of the paid musical employment in the country. It is further estimated, though on data less subject to verification, that the cinema is the sole, or at any rate the chief, avenue by which music reaches three-quarters of the potential audience in the population. For about fifty-nine hours weekly, music is being performed in upwards of three thousand cinemas, and for shorter periods in perhaps a thousand isolated halls. Setting aside all aesthetic considerations in favour of a purely objective view, one may say that the cinema is at present the most important musical institution in the country.[5]

A similar view about its musical importance had been expressed two years earlier in the short-lived magazine *The Music Box*, which claimed that the cinema provided 'the best medium through which the British public as a whole can be educated to a higher musical sense'.[6]

Cyril Ehrlich has quantified Evans' generalisations about employment as the equivalent of some 16,000 full-time jobs, which, in terms of the number of performers would take the figure to at least 20,000.[7] And, of course, for the music industry at large the cinema spawned more than just jobs for orchestral players, pianists and theatre organists. For example, a silent film of an hour or an hour-and-a half would usually need some hundred musical extracts to fit the changing moods and action on the screen. Accordingly, musicians were needed to arrange countless classical and light-music pieces, from which snippets could be taken at the performance. Similarly, there was often a call for 'original' pieces of music. *The Music Box*, noting in 1927 how the standard of music in the cinemas had improved greatly over the years, also pointed to the opportunities opened up by the silent films to composers of all nationalities, observing sadly that few British composers were taking advantage of such opportunities, leaving these to foreign musicians.[8]

Arrangements of music also needed to be published, and collections suitable for playing with the silent movies were built up by musical directors, theatre owners and sometimes by public libraries.[9] Such a collection was the Lyra Edition

---

5 Edwin Evans, 'Music and the Cinema', *Music and Letters*, January, 1929.

6 'Music and the Film', *The Music Box and British Entertainer incorporating 'The Entertainment World' – a publication dealing with all that matters in the Realm of Entertainment*, August, 1927.

7 Cyril Ehrlich, *The Music Profession in Britain Since the Eighteenth Century – a Social History* (Oxford, 1985), p. 199.

8 'Music and the Film', *The Music Box*, August, 1927.

9 Ehrlich, 1985, p. 197.

of *Orchestral Music for Cinema, Cafe, Hotel and Restaurant*, comprising movements from the works of Wagner, Tchaikovsky, Rubinstein, Poldini and others, 'suitable for any number of performers, from three or four upwards'. For keyboard players a useful collection was Erno Rapée's *Motion Picture Moods for Pianists and Organists*, published in the USA by Schirmer in 1924, featuring nearly 400 pieces mostly written by the classical masters. In this monumental collection Rapée describes how in the larger silent movie houses in the USA some half a dozen or so musical experts under a Music Director worked hard to find the music to fit the action on the screen for each movie and get it ready for the orchestra to rehearse. (Hence his collection to make it easier for the single individual at the piano or organ to find the right pieces for 'the quickly changing scenes, different psychological situations chasing each other, back-shots, close-ups, close-ins, etc., etc.') Of course, an ability to improvise at the keyboard was usually the mark of the skillful cinema pianist or organist, but in terms of printed music the silent movies underpinned a strong publishing industry.

That much of the music heard in the smaller, poorer cinemas of those days was as banal as the playing was wretched there can be no doubt; yet it becomes clear that there was also a remarkable amount of well-performed good music that had, in spite of all, found its way into the cinema. There were even a number of silent films of opera – *Carmen*, for example – which demanded an expert orchestra to play the music. Especially in the capital and the larger provincial cities there were establishments that prided themselves on their music, and which offered their patrons performances by excellent orchestras during the main film and during interval. One of the essential accomplishments demanded of a cinema orchestral musician was the ability to read any music at sight, for there were usually no rehearsals. At the beginning of the week the musical director viewed the feature film, decided on the segments of music appropriate for it, and had it ready for the musicians to play at the first showing. As a result of this practice of performance-without-rehearsal in the cinemas, as well as in the restaurants, and also because of a system which long prevailed in the concert orchestras that allowed players to be replaced by 'deputies' at rehearsals, orchestral performers in England established a remarkable reputation for their sight-reading and musicianship.[10] The conductor Eugene Goossens recalled the 'feats of sight-reading performed in a minimum of rehearsal time' in the 1914 season of Russian opera and ballet at Drury Lane, the programme including four English premieres of Russian operas and three new ballets specially commissioned by Diaghilev, much of it in what was then an unusual idiom that presented the players with ever-varying problems of style and technique.[11] (Providing music for the silent

[10] Why this should have placed British orchestral players ahead of their continental and American colleagues when presumably they all experienced similar working conditions is a question that has not been studied.

[11] Eugene Goossens, *Overture and Beginners* (London, 1950), pp. 106–7.

movies was not an unknown task for Goossens. In 1922 he had been invited by the head of United Artists in Hollywood, Walter Wanger, to arrange and conduct the music for the London premiere of *The Three Musketeers* starring Douglas Fairbanks, Snr, to be played by sixty-five members of the London Symphony Orchestra, the season taking place in no less a 'cinema' than the Royal Opera House, Covent Garden.[12]) Successful conducting for the silent movies was no easy task. It depended upon a split-second sense of timing with eyes both on score and screen and a firm control of tempo as one piece moved without a break into the next. There can be no doubt that much of the success of the best silent movie houses depended upon the skill of conductor and players, their performances helping overcome the obvious limitations of the medium.

For Romeo to gain the position of conductor at the Globe, which had opened only two years earlier, was thus no small achievement, particularly for one, who, like his wife, spoke very little English at that time. And although the move from the pit at La Scala, Milan to that of the Globe Cinema, Coventry might on the face of it seem a steep fall from musical grace – and perhaps it was – nevertheless Romeo Campoli was far from being the only fine musician to gain employment in a cinema. As for conducting a 'Ladies' Orchestra', we need to see this in perspective too.

Ladies' orchestras began to appear in Britain towards the end of the nineteenth century, but essentially as amateur groups.[13] From the beginning they were disparaged by the professionals who, as men, saw in these ensembles the possibility of a threat to their own livelihood, and who, accordingly, placed every obstacle in their way to gaining the kind of orchestral experience that could turn the threat into reality. And this despite the proven ability of women to become first-rate players. As the need for orchestral musicians grew with the demands of the silent movies, ladies' orchestras became a frequent sight, particularly during the 1914–18 war when so many men were at the front, and it was at that time, 1916, that Romeo Campoli was engaged to direct such an orchestra at the Globe Theatre in Coventry. There is no reason to believe that they were an inferior group of performers.

The orchestra was part of the improvements to the Globe Theatre that the new management put into place in April that year. Opening in the previous year, this theatre, together with another cinema in Coventry, The Crown, had been taken over by the Midland Amusement Company of Birmingham, which had engaged a Mr Frederick J. Studd as Resident Manager at the Globe. A man of considerable experience of theatres in various parts of Britain, his appointment was made in anticipation that under his management the Globe Theatre would be able to beat the intense competition from other cinemas in Coventry, particularly The Empire Theatre, which, as though in answer to the Globe's new improvements, secured

---

12 Goossens, 1950, pp. 182–3.

13 Ehrlich, 1985, p. 159.

the rights in June to show one of the most celebrated of all silent movies: D.W. Griffith's saga of the American Civil War – *Birth of a Nation* – with its cast of 18,000 people and 15,000 horses. To accompany this film the management of The Empire Theatre engaged a '30-piece Symphony Orchestra' from London's Drury Lane to play the orchestral excerpts that were required.

Improvements to the Globe Theatre announced in April 1916 included an additional projector and a contract for 'a large number of the very best films now being manufactured, including Famous Players, Metro, New Chaplins, Jurys London, and finest all-British subjects'.[14] At the same time, the management was able to announce 'the very expensive engagement of Signor Romeo Campoli and his Ladies' Orchestra'.

As well as providing background music to the films, his orchestra also played after the film had finished. An advertisement in the *Midland Daily Telegraph*, for example, announced on 24 April that at the end of each performance, if time permitted, 'Signor Romeo Campoli, the Wonder Violinist and Leader, will play "Cavalleria Rusticana" by Mascagni', adding that 'it would be possible to arrange performances of patrons' favourite selections if the management were informed in time'. At the end of that month, in its advertisement for the film *Ultus* (dealing with the adventures of two British prospectors in Australia) the management was pleased to report that the musical programme presented each night by Signor Campoli had become a feature of the Globe. In less than two months, however, Mr Frederick J. Studd was replaced by Mr E. Parker Hides, who, while retaining the services of Romeo Campoli and his Ladies' Orchestra, announced that he himself would be playing the newly-installed organ. What effect this had on his highly-professional musical director we do not know, but by mid-October the management announced that Mrs Jack Allan's London Ladies' Orchestra would now be providing music at the Globe, and no more is heard of Romeo Campoli in Coventry. Nor do we know whether those six months at the Globe gave Romeo his first experience of conducting a cinema orchestra. If so, it stood him in good stead for similar work in London.

This may well have been, at least for a time, at the Palladium cinema in Clapham Road, Stockwell, which from November 1916 became for a few years the most popular cinema in the district. Although a Madame Walter was conducting its orchestra when Romeo returned from Coventry, eighteen months later the management announced the formation of a new and augmented orchestra which was soon winning favour with the audience.[15] Alfredo recalled playing in his father's cinema orchestra as a child in London (unfortunately never mentioning it by name), sometimes even conducting when his father was ill.

At the same time Romeo continued teaching at his private 'academy' where his most brilliant student was, of course, his son.

---

[14] *The Coventry and Warwickshire Graphic*, 7 April 1916.

****

Soon after their arrival in London the Campoli family, Alfredo now being aged five-and-a-half, had settled in the suburb of Mitcham where they established a private school of music in their home, although their inability to speak English must have been a serious obstacle for their students. As far as teaching his son was concerned, Romeo was a stern – indeed, harsh – disciplinarian, his bow strokes not confined to his instrument. Alfredo recalled hiding under the table to escape his father's wrath during some lessons, and it says much for the young boy's innate musicality that he remained so passionately engaged with music, despite the rigorous demands placed on him as a child. Nor did these weaken the strong filial attachment he showed to both his parents all their lives.

Romeo remained his only teacher, although Alfredo had some lessons with the celebrated French-born violinist Emile Sauret (1852–1920) who, in the last years of his life, was teaching at the Trinity College of Music in London. Despite Sauret's reputation as a fine performer and teacher, his methods displeased Romeo, who could not understand how rhythms could be taught to a violinist by clapping them, and Alfredo was soon withdrawn.[16]

Judging by a photograph taken before the family migrated to England, Alfredo may have begun his first violin lessons before the age of five. By the age of nine he was displaying such skills that his father seems to have been prepared to let him perform in public – apparently at Coventry, and probably at the Globe Theatre. This has undoubtedly been the basis of some later biographical comments that Alfredo Campoli made his 'début' in Coventry. If it indeed took place there, it went unnoticed by the local press. But at that time Coventry (as elsewhere) had more serious matters to read about, for 1916 was the year of the Battle of the Somme, and Coventry newspapers were increasingly filled with photographs of the many young men from that region either killed or maimed in France. The horrors of that battle came to Coventry eyes when both the Globe and Empire Theatres simultaneously showed the official pictures of the British Army in France (at the Globe, to music specially selected by Romeo). Moreover, during the time of Romeo's engagement at the Globe, Coventry experienced its first bombing from zeppelin raids.

The horrors of the war also came to young Alfredo's eyes, not at Coventry but at Dover where, through the YMCA, he played a number of times in hospitals for wounded soldiers returning from the French trenches, a traumatic experience that he recalled all his life. 'I was playing to wounded troops who had survived the carnage of the Somme and Verdun battles. I remember playing the *Ave Maria* in

[15] See various issues of the *Clapham Observer, Tooting and Balham Times*, 3 November 1916 to 25 January 1918. That its new conductor was probably Romeo Campoli is suggested by comments in a letter quoted on p. 11.

[16] This was recounted to Belinda Bunt by Campoli when she was studying with him during the 1970s.

a hospital and at the beginning seeing two men enjoying it. By the end they had died.'[17]

It seems unlikely that the family as a whole had moved to Coventry. Romeo was there for only six months, and probably Alfredo visited his father during holidays from his school in Balham, a suburb where his parents had set up a new Studio of Violin and Singing in their home at 216 Balham High Road. Balham, situated in London's south-east, was at that time a thriving suburb largely developed in the later years of the nineteenth century, attracting both aspiring middle and working class families. Many people were drawn to the area by its high elevation and the open spaces like Wandsworth, Clapham and Tooting Commons that surround it. Four years before the Campolis came to Balham the train line from Victoria had been electrified and before they left the Underground had arrived. Their house in the wide, busy commercial High Road was very close to both stations. It was obviously a promising place to open a music studio, especially at a time when the culture of 'learning music' was strong in middle-class society.

Alfredo first attended the Cavendish Road School (later called the Henry Cavendish School); strangely, there is no official record of his enrolment although there is no doubt that he was a pupil there.[18] Two months before his twelfth birthday he was enrolled at the Roman Catholic School in Nightingale Square (now called the Holy Ghost School). Before changing schools, however, Alfredo's extraordinary gifts as a child violinist were beginning to attract attention.

He was involved in a concert at Balham on Wednesday 9 May 1917 at the home of a Miss Feeney, aunt of another extraordinarily gifted young musician of those days – Birmingham-born Dorothy Howell, then aged nineteen – who performed at the same concert. Two years later she was to make her début as a pianist at the Aeolian Hall in London, her programme including six of her own compositions. In that same year Sir Henry Wood conducted her symphonic poem *Lamia* at the Proms, where later he also introduced her ballet *Koon Shee*, a piano concerto (with her as soloist) and an Overture *The Rock*. While still in her twenties she was appointed a professor of Harmony and Composition at the Royal Academy of Music and elected a Fellow of that institution in 1928. Despite her achievements as a solo pianist and – especially – as a quite prolific composer, her name is largely forgotten today, although there are signs that recognition is slowly reviving.[19]

---

[17] Interview in *Review and Express*, 11 October 1979.

[18] The School Register for his second school states that he came from the Cavendish Road School. Moreover he is remembered as being there by one of his fellow-students (personal communication). The Cavendish Road School records from those years are now housed in the London Metropolitan Records Office.

[19] The Dorothy Howell Trust has now been set up, and during 1998 there were a number of performances of her works celebrating the centenary of her birth.

The concert at Balham seems to have been a charitable one, either to raise funds for the war effort or for the local church. (Like the Campolis the Howell family was Roman Catholic.) A typed programme has survived.[20] As well as 'Signorino' Alfredo Campoli and Dorothy Howell (who at this concert played Chopin, Paderewski and Saint-Saëns rather than her own piano pieces some of which were already published), the performers included piano duettists, a harpist and three singers, one of whom was Elvira Campoli, who in *Ave Maria* was joined by her son playing the violin obbligato. The whole programme finished up with Alfredo playing Silesu's *Un peu d'amour* and the Intermezzo to Mascagni's *Cavalleria Rusticana*.

Alfredo was, in fact, appearing at this concert fresh from his triumph two months earlier at the South and West London Musical Festival. The ten-year-old had won First Prize and High Commendation in the section for his age group, the adjudicator being the well-known violinist and teacher W.H. Reed, at that time leader of the London Symphony Orchestra. The same story of success was repeated in 1918, but the following year Romeo received a letter from the Secretary of the competition pointing out that there were protests against his son's entry in the 1919 Festival:

> Dear Sir, I regret to inform you that I have received two letters protesting against your son Alfredo competing as an Amateur at our Festival. There is, of course, nothing to prevent him entering for the Gold Medal even if he is a professional, but my Committee wish me to write frankly to you to ask one or two questions.
>
> The lst is Does your son still go to school? 2nd. Which school does he attend? 3rd. Is he a regular member of the orchestra at the Stockwell Palladium or elsewhere?
>
> It was also alleged that Alfredo enters classes for which he is over the age. I do not believe this but, as the charge is made, I have to investigate it. Will you do me the favour of sending the boy's birth certificate, so that I can refute any charge that may subsequently be made upon this subject.
>
> I may just add that it is also stated that your son receives a salary of £4 a week. Is this correct, is it a permanent engagement?
>
> Your reply in due course will oblige.
>
> I am Yours faithfully T Lester Jones.

It was not surprising that his age was called into question, for he was taller than average and his body, despite the slenderness of its bone structure, was

[20] Found in the archives of The Dorothy Howell Trust. More information might have come from Dorothy Howell's own diary (which she kept throughout most of her life), but for the fact that in 1917 her oldest brother was killed in action, an event which so devastated his sister that the diary for that year is incomplete. (I am indebted to Miss Merryn Howell and to Mr Michael Jones – who played some of Dorothy's works during the 1998 centenary – for sending me the Balham programme and other information.)

already beginning to show the tell-tale signs of his mother's skill at cooking pasta. However, as well as furnishing the necessary birth certificate, Romeo was able to rebut the other charges to the satisfaction of the committee, and his son went ahead to win that year's competition, both for solo and duo playing, and gaining a gold medal.

The following year he entered two more competitions, one of which gained for him at the age of thirteen the gold medal for the 'open' section (for any age). This was presented to him by Princess Mary at the Prize-Winners' Concert on the afternoon of 27 March 1920 at Westminster Hall. There were three other gold medallists: Lilian Mann and Mary Dyke (soprano and contralto respectively) and a seventeen-year-old pianist who was to make a fine career for himself: Sidney Harrison, who played a Concert Study by Edward MacDowell. Alfredo played the first movement of the Mendelssohn concerto, a work that he was to make peculiarly his own during his long career. W.H. Reed's adjudication sheet for Alfredo's entry has survived:

> Posture 4/4; Intonation 19/21, Tone (Quality, Volume, Gradation) 6/6, 5/6, 5/6; Facility in Varied Bowing 12/12; Dexterity of Fingering 11/12; Strictness of Time and Choice of Tempo 12/12; Phrasing, Accent and Artistic Excellence 20/21. Total 94. Remarks: Tone and expression good, some of the glissades a little forced. Plays very musically & with much Temperament. 2nd Piece bowing very good.

Such was the prestige of this Festival and the interest aroused in Alfredo's achievement that the *Daily Mirror* published a photograph of father and son on its front page of 23 March with the caption 'Wonderful Boy Violinist', and to mark the occasion the pupils at Nightingale Square School were given a holiday. Letters of congratulation sent by his schoolmates (all in beautiful copperplate writing) reveal a great affection for 'Alf', some saying how much they missed him playing football. As far as games were concerned, his father now forbade him to play them in case of a hand injury, but bought him a billiard table to compensate for this. As with all activities that Alfredo took up, he became very skilled at billiards, especially after his lessons with the champion player Joe Davis, eventually winning the South London Amateur Cup in 1932. It was the perfect game, he once said, for improving and keeping the wrists supple.[21]

His success in the Open Section gave a clear signal to his father that Alfredo was destined for a professional career, and two months later permission was given for him to leave school on 28 May 1920, despite his being under age.[22] The school Register notes that permission was given because Alfredo 'has a private tutor'. This was obviously his father, who, in the three years leading up to

21 *Daily Telegraph* (Sydney), 5 June 1950.

22 The Education Act of 1918 stipulated fourteen years to be the minimum school leaving age. Alfredo was five-and-a-half months short of this.

Alfredo's début at Wigmore Hall was grooming him for that important occasion. Like many of his school friends Alfredo's studies had already been somewhat disrupted in the last year of the war, all prizes having been suspended by the London County Council for the educational year 1917–18. In their place, certificates were distributed at the end of the war, Alfredo receiving one for 'good conduct and meritorious work' at the Nightingale Square School soon after he had enrolled there. Yet, however desirable it may have been to gain further technical mastery and acquire a large and demanding repertoire and to polish the works for his début three years later, what had clearly been a dislocated education left its mark on him in later life.

When not practising, Alfredo's musicianship was developed through constant listening to recordings (primitive as they may have been) of the great singers of the day – Caruso, Tetrazzini and many others – so that he could learn the art of phrasing and reproduce on his instrument the alluring style of bel canto singing.

Shortly before Alfredo's début took place he and his mother gave a charity concert to raise funds to extend the buildings at the Nightingale Square School. It was held in a building, built in 1900, which was known at different times as the Balham Music-Hall, Palace of Varieties, Theatre De Lux, and Balham Pavilion.[23] Not unusually at the time for an entertainments building, it doubled as a cinema, a public meeting place and swimming baths (over which in the colder months was placed a floor). Thus it was that Alfredo and his mother gave their charity recital in what was advertised as the Balham Baths, Elvira singing excerpts from *Cavalleria Rusticana*, *Tosca* and *La Gioconda*, Alfredo playing the César Franck Sonata, movements from Lalo's *Symphonie Espagnole* and Mendelssohn's Concerto, as well as a number of encore-type pieces which were to feature in many of his later programmes. For this concert he was accompanied by Elsa Myers who was also to partner him in his début a few weeks later. And on Friday evening, 18 May 1923, sixteen-year-old Alfredo Campoli, in a white open-neck tennis shirt, stepped on to the platform of Wigmore Hall to give the first of three recitals which were to set him on his career.

Prompted by the experience of the 1919 competition, and by the fact that he now looked considerably older than his years, his birth certificate was prominently displayed in the foyer of Wigmore Hall. But, as the critic of the *Daily Express* said, 'musicians are not interested in prodigies as such for the good reason that few of them justify their promise in later years'. In the case of the young Alfredo Campoli this critic had no doubts that his talents seemed likely to be of 'an enduring kind'. Indeed, the opinion of those critics representing the leading newspapers who attended the recital was that here was a young violinist who combined fine technique with remarkable musical maturity.

---

[23] See Graham Gower, *Balham: A Brief History* (Wandsworth, 1990, reprinted 1996), pp. 40–41.

> Alfredo Campoli is a boy of 16 who played the fiddle at Wigmore Hall on Friday with an assured manner and, what is more important, an excellent tone and a faultless ear . . . (*The Times*)

> It was not as a prodigy but as a mature artist that Mr Alfredo Campoli . . . came before his audience last night . . . (*The Morning Post*)

> Mr Campoli had no difficulty in proving that his study of his instrument has not stopped short at the solution of technical problems (*The Daily Telegraph*)

For his first programme he played 'The Devil's Trill' Sonata (Tartini), Adagio and Fugue from Bach's unaccompanied Sonata in G minor and 'Air on the G string', Violin Concerto No. 1 by Max Bruch, *Perpetuum Mobile* (Ries), *Scherzo Tarentella* (Wieniawski), and *Ave Maria* (Schubert-Wilhelmj). For the second recital at the Wigmore Hall, which took place the following month on Saturday 23 June, the programme included the G minor Sonata 'Dido Abandoned' (Tartini), 'La Folia' Variations (Tartini-Kreisler), Chaconne from the D minor unaccompanied sonata (Bach), Violin Concerto (Mendelssohn), Four Caprices (Paganini), and *La Ronde des Lutins* (Bazzini). This second recital, declared the *Morning Post*, reinforced the impression gained from his first. It led to one of his earliest professional engagements: a recital at Norfolk House for the Duchess of Norfolk. The third recital, on the 22 October (two days after his seventeenth birthday), included works by Nardini, Beethoven, Elgar, Grieg and Paganini. By any measure, it was an impressive beginning to a young violinist's career.

His repertoire was extraordinarily extensive for one so young. According to one press report, at the time of his début he had already memorised ten recital programmes, and the publicity brochure put out by his agent at the end of that spectacular year lists thirteen major works that Alfredo was ready to play with an orchestra: Concerto in E minor (Mendelssohn), Concerto in D (Beethoven), Concerto in D (Paganini), Concerto in D, Op. 121 (Mozart), *Symphonie Espagnole* (Lalo), Concerto No. 1 (Bruch), Concerto (Elgar), Concerto No. 3 (Saint-Saëns), Concerto in A (Vivaldi), Hungarian Dances (Ernst), Introduction and Rondo Capriccioso (Saint-Saëns), Fantaise Caprice, Op. 11 (Vieuxtemps), Ballade and Polonaise (Vieuxtemps).

Alfredo's début coincided with an ebullient period in English musical life. Society, bent on forgetting the horrors of the recent war, set about enjoying itself, helped in no small measure by the discovery of American jazz and a craze for dancing. There was seemingly endless work for orchestral musicians in cinemas, theatres, restaurants, concerts and opera. Beecham, Sargent and Wood commanded the orchestral field, and English composers were now a growing voice in the land. It was also the period when the miracle of broadcasting moved out of the experimental stage to become, through the British Broadcasting Company (later Corporation), the most potent force in Britain in fashioning public taste and offering a style of patronage to arts and entertainment unknown before that time. It was during that decade, too, that electrical recording superseded the old acoustic type, and, like radio, became an indispensable part of musical life. Alfredo Campoli was to establish his name in almost all these activities at different times in his career.

The vitality of that decade was reflected in the International Celebrity Subscription Concerts organised each year by Lionel Powell, the agent who placed Alfredo on his books for his début and later recitals. Lionel Powell & Holt was one of the most successful concert agencies in London at that time, operating a country-wide network that brought the world's most celebrated artists to London and to the major provincial musical centres such as Leeds, Manchester, Liverpool, Birmingham, Glasgow, Edinburgh and other cities. Its list of artists presented during the decade is a roll-call of those who have became the musical legends of our century. The series commenced in the concert season (i.e. winter) 1919/20 and was overwhelmingly successful, encouraging similar series throughout the decade and to as many provincial centres as possible. Indeed, it would seem that Lionel Powell had so underestimated the appeal of the first series that thousands of music-lovers in the provinces had been unable to obtain admission. For the second series, Birmingham music-lovers, for example, were assured of five subscription concerts for which

> . . . Only the World's Most Celebrated Artists will take part in these Concerts as heretofore, and it is the intention of the Director to present to his Subscribers the greatest combinations of World Famous Artist [*sic*] at each Concert ever produced in the provinces – as opposed to the old-fashioned method of engaging only one Star Artist for the whole series. MR. LIONEL POWELL is in the unique position of sole manager, with very few exceptions, to all the World Famous Artists of the present day. . .

Provincial music-lovers would, of course, hear only a selection of the many artists engaged for the International Celebrity series, but the offerings held some enticing possibilities. Amongst the thirty artists appearing in Britain for the second series were the violinists Jan Kubelik, Eugène Ysaÿe, Bronislaw Huberman and Efram Zimbalist; the singers Nellie Melba, Clara Butt and Maggie Teyte; the pianists Vladimir de Pachmann and Ferruccio Busoni.

It's not surprising that in the sleek brochures issued each year by Lionel Powell the name of Alfredo Campoli does not appear. He was still young and unseasoned, and when he toured for Lionel Powell it was either in the role of an assisting artist – he recalled playing for Melba, Clara Butt, Rosina Buckman and Kennerley Rumford – or in recitals that were of the less glamorous kind: in London to share a programme given by the Lavender Hill Temperance Choir, or at Miss Margaret Lichfield's Dance Recital at the Aeolian Hall; at the Pavilion in Bournemouth assisting the 'the famous Australian dramatic contralto' Lily

Payling, or with another Australian musician – the pianist Betty Beattie; in Belfast sharing the programme with the city organist and with the London singer Topliss Green, or in London playing at the Annual Dinner of the Publicity Club held in the Hotel Cecil. Not producing a brilliant career as yet, these years seemed to have offered 'journeyman' experiences that might lead eventually to the status of master musician, like that of the violinists he deeply revered – Kreisler, Heifetz, Ysaÿe.

Moreover, he was not the only very gifted young violinist of those days. In November of the same year that Alfredo made his début at the Wigmore Hall a thirteen-year-old violinist was making a great impression up in Leeds (one of the most musically sophisticated cities outside London at that time). It was Harry Blech who was later to contribute so richly to London musical life through his String Quartet and his founding of both the London Wind Players (1942) and the London Mozart Players (1949). In the following year the Leeds Tuesday Evening Concert Series offered, as usual, not only established artists such as John Coates, Andersen Tyrer, Mark Hambourg, Julius Harrison and others, but also a Master Norman Walker, billed in the *Yorkshire Post* as 'the great violinist'.[24] In the eyes of some, however, 'Signor Alfredo Campoli, the Italian violinist' as he was so often described in publicity and reviews, enjoyed the advantage of being 'foreign' – which, of course, technically he was – up until 1947. Certainly, during the Great War foreign musicians had had a hard time of it, not only the Germans, most of whom had to leave the country, but even the Italians who in that war were fighting on the side of Britain.[25] It was xenophobia at its most depressing. The Campolis had come to England some two years before the war and before foreign musicians were banned from immigrating there – a union and government attempt to protect the livelihood of the locals.[26] Yet there seems to have been no vendetta against Romeo in Coventry during the war where, as we have seen, his Italian background was proudly vaunted by the Globe Theatre management. By the time Alfredo was beginning his career in 1923 the world had changed again, and the old mystique of the foreign-born once more held some audiences in thrall. Elgar had once said of the violinist Arthur Catterall that if he had not been an Englishman, he would have been acclaimed as one of the greatest violinists of the day.[27] Albert Sammons was another whose reputation amongst the general concert-going public suffered through being 'home-grown', despite being regarded by Heifetz, Szigeti, Stern and Ysaÿe as their equal.[28] Of course, the

[24] Not to be confused with the singer of the same name.

[25] Ehrlich, 1985, p. 188. Ehrlich's *The Piano – A History* (London, 1976), pp. 159–63, reveals how the hatred for all things German at this time led to the virtual embargo on the sale of Steinway and Bechstein pianos or their use at recitals in Britain.

[26] Ehrlich, 1985, p. 187.

[27] Quoted in *Radio Times*, 10 December 1943.

[28] For a biography of this violinist see Eric Wetherell, *Albert Sammons* (London, 1998).

Italian 'mystique' surrounding Alfredo Campoli was somewhat dissipated by his broad London accent acquired in Balham. To this day there are some who believe that he was not Italian at all, and that his real name was Alfred Campbell or Alfred Camp, a belief given some credence by the fact that during the 1930s his close friends and colleagues all called him 'Camp'. But, indeed, Alfredo was proud of his Italian blood and temperament, and throughout his career conveyed it in every phrase he played.

When not giving recitals, Alfredo assisted his father with the cinema orchestra and with his teaching. Romeo's Academy, by then located at 187 Mitcham Road and re-named The York House College of Music, was now advertising in much more ambitious terms than before, and with indirect but pointed reference to his son's success:

> **PROFESSOR ROMEO CAMPOLI/**
> The well-known Violin Teacher, late of Royal Academy, Rome.
> Eminent Professors in attendance for all Branches of Music. Prospectus will be given on application to the Secretary.
> In the last few years many pupils have been successful Recitalists at Wigmore and Aeolian Halls, in addition to Gold Medals, First Prizes, Honours and Certificates being gained.
> PHONE FOR APPOINTMENT Students prepared for all Examinations and Competition-Festivals and also for a Professional Career.

Romeo's description of himself as being 'late of the Royal Academy, Rome' was an understandable professional liberty. There has never been, in fact, such an institution in that city. The Liceo Musicale, founded in 1876 by Sgambati and Pinelli and taken under the wing of the Accademia di S. Cecilia, did not become a State Conservatory until 1919, some seven years after the Campolis had left Italy, and to the present day the Accademia di S. Cecilia and the Conservatorio di S. Cecilia are related but different organisations, easily confused by the outsider. Romeo may have felt that at least the term 'Royal Academy, Rome' would resonate in popular imagination with the 'The Royal Academy of Music, London', better than the cumbersome and confusing Liceo Musicale of the Accademia di S. Cecilia. His self-applied title of 'Professor' was, of course, no more than what most European teachers called themselves (and still do), but what teaching duties at the Liceo Musicale he undertook are unknown. He may have been a teaching assistant to his own great teacher Pinelli. Nor is there any record of Romeo playing in the celebrated orchestra of the Accademia di S. Cecilia, so we must assume that it was the conservatory orchestra that he sometimes led. This is not meant to suggest that Romeo deliberately misled his son or his students; rather, it was merely a 'translation' of terminology. What is not in doubt, however, is the fact that he was a very fine teacher, as constantly attested by his son throughout his own career. It is understandable that many years later as an established concert artist Alfredo should refer in exaggerated terms to his parents' careers. Menuhin could point to great artists like Enescu and Adolf Busch who had helped shape his musicianship and style. Alfredo's mentors were his parents; their achievements had to be the foil to the reputation he had established in light music.

Those early recitals of Alfredo's were invariably greeted with enthusiastic reviews and pointed to a rosy future. But the decade of the 1920s which began so confidently – indeed, recklessly – ended in economic collapse with news of the Wall Street Crash at the end of 1929. For countless musicians, however, economic collapse had already occurred, for in 1927 Warner Brothers in the USA produced the world's first talkie. *The Jazz Singer* inaugurated a new era in the movie industry, but in so doing destroyed the livelihood of thousands upon thousands of those who had played music in front of the silent screen.[29] Ehrlich estimates that the final figure of those thrown out of work because of this development alone could have been as high as 10,000.[30] This catastrophe and the effects of the Great Depression undoubtedly hit musicians hardest of all, for there were now so few opportunities for them. Statistics from 1931 show that the music profession – players and teachers – in London dropped to a third of what it had been ten years earlier.[31] It was now the survival of the fittest.

On 7 March 1930 Alfredo gave the first of two recitals at Wigmore Hall with London's leading accompanist, Ivor Newton. One critic only (from *The Times*) turned up to review it.

> Mr Alfredo Campoli, who made his reappearance on Friday, giving the first of two recitals in the Wigmore Hall, is, unquestionably, a very competent violinist. He has a clean technique, plenty of tonal variety, and true intonation. In interpretation, however, his style is rather limited, and we did not feel that either the 'La Follia' variations of Corelli or the Chaconne of Bach were given with nearly enough breadth and dignity. This was chiefly on account of an excess of sentiment in the expression, carried to the point of gravely interfering with the rhythmical flow of the music. Otherwise his playing was accurate and assured.

No critic seems to have come to the second recital.

It was hardly encouraging for a young man whose career had begun with such promise, but who now faced an uncertain future in troubled times. And how to support his parents, now that Romeo was as hard hit as any musician by the triple disaster of the demise of the silent cinema orchestra, the Depression and the

---

[29] In the more affluent places the move to talkies would have happened fairly quickly, but the fact that Edwin Evans's article (see fn. 9) makes no mention of this development suggests that the new sound system was not widely installed even by 1929.

[30] Ehrlich, 1985, p. 210.

[31] Ehrlich, 1985, p. 237 (Table IV).

disintegration of the culture of the 'music lesson'? The answer lay in the direction that many brilliant classical performers were beginning to take. Alfredo was far from alone in moving into a field where success in playing music in restaurants, hotels and theatres, and making recordings and broadcasts of light music, might lead not only to secure employment, but also, for those at the top, to financial affluence. An indication of his success in this is that in the next decade 'Alfredo Campoli and his Salon Orchestra' became a household name.

Chapter 2

'Alfredo Campoli and his Salon Orchestra'

Paradoxical as it may seem, during the years of economic depression in Britain London restaurants and hotels so flourished as to provide many fine musicians with a good livelihood, for it seem that London and the South were not affected as profoundly as the industrial areas. In some places the standard of living actually rose.[1] Certainly, Alfredo was to enjoy a good income and life-style when he moved into the field of light music.

Nevertheless, he had mixed views about the change in his career during the 1930s. He was keenly aware of his father's disappointment over the decision to extend his playing into light music, for it was not unlikely that Romeo had envisaged early hopes for his own performance career fulfilled in his son's. Yet, Alfredo's career was far from being exclusively devoted to light music. He led, as he used to say, 'a double-life', as did many of those who were treading the same path with him.

His 'fellow-travellers' included many who were able to establish themselves exclusively as concert artists after the Second World War: Reginald Kell, who became the recognised leader of a new school of clarinet playing in Britain and who filled the principal desk in leading orchestras there, as well as in a number of international ones; Jean Pougnet and David McCallum, both outstanding orchestral and solo violinists; William Primrose, for whom Bartòk wrote his viola concerto; Anthony Pini, who established a fine reputation as both solo cellist and chamber music player. Others became well known as conductors: Stanford Robinson, Walter Goehr, Rae Jenkins and Hugo Rignold. These are just a few of the better-known musicians whose careers, like Alfredo's, were shaped by the forces at work at that time. Of them, Hugo Rignold is a striking example.

Born in 1905, Hugo Rignold enjoyed a solid musical training at the Royal Academy of Music in London, studying violin with Hans Wessely, viola with Lionel Tertis and oboe with Leon Goossens. Like Alfredo, his musical interests were as wide as those outside it (he is reputed to have been trained by Jack Dempsey as a boxer, and was also a passionate racing driver[2]), and his early career was in light music. His name, for example, figures in the list of dance bands given below. One of the original members of Jack Hylton's Dance Band, his own was featured regularly in BBC broadcasts during the early years of the

---

1 See D. LeMahieu, *A Culture for Democracy – Mass Communication and the Cultivated Mind in Britain during the Wars* (Oxford, 1988), pp. 235 ff., which also includes a list of important literature about the economics of the 1930s.

2 *Radio Times*, 26 April 1940.

Second World War. After the war he was appointed conductor of the Sadler's Wells Ballet Company of Covent Garden in 1945, and three years later became principal conductor of the Liverpool Philharmonic Orchestra, then joining the Royal Ballet as Musical Director in 1957. After three years with that company he was appointed principal conductor of the City of Birmingham Orchestra. He made many international tours and conducted Alfredo's concerto performances from time to time.

The restaurants were a thriving scene for music, their bands and orchestras seemingly as important as the food they served. In the middle of the 1930s the smartest restaurants in Mayfair and the West End were making a feature of their music as many had done before the war (see list below).[3]

To that list of dance bands must be added the many salon and palm-court orchestras that provided an elegant ambience in leading hotels and restaurants. One of the most famous of these had been the De Groot Trio, which had set a standard to which all such later trios aspired. Like so many other musicians who had come to London before the First World War de Groot was Dutch, and those he engaged to play with him in his various ensembles were almost invariably from Holland – with the exception of the young English pianist Ivor Newton who, at the age of seventeen, became his accompanist for a few years. At that time de Groot was musical director for the luxurious Piccadilly Hotel, social focal point in London for the world's rich and famous. As well as playing with and conducting his orchestras (all in evening dress), de Groot also performed as a soloist, standing on the edge of the platform, leaning out towards his audience with his treasured Stradivarius, his slim figure, aristocratic bearing and eloquent playing holding all under his spell. As Ivor Newton recalled 'nobody could have regarded what we played as "background music"; guests were free to talk during

[3] Grosvenor House, Park Lane (Sydney Lipton), The Dorchester, Park Lane (Jack Jackson), Lansdowne Restaurant, Berkeley Square (Brian Lawrance), Mayfair, Berkeley Street (Michael Flome), The Ritz, Piccadilly (Joe Kaye), The Berkeley, Piccadilly (Al Collins), Embassy, Old Bond Street (Jim Clayton), Prince's, Piccadilly (in the restaurant Norman Colc, in the Grill Room Jerry Hoey), Odeninnos, Regent Street (Roy Wallace), Cocoanut Grove, Regent Street (Oscar Grasso), Paradise, Regent Street (Arthur Roseberr), Murray's Club, Beak Street (Norman Stanley), Quaglino's, Bury Street (Van Stratten and Frank Gregori's Quintet), Cabaret, Beak Street (Tony Kanzello), Trocadero, Shaftesbury Avenue (Adam), Havana, Denman Street (Cuban Band), Casino, Old Compton Street (Bert Firman and Hugo Rignold), The Astoria, Charing Cross (Joe Loss and Jack White). Frascati's, Oxford Street (Manuel Raymond), Ciro's, Orange Street (Jack Harris), Holborn Restaurant, Kingsway (Edward Dennis), Haymarket Brasserie, Piccadilly (Archie Alexander), Hungaria, Regent Street (Tzigane Orchestra), Romano's, Strand (Romano's Band), The Savoy, Strand (Carroll Gibbons and Geraldo), Bag of Nails, Kingly Street (Swing Band and Buskers), Palm Beach, Frith Street (Ike Hatch), Midnight Room, Albermarle Street (Len Newbury), Hell, Gerrard Street (Al Craig), The 400, Leicester Square (Tim Clayton). Taken from a list kindly provided by The Dorchester Hotel, Park Lane. Unfortunately some names of restaurants and bands were undecipherable and have not been included in the above list (such as Café Anglais).

the long intervals between our pieces, but as soon as he picked up his violin, de Groot imposed silence upon them'.[4] De Groot's solo programmes, as well as those for his Trio, were taken from the light classical repertoire. Asked in 1927 about his views on 'syncopated music' (modern dance music and jazz) he replied 'I have been playing straight music here consistently now for nineteen years. Is that not my greatest argument against syncopated music? I am proud to think that year after year as I have climbed the ladder of fame and success I have stuck to the old masters and to, as some folk call it, highbrow music.'[5] His impeccably high standards were such that the conductor John Barbirolli, who was a fine cellist in those days, regretted that, although he had played in every theatre pit in London, he had never had the chance of playing with de Groot.[6] When Alfredo formed his Campoli Trio for the BBC in 1934 the *Radio Times*, announcing its first broadcast appearance on 4 November, described it as 'playing the melodious and irresistibly appealing music in the tradition of the ensemble made famous by de Groot'.

It seems that Alfredo's first engagement as a restaurant musician was towards the end of the 1929. In publicity leading up to the first of his two recitals in Wigmore Hall (described in the previous chapter) the *Daily Mirror* had written on 4 March 1930: 'This young musician (who is now twenty-three) is director and soloist in the grill-room of a West End restaurant, and is by no means new to London. Regular concert-goers may recall being delighted by his playing a few years ago.' That West End restaurant was the smartest of the Lyons Corner Houses, the Trocadero in Shaftesbury Avenue. When he decided to leave the Trocadero Alfredo turned, like a number of other Italian musicians to Emilio Colombo for help, for if as a recitalist he had needed an agent, for work in the hotels and restaurants he needed a 'fixer'. Colombo was one such man.

At this distance an elusive shadow, Emilio Colombo was in his day a gifted and popular violinist whose early life reads like a romantic novel. Born in 1874 in Magenta, Italy, at the age of six he entered his father's orchestra which was to tour Europe and Russia. Here he came to the attention of Tchaikovsky on whose advice he was sent to Liège in Belgium to perfect his technique. In 1910 he settled in Petrograd where he was appointed solo violinist at the Tsar's court. At the outbreak of the Revolution Colombo fled Petrograd, making his way through Russia while enduring great hardship, eventually reaching Vladivostok penniless. However, the proceeds of a concert there enabled him eventually to reach England via Tokyo (where he was invited to play before the Japanese Imperial Family), Hong Kong, Singapore, Indonesia and Canada. He made his London début at the Aeolian Hall in 1920. Already no stranger to royal patronage, Colombo attracted the attention of the Duke and Duchess of York (later to take

4 Ivor Newton, *At the Piano* (London, 1966), p. 30.

5 *The Music Box*, July 1927, p. 7.

6 Newton, 1966, p. 31.

the throne), the Prince of Wales and other members of the Royal Family who regularly invited him to play for them. His career was that of a restaurant violinist and it was indeed while playing in the Savoy Hotel Grill Room that he collapsed and died on 24 November 1937.[7]

He was also an influential figure 'behind the scenes'. When wanting to engage a salon or palm-court orchestra it was to Emilio Colombo that hotel and restaurant management often turned. He auditioned Italian musicians (or those of Italian origin) and hence Alfredo was soon on his books – as was Mantovani. Morris Taylor, then a seventeen-year-old violinist recalled his first meeting with Colombo.[8] Like hundreds of other unemployed musicians at the beginning of the 1930s, Morris Taylor was waiting outside the Musicians Union office in search of a job when a friend saw him and suggested he should see 'Mr Colombo'. Fortunately for the young man, his sleeked-down black hair and side burns gave him a decidedly Italian look and Colombo asked him to play in an ensemble at the Victoria Hotel the next night, this in the nature of an audition. This went on for several nights until Colombo told him that there might be something for him if he were to turn up at his flat in Grape Street next day. There Morris Taylor found Alfredo (whom he had never met) and four other Italian musicians (on accordion, guitar, cello and bass) rehearsing for their first appearance at the elegant new Devonshire House restaurant behind Green Park tube station. Morris Taylor joined that ensemble,[9] playing second violin to Alfredo, both at Devonshire House and in the restaurant that was to establish Alfredo's reputation firmly in the field of light music: the newly constructed Dorchester Hotel in Park Lane.

The building of The Dorchester was seen as a bright light amidst the deepening economic gloom in Britain. Its construction gave employment to many workers, and through its luxurious appointments it was hoped that the hotel would attract many visitors from America, the Continent and from what were then called the Dominions, thus bringing much-needed currency into the country. In its issue of 20 April 1931, the architectural correspondent of *The Times* described the splendour of the interior, and writing about the restaurant and its adjacent rooms he said

> The general tone of the restaurant, which has an elliptical ceiling light, is primrose, enriched with gilding. The pilasters are faced with a composition called 'lap', an imitation marble with veining of English gold introduced

[7] This account is taken from an obituary in *The Times*, 15 November 1937.

[8] The following is indebted to Mr Morris Taylor, whose recorded interview with the author provided an invaluable source of information about this period.

[9] Morris Taylor recalls being asked by Alfredo to put in 'some thirds'. 'Si, si' agreed Colombo. Puzzled by Colombo's words the young man obligingly played the notes C C to a burst of laughter from Alfredo who insisted that Morris should get the job even though he wasn't Italian.

> in casting. The wall lights are screened with apricot. Here, as elsewhere, a feature is made of mirrors which the chief reflecting surface gives a flesh tint and the surrounds are composed of overlapping plates in three tones of black. The scheme for the ballroom which is 91ft by 75ft to the ends of the transepts is in 'oyster', against which the generally grey tone of the mirrors produces a very charming effect. In the ceiling are two polygonal lights with in-curved sides, the curves being picked up happily by the chairs in sycamore. The reception-room for the ball-room is oval, with a dome of bronze gold. From the first bay of the lounge suite, described as the inner hall, one enters the grill-room which has a separate entrance, with sherry bar, from Deanery Street. All the details throughout the public rooms are very carefully designed to give the maximum of return with the minimum of aggression, so that the general effect is that of luxury being taught good manners.

It was in this elegant ambience that Alfredo was invited to direct a salon orchestra that the hotel had engaged to entertain the patrons as they dined. For those who wished to dance there was the Dorchester Dance Band under the direction of Melville Gideon.

The ceremony to open The Dorchester took place on Saturday 18 April 1931 at a luncheon for 672 guests who were served in the Ballroom and in the adjoining Gold and Silver rooms. For the next six months Alfredo was to give performances with The Dorchester Hotel Orchestra at lunch and afternoon-tea, his solos, of course, a highlight, especially at afternoon-tea when many a musician would come to hear him play.

The next month The Dorchester inaugurated a series of Sunday After-Dinner Recitals at which some of the most celebrated performers of their day appeared: Kreisler, Chaliapin and the pianist Ania Dorfmann. They were reviewed as serious musical events by *The Times*. Naturally, for Alfredo the highlight was the recital given by Fritz Kreisler, and he begged the management to allow him to turn the music over for the accompanist. They, no doubt feeling that it was somewhat undignified for the conductor of their orchestra to be seen in this role, assigned the task to the youngest member of it, Morris Taylor. Alfredo did not even meet Kreisler at that appearance; this had to wait for some years.

Following those recitals another series commenced in October, but it was the last. The recitals appear not to have been the success envisaged for them. In any case, by that time Alfredo was no longer appearing at The Dorchester, his career having become increasingly busy through the impetus given it by the hotel, He soon had several orchestras under his own name playing permanently in different restaurants. Both the Gaumont British and Paramount film companies contracted Alfredo Campoli and his Salon Orchestra to appear in stage presentations at their chain of 'super-cinemas' throughout the country.[10] The major boost, however, was a recording contract with Decca.

10 *The Monthly Pictorial*, May, 1933.

It had been a mere six years since the first commercial electrical recordings (issued by Victor and Columbia in the USA) had superseded the acoustic type, revitalising what had become a rather moribund period in the recording industry, although in Britain the innovation encountered some hostility over what many thought to be an ear-splitting sound.[11] The music-critic of the *Sunday Times* Ernest Newman, however, warmly welcomed the new technology which was to usher in an era comparable to that of the talkies two years later. While it is not possible to identify any precise dates, it would seem that Alfredo had already recorded a little for Edison Bell and for Brunswick Panatrope. His association with Decca, however, was to last thoughout his entire career, and was the direct result of The Dorchester Hotel engagement.

Decca produced its first recordings at the same time that Alfredo was embarking on his career in light music. Before 1929 the name Decca – no-one seems to know its origins – was associated only with a well-known portable gramophone made by Barnett Samuel and Sons, manufacturers of musical instruments. At the end of 1928 that manufacturing firm was put up for sale, and a new public company formed from it called the Decca Gramophone Company. At that stage the new directors had no thought of producing recordings, especially as there were such powerful companies already doing this as the Brunswick Record Company, the Columbia Graphophone Company, and the Gramophone Company (HMV), as well as Edison Bell, Vocalion, Crystalate, Metropole and others, producing between them millions of recordings. Many of them survived for only a short time.

It was E.R. (Ted) Lewis who had originally brokered the deal between Barnett Samuel and Sons and the new company, and who so strongly believed that the future of Decca lay in producing records as well as equipment that he formed a syndicate to buy up the record factory of the floundering Duophone Company and (with more difficulty) to buy out Decca with a public flotation of shares. This was accomplished only a matter of weeks before the Wall Street crash and the ensuing Great Depression, and it was not until 1945 that those original subscribers obtained a profit on their holdings.[12] Indeed, disaster stared at the directors almost immediately, and but for the extraordinary skill and efforts of Ted Lewis the Decca Company might well have ceased to exist. Its first recordings were by the dance-band conductors Ambrose, Billy Cotton and Jack Hylton. Alfredo was soon to join them on an exclusive contract for five years, his first recording, in 1931, being selections from *The Chocolate Soldier* (Oscar Straus) and *The Quaker Girl* (Lionel Monckton) played by his Dorchester Hotel Orchestra. By the beginning of the next year eight recordings by the Dorchester Hotel Orchestra had been released, including Heykens' Serenade No. 1, which became a best-seller at a critical time in Decca's fortunes. Eighteen months after

[11] Roland Gelatt, *The Fabulous Phonograph* (London, 1956), pp. 176–7.

[12] E.R. Lewis, *No C. I. C.* (London, 1956), p. 20.

its release that record is reported to have sold 85,000 copies, while by May 1933 the total sales of Alfredo's recordings had reached 350,000.[13]

In order to compete in the depressed market Decca had been one of the first recording companies to exploit bargain prices, the F series (10-inch double-sided Blue Label) selling for one shilling and sixpence, the K series (12-inch double-sided Black Label) selling for two shillings and sixpence, prices well below those of its competitors. From 1936 he was also taken up by HMV and Columbia, and by the beginning of the war 117 of his recordings had been released. Sprinkled through them were short solo pieces from the standard concert repertoire, as well as Max Bruch's Violin Concerto No. 1, conducted by Walter Goehr. The majority, however, featured light music, with ensembles that went under a variety of names: Alfredo Campoli and his Salon Orchestra, Alfredo Campoli and his Novelty Orchestra, Alfredo Campoli Grand Orchestra, Alfredo Campoli and his Old-Fashioned Waltz Orchestra, Alfredo Campoli and his Marimba Tango Orchestra. (See Appendix 1 for a chronological listing of his complete recordings.) At the same time his name was even more widely known through another medium: that of broadcasting.

When Alfredo made his début at Wigmore Hall in 1923 the BBC (then called the British Broadcasting Company) had only been on air for six months. At that time it was only a conglomerate of companies manufacturing radios and component parts, and permitted to broadcast at specific times under strict lines laid down by the Post Office. By the time Alfredo auditioned for it, it had become the British Broadcasting Corporation and under its Director-General John Reith had established itself as one of the most potent forces in Britain. Reith's attitude towards broadcast music was that there should be no divisions between its various forms. Those whose natural predilections were towards light music might also be encouraged to enjoy more 'serious' music simply by hearing it, while devotees of the classics might occasionally want to listen to music of a more relaxing kind. It was in Reith's view a process of education both ways. Moreover, as the historian of the BBC, Asa Briggs, has noted, it was an attitude that saw the versatility of the artist as a reflection of the 'roundedness' of the listener.[14] Thus, the very versatility of a Campoli, a Rignold, or any of those mentioned earlier was obviously an advantage for those lucky enough to be taken up by the BBC.

It seems likely that Alfredo auditioned for the BBC sometime in 1931, playing Brahms's Second Violin Sonata in A major to B. Walton O'Donnell, conductor of the BBC Wireless Military Band since 1927. Walton O'Donnell was a remarkable musician – cellist, pianist, composer and conductor. Born in Belfast he was one of three brothers who were all bandmasters. At the age of fourteen he won a scholarship to the Royal Academy of Music in London, where later he was to teach composition and military music, and conduct the Academy orchestra when

13 *The Monthly Pictorial*, May, 1933.

14 Asa Briggs, *The Golden Age of Wireless* (London, 1965), p. 122.

Sir Henry Wood was absent. Before joining the BBC he was Director of the Royal Marines Band at Deal. After Alfredo's audition Walton O'Donnell invited him to appear as a guest artist in a programme given by the BBC Wireless Military Band broadcast on the evening of Wednesday 6 January 1932.

Nothing could reflect better the bringing together of light and more serious styles championed by Reith than that particular broadcast. In this programme Alfredo's solo pieces, accompanied by an unnamed staff pianist, were *Tango* (Albeniz), *Valse Bluette* (Drigo, arr. Auer), *Variations on a Theme of Corelli* (Tartini, arr. Kreisler), *Ave Maria* (Schubert, arr. Wilhelmj) and *La ronde des lutins* (Bazzini). The Band played the Overture to *Die Fledermaus* (Strauss), *Two Slavonic Dances* (Dvorák), *Welsh Rhapsody* (German), Two Dances from *Faust* (Gounod), and some incidental music by Coleridge-Taylor. That year Alfredo was to broadcast similar programmes with two other bands (the Luton Band and Callender's 'A' Band), but on Sunday 6 November was at last given his own recital. This consisted of the Sonata in G minor (Tartini), the second and third movements of Mendelssohn's violin concerto, Nocturne in E flat (Chopin, arr. Sarasate) and *Moto Perpetuo* (Paganini). In 1933 he gave six more broadcasts, three with the bands mentioned above, and three solo recitals. But, undoubtedly, the most significant broadcast that year came from The Pavilion in Bournemouth where Sir Dan Godfrey conducted him in a performance of Brahms's violin concerto on the afternoon of Wednesday 11 October.

The Bournemouth Municipal Orchestra had gained its name and permanency when, in 1896, the Bournemouth Corporation took over an orchestra that had been formed by Dan Godfrey (1868–1939) the previous year. Godfrey established a symphony concert series that has lasted to the present day, and in which were featured works by modern composers, particularly British, as well as the classics. The concert series first took place in the Bournemouth Winter Gardens until the Pavilion was built. It will be recalled that Alfredo had already performed there with the Australian contralto Lily Payling.

The broadcast of Brahms's violin concerto aroused considerable interest, the *Radio Times*, for example, highlighting it in its column 'Picked from the Programmes' and reproducing a photograph of Alfredo in its pages. The programme included Franck's Symphony in D minor and movements from Rimsky-Korsakoff's suite *Antar*. Typical of a Dan Godfrey programme it also included a work by a British composer whose name – O'Connell Morris – and work – *Heroic Overture* – have slipped from musical history. Alfredo's playing was reported as displaying 'a delightful silvery tone [and] admirable feeling for the lilt of the rhythm in the gypsy-like theme of the finale'. The critic spoke of the infinite pleasure given by Alfredo's beauty of tone in the more reflective passages and concluded that 'the masterful technique of the soloist enabled him to sustain unbroken attention on the beauties of the music'.[15]

[15] *Bournemouth Daily Echo*, 13 October 1933.

As a broadcast artist Alfredo was thus first known as a 'classical' violinist, but from 1934 his name became increasingly associated over the radio with light music, for on 3 March that year his Salon Orchestra made its broadcast début, followed eight months later by the appearance of the Campoli Trio. Both ensembles were to be heard frequently over the air until the early years of the war; from March 1934 until April 1940 they gave a total of 183 broadcasts.

Light music over the BBC, in fact, took up more broadcast hours than any other kind of programme. On the National Programme there were more than twice as many hours given over to light music as to 'classical' music, while on the Regional Programmes this rose to almost three times as many hours.[16] Clearly, light music was a good field to be working in if engaged by the BBC.

Alfredo now needed no Emilio Colombo; his own reputation guaranteed engagements and he chose his own musicians. Unlike most of the restaurant orchestras, Alfredo's salon orchestra rehearsed rigorously. For its broadcasts it usually consisted of eight to nine players, but this was only part of a larger salon orchestra of some twenty-two players, including brass and wind. When it gave its first BBC broadcast it had already fulfilled a number of engagements in Europe, including a series of broadcasts in Holland from the Hilversum station. This combination of broadcast and live performance, typical of its schedule, was of utmost importance in Alfredo's mind, believing as he did that 'a successful radio combination should keep in the public eye with other forms of entertainment'.[17] He engaged the best that London could offer. They included Arthur Gleghorn, whom Alfredo always maintained was the finest flautist in England; Rae Jenkins (viola) who became conductor of the BBC Midland and Welsh Orchestras and who was to conduct Alfredo from time to time in the last years of the war and after it; John Russell (violin); John Cockerill, who became chief harpist of the London Symphony Orchestra for many years; James Merritt (bass); Michael Krein (saxophone and arranger) whose Fantasy on the Sailor's Hornpipe was a brilliant and popular piece. Alfredo made a number of arrangements himself, as did his regular pianist Sidney Crooke, but it was Fred Hartley whom he felt was the best of all his arrangers. Moreover, Hartley in those days was prepared to have his arrangements played without fee so that they could be heard by the large radio audience.[18]

The first programme over the BBC given by Alfredo Campoli and his Salon Orchestra was typical of those to follow, not least in featuring a guest artist, in this case the soprano Alice Lilley. It comprised

---

[16] Percentages of all kinds of programmes are given by Briggs, 1965, p. 51.

[17] *Topical Times*, 1 September 1934.

[18] Campoli in a recorded conversation with John Allt, May 1985.

Orchestra	*Memories of the Ball* – in rhythm style (arr. Crooke). *Melody in F* (Rubinstein); *Her First Dance* (Heykens).
Alice Lilley	*Three Songs of June* (Haydn Wood).
Orchestra	*Serenade No. 2* (Heykens); Trio: *Softly Awakes My Heart* (Saint-Saëns); *Hiawatha* (Moret); *Smilin' Through* (Penn); *Kasbek* (traditional).
Alice Lilley	*This Lovely Rose* (Ramsay); *O Happy Childhood* (Carse); *Love the Jester* (Phillips); *Castles in the Air* (Lincke).
Orchestra	Selection of Viennese Waltzes – in rhythm style (arr. Robrecht).

When the Campoli Trio came to air later in the year, at 1.15pm on Sunday 4 November, like the Salon Orchestra, it had already been playing for some years in restaurants and on stage. Early in 1933, for example, the Campoli Trio had appeared at London's Winter Garden Theatre in a production of Laddie Cliff's *Rhyme and Rhythm* and was regarded by many London critics as 'the hit of the show'. For his Trio Alfredo chose Sidney Crooke as pianist and Reginald Murray as cellist. As with the Salon Orchestra, its broadcasts often included a guest artist; for its first programme it was joined by the tenor Leonard Gower. It will be seen that there was considerable overlap in style between the two ensembles, even though the Trio tended towards the slightly more serious works.

Trio	Selections from *Madame Butterfly* (Puccini); *Serenade No. 1* (Heykens); *Serenade* (Drigo).
Leonard Gower	*I Know a Bank* (Martin Shaw); *Sealed Orders* (Willeby); *Now Sleeps the Crimson Petal* (Quilter); *Phillida* (Fisher).
Trio	*Si mes vers avaient des ailes* (Hahn); *Dear Love, My Love* (Friml); *La Paloma* (Yradier); *Until* (Sanderson).
Leonard Gower	*An Eriskay Love Lilt* (Kennedy-Fraser); *Doloroso* (Phillips); *Fifinella* (Oliver).
Trio	*Elegy* (Massenet); *First Flowers in the Garden* (Heykens); *Imitations des petits tambours* (Poliakin).

Still another light music ensemble was to be formed in 1938, this time purely for broadcasting and at the invitation of the BBC itself. It was formed to play light music, including movements from popular classical quartets. Named the Welbeck Light String Quartet (after a street near the BBC) it comprised Alfredo (leader), Maurice Linden (second violin), Rae Jenkins (viola), and on different occasions Cedric Sharpe or Douglas Cameron (cello). It gave its first broadcast on 1 January 1938, playing *Kentucky* (Moore), *Tambours* (Gossec, arr. Sharpe), *Träumerei* (Schumann, arr. Douglas), *Bosnian Legend* (Komzak) and *Perpetuo Mobile* (Ries). Only four more broadcasts were to be heard because of the intervention of the war.

The name of Alfredo Campoli was now so well-known over the air that one might have imagined that he was a member of the BBC itself. And there were also countless broadcasts that he took part in when his name was never mentioned, as when he was leading violinist in the Serge Krish Septet, Fred Hartley's Novelty Quartet or Leslie Bridgewater's Quintet – although, such was the well-known lustre of his tone that the veil of anonymity could be pierced by the discerning listener.[19] The oboist Evelyn Rothwell (later Lady Barbirolli) regularly broadcast with Alfredo in a small ensemble run by the pianist Reginald King during the mid-1930s and recalls the very high standard of performance reached by this group.[20] Then there were the orchestras he anonymously led for films and recordings, including, on one occasion all of those for Richard Tauber, a performer with whom he had much in common, the tenor moving between opera and operetta as easily as Alfredo moved between palm-court and concert stage. It was Alfredo who led the orchestra in the Flesch/Szigeti recording of Bach's Double Concerto. In later years he recalled how during some periods he was at HMV studios almost every day.

His Salon Orchestra was featured in a film series 'Famous Light Orchestras' (Inspirational Film Production), while he himself also took part in two commercial films. The first of these was a Fox British production called *His Majesty and Company* in which he had an extensive speaking and playing part. A still from it shows an orchestra placed on an elegantly sweeping staircase conducted by Alfredo in period-costume! The other, appearing during the war years, was called *Dreaming*, and despite its name, was a far more down-to-earth film, a slap-stick comedy. Its publicity reads

> You certainly get plenty for your money in the musical comedy farce which deals with what happens when Budd Flanigan gets a direct hit on the head from a heavily-laden bag. Apart from the drolleries of Messrs Flanigan and Allen you hear Teddy Brown, Reginald Foort and Alfredo

[19] One such discerning listener was the violinist and teacher Doris Faulkner of Swadlincote near Derby, who could always detect the presence of Campoli in BBC broadcasts during the 1930s and early part of the war (personal interview).

[20] Personal communication with the author.

> Campoli [playing part of the last movement of the Mendelssohn Violin Concerto] and you get a glimpse of Ascot and the African jungle.

The years 1936–38 were also busy for Alfredo as a concert artist. He was heard over the BBC playing concertos by Richard Strauss, Saint-Saëns, Max Bruch, Rimsky-Korsakoff's *Fantasia on Russian Melodies*, and Vieuxtemps's *Ballade and Polonaise*. The performance on 22 July 1936 of the Max Bruch Concerto No. 1 (from Bournemouth) gained a glowing review from the critic of *Musical Opinion*, who contrasted it with the many insensitive performances suffered by that work. From Bournemouth also came a broadcast of his performance of Lalo's *Symphonie Espagnole*. During this period he gave solo recitals for the BBC and two large-scale solo recitals at Wigmore Hall, which included sonatas by Beethoven, Brahms and Dohnányi. The crowning moment of this period was, however, his appearance at the Proms under Sir Henry Wood on Saturday, 20 August 1937.

By now it was ten years since the BBC had rescued the Proms from collapse following the death of Robert Newman, manager of the Queen's Hall who, with Henry Wood, had established this famous series in 1895. It was the forty-third season that saw Alfredo's appearance in Kreisler's arrangement of the first movement of Paganini's Violin Concerto No. 1. The original had been given its first performance in Naples in 1819 when the thirty-seven-year-old violinist was making his first major tours throughout Italy, creating the start of a legend attributing supernatural powers to his playing. Yet, while this concerto provided ample opportunities for Paganini's extraordinary virtuosity, it is also nevertheless a well-constructed piece, for he had been quite rigorously trained in his youth as a composer. To ensure that the soloist stood out against the orchestra Paganini required the solo violin to be tuned half a tone higher than normal, the extra tension on the strings producing a more penetrating sound. Thus, although the soloist's part was written and fingered in D major, like the orchestra, it sounded in the higher key of E flat major. The concerto became very popular and, in one form or another, has been published in almost forty different editions, the most recent in 1993. The later editions dispensed with Paganini's higher tuning of the solo part, and with the orchestral part transposed down, the key of the work is now regarded as D major.

Alfredo had already performed the concerto with piano accompaniment at the third of his début recitals in 1923, but it is not clear which arrangement he used. It could have been that by Emile Sauret (with whom, it will be recalled, he had had a lesson or two), whose edition came out in 1919. Or it could have been the better-known arrangement by August Wilhelmj, which had appeared in both orchestral score and piano accompaniment versions in the last years of the nineteenth century. Wilhelmj arranged the first movement only. Kreisler's arrangement, also only of the first movement, had been published in New York just a year before Alfredo gave its performance in London. He had arranged it while on board ship bound for the USA in 1934, playing it for the first time in St Louis where the critics declared it to be a distinct improvement on the original.[21]

Both Wilhelmj and Kreisler took liberties with the original that nowadays would be considered outrageous. Although the violin part was kept largely intact, their changes to Paganini's original included excisions, additions and modifications on a large scale. Their orchestral introductions – a third of the length of the original – bear little resemblance to Paganini's, Wilhelmj's being entirely his own work (except for the occasional appearance of the original opening figure), Kreisler's at least musing on Paganini's second lyrical theme for a time before launching into his own invention. Some of the orchestral interludes in both arrangements are completely rewritten and out of character with the original; in fact, it would be fairer to describe them as compositions 'based on' Paganini. Yet in performance Kreisler's version, despite the presence of material alien to Paganini's style, does not sound strikingly inconsistent because his re-orchestration is so rich that it casts a romantic sheen over everything. One of the biggest changes was the addition of a harp, which features, not only as an orchestral instrument, but also by itself as an accompaniment to the soloist. Yet it is not so much the changes to Paganini's instrumentation that make the difference in sound as the way he uses the instruments: doubling parts, adding orchestral counter-melodies and often transforming Paganini's simple strumming accompaniments to more rhythmically subtle ones. In a word, the classical clarity of Paganini's orchestration gives way to a late nineteenth-century overlay. Ironically, when Alfredo played Kreisler's arrangement in its piano accompaniment version (as he often did) he usually asked the pianist to leave out as many notes as possible from the now complex keyboard part, and, in a sense, return to Paganini's lighter, cleaner texture.[22] (Alfredo's preference for the Kreisler arrangement meant, unfortunately, that he did not play the two very attractive remaining movements of the concerto, both of which would have suited him admirably.)

Like the St Louis critics, Alfredo much preferred Kreisler's arrangement to the original, particularly because of its colourful orchestration. But, after all, this was in the tradition of those kinds of arrangements that he had grown up with and which were played by most of the great concert violinists of the day, particularly those of the generation before his. And there is no doubt that Kreisler's arrangement, strongly underlining the concerto's lyrical moments, is beautiful in its own way. Moreover, Alfredo felt closely identified with the arrangement, as his seems to have been the first performance of it in Britain. He was to make two recordings of it: with Victor Olof and the National Symphony Orchestra in 1947 and with Piero Gamba and the London Symphony Orchestra in 1957 – both for

---

21 Louis P. Lochner, *Fritz Kreisler* (London, 1951), p. 282.

22 Recalled by the New Zealand pianist Maurice Till who accompanied Campoli in this work a number of times in New Zealand and Australia.

Decca. On his tour of Russia in 1956 he chose to play it in recital, accompanied by Gerald Moore.

At his début in 1923 Alfredo can scarcely have imagined into what varied paths his career would lead him in the following decade. Not only had he become a well-known and sought-after violinist in his own right, giving recitals and performing concertos as well as playing in theatres and restaurants, he was also busy engaging arrangers and players (sometimes up to fifty or more musicians a week) for his many live, broadcast and recorded performances of light music. For his recordings at that time no royalties came to him; he was given a fee from which he also paid his players and arrangers. With so many engagements for which to find good players Alfredo had now become his own 'fixer'.

In the midst of this busy and demanding life he also threw himself into activities outside music. His prowess at billiards has already been mentioned. Towards the end of the 1920s he had been introduced to a game which remained a passion until, quite literally, the day he died. By all accounts he was an unpromising player until 1932, when he joined the London Duplicate Bridge Club in Berkeley Square and met the famous Sharples twins who took him in hand. His later success as a bridge player owed as much to their tutelage as to his own assiduity. Another game he loved and practised was tennis, and in this, too, he displayed great skill, not merely in social tennis, but also as a competition player. A 'newsworthy' musical celebrity, Alfredo excited much interest from the press when he appeared on the court on 1 April 1936 in the London Lawn Tennis Tournament at Paddington, meeting with much journalistic ribbing, such as his taking up 'another stringed instrument', and so on. His appearance in the same competition two years later sparked off an amusing cartoon in the *News Chronicle* of 30 March 1938, by the well-known cartoonist Mercer. He was also adroit at table tennis and skilled in the challenging game of croquet.

Newsworthy also was his income, estimated by most newspapers to be £2,000 a year, which was twice as much as a principal civil servant at that time.[23] He was thus not only amongst the elite of performers making a very good living; he was also in the higher reaches of professional income generally. Quite early in the 1930s he bought a large Victorian house on the corner of Brodrick Road and St James Drive near Wandsworth Common, enabling the family to move out of busy, noisy Balham High Road into a much quieter and more attractive area. A few years later they moved to the northern suburb of Golders Green in the leafy area of Park Drive.

As early as April 1934 one gossip magazine ran an article on the musicians Carroll Gibbons, Harry Roy and Alfredo Campoli, reminding its female readers that these three radio celebrities were still unmarried. Alfredo was a strikingly handsome twenty-seven-year-old. A sensitive face, distinctly Italian, and set off by dreaming dark eyes, radiated the artist within; but there was also his zest for

[23] Erhlich, 1985, p. 207.

living, his boundless enthusiasm for the things he loved: music, motoring, sports and recreations, good Italian food and the pleasure of friends. He was 'untemperamental', his brilliant and reliable technique (at which he worked unceasingly) giving him no cause for nervousness. Those who worked with him over the years invariably spoke of his essentially genial nature, with only the occasional outbursts. Indeed, at his very début critics noted his 'boyish, fresh and unaffected personality', which was to mature into an artist who endeared himself to orchestras and audiences alike. Evelyn Rothwell (Lady Barbirolli) remembers how extraordinarily helpful he was to younger and less experienced players – as she was then – and how generous he was in his opinion of others. Those ten years in light music were to build up a sense of camaraderie between Alfredo and his fellow-musicians that passed over into his later career, not least amongst them some who, having themselves worked in light music, were to conduct his concertos when they also moved exclusively into the concert world. Despite his attractive looks and personality, Alfredo's heavy professional commitments and sense of filial duty seemed to hold romance at bay – until 1937, when Leslie Bridgewater of the BBC's Light Music unit asked his secretary Joy Burbridge to take some music down to a theatre in Shaftesbury Lane where Alfredo was playing.

Joy was born in York on 17 September 1912, to Ella and David Burbridge. Her brother Stanley was born two years later. At the outbreak of war in 1914 her father, a mechanical engineer by training, enlisted in the Royal Army Service Corps and was eventually posted to Tanganyika, then part of German East Africa. In 1916 word came from the War Office that he had died on active service and was buried in Dar es Salaam, which the British troops had captured. He was thirty. With nothing to keep her in York, the young widow took herself and her two children to the market town of Thame near Oxford, where her mother lived. The town was to play a significant part in the lives of both Joy and Alfredo.

Joy's grandfather had lived and worked there, starting a bicycle shop and then moving on to motor cycles and cars. His life came to a tragic end when he was killed in a road accident at the age of forty-nine. Thame remained his widow's home, as it was to be for his widowed daughter, Ella, for whom a further tragedy was waiting. Within a few weeks of arriving in Thame Stanley caught double pneumonia and died at the age of two. At a time when there was little financial assistance for war widows it was imperative that Joy's mother find full-time employment, which she did in Barclay's Bank in Oxford. But the relatively easy solution to that problem led to another.

Ella's widowed mother already had her own family to look after, so with Ella working all day in Oxford Joy was first enrolled as a day student at a school in Oxford at the age of four. Two years later she became a boarder at Thame Girls' Grammar School, where as one of the youngest boarding pupils there, she was allowed a special concession. If she behaved herself she could be collected once a month on a Sunday afternoon to spend a few hours with the family before being returned after tea-time for church. Her mother had to check a week beforehand to see if Joy would allowed to enjoy this special favour. Poor behaviour meant not merely a postponement of the Sunday outing, but a cancellation for that month.

At fifteen she had completed her schooling, but was too young to begin training in what was her chosen career: secretarial work. Her mother decided that a year in France would fill the gap between leaving school and entering a secretarial college. Having heard of a 'finishing school' near Fontainebleau outside Paris, Joy's mother enrolled her there and the two of them set out for France. It was no small shock for Joy's staunchly Methodist mother when the door of the establishment was opened by a catholic nun. But the fees had been paid and there was nothing for it but to accept the situation gracefully. Her mother's fears that her daughter might be converted to the Roman faith were nothing to what she might have felt if she had known that every Saturday afternoon the girls were taken into Paris by nuns who then left them by themselves at a Thé Dansant which they were free to enjoy if they so wanted. While in France Joy also had piano lessons at the Paris Conservatoire, although she never regarded herself as a true musician.

On her return to England she began her secretarial training at a college in Piccadilly, gaining her first job with the Association of British Chemical Manufacturers. It was dull work. One day her eyes fell on a newspaper article describing the construction of the new BBC building in Portland Place; Joy decided to apply for a post with the Corporation, and after an interview she was accepted as a secretary. The BBC had not yet moved to Broadcasting House and she found herself at Savoy Hill with studios and equipment a far cry from those described in the newspaper article. But the move soon came and as the staff assembled in the concert hall of the building they were welcomed by the Director-General. His speech was recorded and it fell to Joy to transcribe it for publication in the staff magazine. Studio recording (as distinct from gramophone recording) was still in a primitive state. Going back to the almost deserted Savoy Hill, she sat down in front of the weird-looking machine called a 'Blattnerphone' imploring the engineers to keep replaying the recording while she attempted to take down Reith's speech, its Latin quotations made more impenetrable by his thick Scottish accent.

One of her earliest tasks was helping to transform the BBC Record Library, which was then in a chaotic state. No policy having been formulated to acquire or catalogue its recordings, this had been largely left to individual departments and the result was a collection unbalanced in its holdings, often with several copies of the same recording. It was thus decided to begin building up a truly representative library to fit the needs of the BBC, and all gramophone companies were invited to send two copies of their available recordings, one to be kept in pristine condition for broadcasting. This catalogue system that Joy worked on was maintained for many years.

As well as her duties in the new Record Library, Joy also worked for Sir Walford Davies in the Schools Department, Sir Reginald Thatcher in Music and, occasionally, Sir Adrian Boult, Director of Music. Part of her time was spent as secretary to Leslie Bridgewater who had been appointed to the BBC Music Department in 1935 in a part-time capacity as a 'technical expert in light music' because of his long experience in theatre, broadcasting, recording and films, and as a conductor and composer.[24] His two ensembles – The Leslie Bridgewater Quintet and The Leslie Bridgewater Harp Quintet – had often been heard over the BBC and for them he was reputed to have made 1,000 arrangements.[25] He was thus a valuable member of the BBC Music Department where he remained until 1942 when he became musical adviser for the Shakespeare Memorial Theatre at Stratford-on-Avon. Although the majority of his pieces were lightweight, just before he left the BBC he also wrote a piano concerto that was given a broadcast, and a string quartet in the twelve-tone system which was not. One of his pieces, *Caprice-Alla Toccata* for violin and piano, was played by Alfredo at a Wigmore Hall recital on 2 October 1937.

Bridgewater's work outside the BBC was as musical director for the huge theatre empire of H.M. Tennent. Operating from the Haymarket Theatre he arranged or composed much of the music played by theatre orchestras at the beginning of the show or during interval, engaging the necessary musicians for any theatre presenting a Tennent production. The company paid well for the best musicians and Alfredo was one whom he often invited, on the understanding that if more important engagements came up Alfredo could install a deputy in his place. Thus it was that Leslie Bridgewater rang up the BBC to ask Joy to bring some music around to the theatre between the matinee and evening sessions. It was a hot day and the musicians, having just come out of the performance, were standing on the pavement outside the theatre. Bridgewater introduced her to them. For Joy it was the interest in seeing the man whose name she had typed out so many times in radio programmes; for Alfredo it was the unmistakable stirring of love.

---

[24] *The Times*, 1 January 1935.

[25] Reported in the *Manchester Guardian*, 1 November 1935.

Chapter 3

The War: Conflicts and Crises

The day following their encounter in Shaftesbury Avenue, Joy received a dinner invitation from Alfredo. It was promptly turned down, Joy imagining that, looking so mature, he was undoubtedly married. He was, in fact, only thirty-three and a devoted son to his parents. When this misunderstanding was eventually cleared up, the invitation was accepted – but not so the gold watch inscribed with her name, which Alfredo produced at the dinner-table. Joy was not so easily won. It was not until eighteen months later that their engagement was announced.

It was now wartime and Joy, still working for the BBC, had been evacuated to Evesham where the administration of the Light Music unit was now located. She had very little time off, and following her engagement found it so difficult to divide what little she had between Alfredo in London and her mother in Thame, that she applied to resign from the Corporation. This was not a simple matter in wartime, for, like all those who were working in organisations of 'national importance' there were restrictions placed on her. As with others in the BBC, she had been handed an envelope – to be opened only in the event of war – listing her in one of three categories: those required to remain in the organisation; those who had to stay in it for the time being, and those who were dismissed to join the forces or work in other areas of national importance. Joy's was the first category. Fortunately special permission was granted her to change this, and she was able to work in another institution which had been evacuated from Westminster to – of all places – Thame, where she became a secretary in the Lord Chancellor's Department now housed in the Oxfordshire County Court.

In the months leading up to the war the BBC, ever-conscious of its looming responsibilities, saw light music as a way of lifting the morale and spirits of the British people, for, as the Director of Music Sir Adrian Boult admitted, it was listened to by considerably larger audiences than those for serious music.[1] Thus in the middle of 1939 plans for an 'emergency' light orchestra were drawn up: the BBC Salon Orchestra, which for safety's sake would be located away from London. In the list of possible players Alfredo's name was put forward as leader. Had he accepted the position it would have meant, of course, that he would no longer be free-lance, but a full-time employee of the BBC. In the event, he did not join it. The new orchestra, which began rehearsing some months before the war, was envisaged as a 'star' group, comprising some of the finest orchestral players in the country. At the outbreak of war they were sent for a short time to Evesham where the administration of light music was to be located, but soon afterwards both the BBC Salon Orchestra and the BBC Symphony Orchestra

---

1 *BBC Year Book*, 1941, p. 69.

were sent to Bristol. This move was part of an extensive plan to decentralise the BBC's activities, the corporation having acquired various properties outside London when war seemed likely.

The BBC Salon Orchestra was placed under the direction of Leslie Bridgewater who had at his disposal some of the finest soloists and orchestral players in the country. Its leader was Jean Pougnet who during the previous year had given a memorable performance of Elgar's Violin Concerto at the Proms, and who had been the leader of the London String Players and the London Chamber Orchestra. He was later to be engaged as leader of the BBC Symphony Orchestra. With him was David Wise, violinist of the New London Trio, who had toured America three times with the Brosa Quartet. Another superb violinist was Victor Olof, a member of the London Symphony Orchestra and leader of his own, well-known light music Sextet. One of the most versatile string players was Rae Jenkins who doubled on violin and viola and whose career, like Alfredo's, covered an extraordinary range of combinations and styles. Principal viola was Frederick Riddle from the London Symphony Orchestra and the Glyndebourne Opera Orchestra who had also been a member of a number of string quartets well-known in their day. The cellists were Douglas Cameron and Anthony Pini – concert soloists in their right as well as orchestral and chamber music players of the front rank. To complete the strings were Victor Watson, principal bass of the London Philharmonic Orchestra, while from the Hallé Orchestra came the harpist John Cockerill. With flautist Arthur Gleghorn, clarinettist Reginald Kell and oboist Leon Goossens, the Salon Orchestra was, indeed, the proverbial 'army of generals'. To complete it were two superb pianists, Sidney Crooke and Dennis Gomm, with Phil Green accordion and arranger and Jack Collings who had played drums in both symphonic and dance bands.

It's therefore not at all surprising that when the well-known and highly-respected writer on music, music critic and regular columnist for the *Radio Times* Ralph Hill visited the Salon Orchestra at rehearsal for its first broadcast on 8 September, he was glowing in his admiration for what he heard – to the extent of pointing out that those 'serious' musicians and music-lovers who disdained listening to popular music were missing out on what he found to be 'a revelation in execution'. His comments are worth quoting at some length.

> I listened to string playing that for beautiful tone and vitality of rhythm was the equal of the finest of chamber-music ensembles. When the melody was transferred to the flute with perhaps a counter-melody on the clarinet, one realised the meaning of a perfect technique being the servant of great artistry. Then the oboe took up the tune, and I thought of Casals and Kreisler, for the oboe tone was unique. In the background was a pianist, whose rhythm and execution were worthy of a great concert artist. And finally, a harp and percussion that added colour and dynamics with a deftness and perfect understanding that were technically and artistically

> the equal of anything presented by the rest of the orchestra. But wait! I had nearly forgotten the accordion, whose admirable playing after three months with this orchestra has already inspired several eminent composers of 'serious' music to write for his instrument.[2]

Equally unsurprising was that this refinement of execution was not to all BBC tastes, some wanting a more robust style of light music than the Salon Orchestra was able to provide during those early weeks of the war.[3] There were a number of suggestions made about how to overcome what was seen as a deficiency, including using outside broadcasts so as to make use of the many light music ensembles still operating in London and the regions. Another proposal was to make greater use of the conducting skills and versatility of Walter Goehr.

Born in Berlin of Jewish extraction, Walter Goehr (1903–60) came to Britain as a refugee from Nazi Germany. Although better known in his adopted country as a conductor of the music of Schoenberg (whose student he had once been) and of the more forward-looking British composers such as Britten, Tippett and Seiber, Goehr was also part of the light music scene before and during the war. When conducting light music he often went by the name of G.Walter. Having met Walter Goehr when he was recording music for a programme called 'The Shadow of the Swastika', Horace Dann suggested to the Music Department that Goehr's Orchestre Raymonde and a group called The Bohemians be revived under Goehr's direction, and even that he replace Leslie Bridgewater as conductor of the Salon Orchestra.[4] This last suggestion, however, was turned down.[5] The Orchestre Raymonde was a larger group than the BBC Salon Orchestra but, as Dann pointed out, if the Salon Orchestra could be enlarged to include second clarinet, first and second trumpet, trombone and drums, then they could share the same repertoire. Permission was given to engage the Orchestre Raymonde in the London studios from time to time, but no mention was made of enlarging the Salon Orchestra.[6] In recommending the revival of The Bohemians Dann made out a strong case for the leader to be Alfredo Campoli 'on account of his inimitable style'.[7]

On the gloriously sunny Sunday when war was declared on 3 September, readers of the *Radio Times*, already distributed for that period, saw that the forthcoming programmes included a broadcast by Alfredo Campoli and his Salon Orchestra. They did, in fact, hear his Salon Orchestra, but not live. Like all broadcasts of music in those first few days of the war, live performances were

---

[2] *Radio Times*, 15 December 1939, p. 8.

[3] DDP (Deputy-Director of Programmes) to DDM (Deputy-Director of Music), 30 September 1939.

[4] H. Dann to ADM (Assistant Director of Music) at Bristol, 10 November 1939.

[5] ADM to H. Dann, 23 November 1939.

[6] ADM to H. Dann, 23 November 1939.

[7] H. Dann to ADM, 10 November, 1939.

cancelled as various players, following instructions issued by the BBC, were now making their way out of London to their new locations and gramophone recordings were substituted. These included Decca's release of his Paganini's *Moto perpetuo*, Francoeur's *Sicilienne* and *Rigaudon*, Chaminade's *Spanish Serenade* and Moskowski's *Guitarre*, as well as recordings of his Salon Orchestra

As well as decentralising its musical (and other) activities, the BBC also re-organised its transmissions. The various regional transmissions which had been slowly evolving during the 1930s had, in the interests of security, to give way to one 'national' transmission: the Home Service. (As the BBC explained to its listeners, wireless transmissions could, in certain conditions, afford direct guidance to enemy aircraft in steering their way to a target.[8]) As well, there were two other transmissions. The first of these was the Empire Service (later known as the Overseas Service), which had begun transmitting in 1932 and which now achieved new importance. By December 1941 it was broadcasting in forty different foreign languages. Music – both serious and light – figured so largely in its programmes that by the autumn of 1940 a special Overseas Music Department was established under the direction of Kenneth Wright, who was joined in the following year by the composer Arthur Bliss.

At the beginning of 1940 an experimental transmission was also successfully tried out to provide programmes for the British Expeditionary Forces and others serving outside Britain. Called 'For the Forces', it could also be heard by the general listening public. Alfredo gave a solo recital over it three weeks after the transmission was established in February, playing some popular violin works: *Liebesfreud*; *Liebeslied* (Kreisler); *Valse bluette* (Drigo/Auer); *Hora staccato* (Dinicu/Heifetz); *The Bee* (Schubert);[9] *Aloha Oe* (Hawaiian/Kreisler); *Variations on a Theme of Tartini* (Tartini/Kreisler). At first, the Forces Programme was only used to transmit those of the Home Service during the evening, but gradually it began to provide special programmes for armed forces, including some from the Home Service, but not those which the BBC believed to be 'unsuitable for active-service listening'. To help it decide what was 'suitable' for those on active-service, the BBC undertook a survey of what the Forces wanted. The result confirmed the view that light programmes were more acceptable, and it accordingly took steps to offer that special group of listeners plenty of variety entertainment (from both studio and theatre), dance-bands, theatre organ, radio thrillers, community singing, students' songs and all possible kinds of sports programmes.[10]

Such fare was certainly not to the liking of all. Letters from soldiers and others to the *Radio Times* complained that the BBC was pandering too much to the lowbrow, 'serving up enormous helpings of poor quality music played by

---

8 *BBC Yearbook*, 1940, p. 43.

9 The composer of this work, though also called Franz Schubert, was no relation of the famous Franz Schubert.

10 *Radio Times*, 16 February 1940.

blaring, discordant dance-bands, with vocal numbers nasally bleated by incompetent singers'. Another pleaded to have 'one decent concert a week with music by Beethoven, Brahms and Mozart'. Nevertheless, despite these (minority) protests, light music dominated the programmes directed towards the armed forces.

Yet it was not only they who were bombarded with 'entertainment' music. In what was described as a 'typical week of broadcasting in the Home Service' towards the end of 1940, programmes that comprised cinema organ, variety, light music (including military and brass bands) took up just over forty-five hours of the total of 129 listening hours in comparison with just over twenty-seven hours of 'serious' music (including orchestral concerts and recitals).[11] This represents about the same proportions as given in the previous chapter, but added to the programmes for the Forces and for Overseas, light music truly dominated the airwaves. Nevertheless, light music programmes were suffering, as were those featuring serious music, from the difficult and touchy question about whether or not to broadcast works from the German and Italian repertoire.

At the time of the First World War the question of whether German music should be performed in concerts and recitals had been a burning issue. Now, for the first time the BBC was confronted with the same question, but with even wider implications when Italy and other countries entered the war on the side of Germany. Moreover, as a broadcasting organisation the BBC was also faced with having to pay royalties on copyright music to composers of enemy nationality, and the idea of British listeners' money (through licence fees) finding its way to enemy countries was repugnant not only to the BBC, but also to the Incorporated Society of Musicians which had first raised the problem with the Corporation.[12] A 'Black List' (the terminology was the BBC's) was drawn up, which, if implemented, would have almost wiped out the major classical repertoire, and would have had a severe impact on that of light music, too. However, it was decided not to take a narrow view, and that exclusion of music by enemy composers who had attained 'classic' status, whether copyright or not, should only occur if a particular work expressed what was described as the 'German spirit'. Hence, Brahms' *Triumphlied* was excluded. Also banned were Sibelius's *Finlandia* and *'Karelia' Suite*, and, of course, the music of Richard Strauss was a bone of contention. A nice distinction was made between Wagner's *Siegfried* and *Siegfried Idyll*, the latter being permitted. Music by composers of enemy nationality who were still alive met with the strongest opposition from those forging BBC policy. In the light music field, Lehar, for example, was banned from broadcast programmes for some time, despite the fact that Richard Tauber was then touring Britain with that composer's *Land of Smiles*. There was even

11 *BBC Yearbook*, 1940, p 45. One BBC listener admitted to turning to German stations in order to hear suitable music (*Radio Times*, 12 April 1940).

12 The source of information contained in this and following paragraphs is File R27/3/2 (BBC Written Archives).

doubt about whether Kreisler's music should be broadcast, and though it was decided that it could go to air, programme compilers were asked not to feature the composer very prominently.

In July 1940 the BBC decided to exclude all copyright music by composers of enemy nationality with the exception of works that 'were so individual, characteristic, and popular as to be practically irreplaceable in any extensive programme scheme'. After six months the policy was to be reviewed. Having never been publicly stated, there was little reaction in the general press to the policy. But within the music press and the BBC opinion was equally divided, those against it sensing a spirit of illiberality uncharacteristic of the BBC, those for it seeing it as an economic measure. The policy was still in force in March 1941, by which time the BBC Music Department was putting up a case for a more flexible approach. As far as choral music, and works for military and brass bands were concerned, they agreed that programming had not suffered unduly because of the large repertoire of British music for these groups. Badly hit, however, were the orchestral and recital programmes, and light music, for which 'great ingenuity has to be exercised in programme building'. They pointed to the danger of excessive repetition as a result of a more limited repertoire and requested that the ban be relaxed so that transcriptions like Bach-Busoni, Rossini-Respighi, etc could be admitted, and that more latitude be allowed when planning 'special feature' programmes which were severely hampered when enemy copyright sources were not available. All decisions, it was assured, would be made only after the Music Department was satisfied that there were no works by British composers or those from 'friendly' nations to fill the gap. The request was turned down.

It was probably inevitable that in the turmoil of war the policy sometimes missed its target or hit the wrong one. Two Jewish composers, Jurmann and Kaper, who had fled Germany and were now successfully working in Hollywood were on the 'black list' to the detriment of their royalties from Britain, as a letter from their publishers to the BBC complained. The bureaucratic mind was most severely taxed, however, over the case of the Dutch composer Heykens, whose charming pieces had been the staple diet of light music orchestras for many years. One of them, *Musical Box*, was, in fact, dedicated to Alfredo, and it will be recalled that it was Heykens' celebrated *Serenade No. 1* which Alfredo had recorded for Decca at the beginning of the 1930s, selling in such numbers that it helped that company through awkward times. But news was that he had joined the Nazi party and in Holland was a named collaborator. To the outraged ears of Dutch listeners to the BBC his music was still being played – for the simple reason that being Dutch he was not of 'enemy nationality' and thus, according to the BBC's own regulations his music should not be banned. Despite continued complaints from Holland, the ban on his music was not imposed until August 1941, six months after the matter had been first brought to the attention of the BBC.

The light music programmes were hit not only by the restricted repertoire but also by the growing shortage of good performers caused by the military call-up, especially in those restaurant and hotel orchestras and bands that were frequently heard either in the studio or through outside broadcasts. Yet, light music was in greater demand than ever before; Alfredo's services would have been a boon to it, but the events of war had now overtaken him.

Alfredo's position as an Italian national living in Britain was not a pressing problem until Italy entered the conflict. He had been granted exemption from Italian military service back in 1926, applied for, perhaps, as a precaution in case he went back to Italy for some reason and found himself called up, a situation not uncommon in some European countries. The certificate of exemption was endorsed by the Italian Consul-General in London in May 1939. Six months before the outbreak of war with Germany Leslie Bridgewater had warned Alfredo of the dangers of retaining his Italian citizenship, for Mussolini's invasion and conquest of Ethiopia in 1935 had already given a clear signal to the world that the dictators in Italy and Germany might eventually form an alliance. When reaching twenty-one Alfredo had, in fact, expressed a wish to become a British citizen. This was opposed by his parents. So attached temperamentally were they to the country they had chosen to leave that they created a small Italian world around themselves in London. Moreover, Romeo's chronic angina was such that Alfredo hesitated to upset him and so had resisted following up the process of naturalisation. Now, however, it was a matter of urgency. Four sponsors – H. Ashworth-Hope of Somerset, P. Woodhead of Buckingham, and two members of the BBC: Kenneth Wright and Leslie Bridgewater – supported his case. Mr Woodhead, questioned by the police at the beginning of 1940, was given to understand that it would only be a matter of time before the application was processed.[13] In the meantime Alfredo continued much as before. Just after the outbreak of war Alfredo recorded some works for HMV with his Salon Orchestra and his Welbeck Light String Quartet. Only the master copies were made, however, for at that time there was a desperate need to conserve shellac (the principal material for gramophone recordings) for the war effort. (In its 1943 catalogue Decca, indeed, put out an urgent call for old recordings to be sent in for melting down to make new ones.)

Once the BBC moved into its new routine with live music coming from Bristol and other provincial centres as well as from the capital Alfredo's two ensembles were heard once again live over the air from London studios. But time was running out for him, for the Home Office had begun suspending all applications for naturalisation, and on 10 June 1940 Alfredo Campoli, once the personification of English light music, was declared an enemy alien.

Those broadcasts of the Welbeck Light String Quartet, his Salon Orchestra and his Trio, heard in the early months of that year, were to be their last and they

[13] Letter from Campoli to BBC, 28 January 1941 (BBC Written Archives).

were never formed again. Alfredo's last broadcast as a named soloist was on 27 May when, ironically, he took part in a programme commemorating the death of the legendary Italian musician whose concerto Alfredo had championed. In 'Paganini – Virtuoso of the Court', Alfredo played the Kreisler arrangement of the Concerto in D, the unnamed orchestra conducted by Gordon Thorne, the concert preceded by a talk about Paganini by Maurice Brown. After that broadcast the name of Alfredo Campoli was not heard over the BBC for two years.

Unlike many others of similar status in Britain, Alfredo and his family were not deported to the Isle of Man for the duration of the war, or even placed under curfew. Instead, following a fruitless search by the police for fascist literature and other incriminating documents, they were permitted to live at home, but radio, camera and car were confiscated, and each week the family had to report to the local police station – much to the amusement of the officers on duty who knew them well and who were pleased to have regular autographs from their celebrated charge. At first, Alfredo was not permitted to work, but, finding no evidence of fascist sympathies, it was not long before the Campoli family were regarded as 'friendly' enemy aliens and the ruling relaxed. Ironically, permission to perform eventually extended to his giving recitals in high-security areas that no ordinary British citizen would have penetrated. The BBC, however, always sensitive to the possibility of public criticism for engaging an Italian national on its programmes, maintained a ban for much longer.

A month after Italy entered the war the ruthless blitz on London began. Romeo and Elvira, now retired and elderly, looked to the possibility of finding somewhere out of London to avoid the bombing. Romeo seemed particularly frail. Through a BBC contact Alfredo was able to locate a small cottage in Oxfordshire, and the three of them moved to Postcombe near Thame. It also brought Alfredo closer to his fiancée.

As well as playing for factories, aerodromes and military camps, Alfredo was also busy as an orchestral leader for film music, often working with the conductor Louis Levy and the composer Charles Williams (who a few years later was to become very well-known through his *Dream of Olwyn*, featured in the film *While I Live*). Seeking some respite from the bombs, Levy and Williams stayed whenever they could find the time at a little farm near the cottage rented by the Campolis. They had been good friends with Alfredo for some years, and on the evening of 20 October came around to where the Campolis were living to celebrate his thirty-fifth birthday. His father had been most unwell, not only with his chronic angina but with a chest infection, probably caused by the damp coldness of the flagstoned cottage. Elvira had made up a bed on the ground floor so that Romeo would not have to walk upstairs and Joy was staying the night with them. Alfredo left early next morning, joining Louis Levy and Charles Williams for another recording session at the Pinewood film studios on the outskirts of London, and soon afterwards Joy prepared to cycle back to Thame. Asking her to wait a moment while she collected some laundry for Joy to take into town, Elvira crept to where Romeo lay still, only to find that he had died during the night. Ringing the Lord Chancellor's Department to beg leave for the day, Joy made the necessary arrangements, comforting and helping Elvira in the countless problems that now confronted her. Not knowing exactly where Alfredo was working and unable to contact him, Joy waited until his return to Postcombe in the evening to break the news. Elvira eventually decided to leave Postcombe and to return to the home at Golders Green with Alfredo for company. Now away from where Joy was living, this move back to London at least placed him in a more central position for his work. This still did not, however, include engagements with the BBC.

Even after the War Office had relaxed its restrictions on Alfredo there was confusion in the BBC as to whether he should be permitted to be perform for it. As late as February 1941 in a long memo dealing with the possible expansion of the light music pool, especially in view of the steadily increasing demands of the Overseas programmes, the name of Alfredo Campoli was still coming up as 'the ideal leader of café groups' to be formed from it.[14] One man anxious to retain Alfredo's services was the pianist and arranger Fred Hartley who, because of the ever-growing needs of the Overseas transmissions (including to Europe), had been appointed to the new post of Artistic Adviser to Light Music. Later, he was appointed Supervisor to it, bringing to that position a wealth of experience.

Unlike many of the extraordinarily gifted performers who worked for the BBC before and during the war, light music was Fred Hartley's chosen field. Born in Dundee in 1905, he studied both violin and piano as a child, coming to London at the age of sixteen to study at the Royal Academy of Music where he made a reputation as a fine accompanist, and also as a soloist, playing concertos by Schumann, Grieg and Tchaikovsky under Sir Alexander Mackenzie and Sir Henry Wood. As a student he sought as much musical experience as he could find. It included playing in the Cirkus Theatre in Stockholm, accompanying singers on stage and playing in popular bands. His studies completed, he returned to Dundee for three years as an accompanist in the Dundee Radio Station before returning to London where his career flourished as a light musician, particularly through his frequent broadcasts over the BBC from 1924 onwards with his various ensembles such as his Novelty Quintet and his Sextet. The latter was described by Kenneth Wright in the BBC as representing 'the high water mark of that type of light music'.[15] Both a brilliant arranger and a gifted composer of light music his best-known song was his signature-tune 'Life is Nothing Without Music', while one of the gems of light music was undoubtedly his 'Twentieth Century Nocturne' recorded for Decca by Alfredo's Welbeck Light String Quartet in 1940 but never issued.

---

[14] This memo, dated 13 February 1941 is almost illegible in parts, including the names of the writer and recipients.

[15] Wright's remarks were quoted in a letter from Bernard Heinze to Charles Moses, 28 January 1939 (Australian Broadcasting Corporation Archives).

Hartley was possessed of a roving spirit. Even at the height of his success in the 1930s he was sounding out possibilities of working in Australia, approaching the Melbourne conductor Bernard Heinze, who was in London in 1938 to see if a position could be found for him in the Australian Broadcasting Commission, either to train an Australian ensemble or to bring out one of his own.[16] It was a proposal that interested the ABC, for they had, in fact, approached Leslie Bridgewater somewhat earlier with the same idea in mind[17] – unsuccessfully, it would seem. The intervention of the war, however, delayed any move to bring Hartley to Australia until the beginning of 1945 when he was offered a six-month engagement by the ABC to prepare a report on the state of its light music throughout the country as well as to form an ensemble to give regular broadcasts.[18] It was the beginning of a long association between Fred Hartley and the Australian Broadcasting Commission during which he visited Australia for a number of years, usually for six months at a time.

Fred Hartley and Alfredo had performed together many times before the war. Now in his new wartime administrative position at the BBC Hartley was anxious to engage him to lead yet another salon-type orchestra, but also leaving Alfredo the freedom to accept outside engagements. Included in the list of suggested performers for this ten-piece orchestra was Hugo Rignold playing second violin to Alfredo.[19] The reaction from BBC officialdom was predictably cool, pointing out that even if no other difficulty existed there would be 'considerable criticism of the Corporation's action in appointing an Italian subject', and suggesting that any action could only be considered after Alfredo became naturalised.[20] Even in the case of British musicians engaged by the BBC for its light music programmes, as well as for its symphony orchestra, there was some doubt at that time as to whether or not they would be called up for military service for, although the BBC had put forward the names of musicians of exceptional ability for deferment, there was as yet no indication of how the War Office would react.[21] The case for Alfredo seemed, at that point, to be hopeless.

By the end of 1940 Bristol had experienced such ferocious bombing as to make the city very dangerous, and the two orchestras were moved away from it: the Symphony Orchestra to Bedford, the Salon Orchestra to Evesham where it

---

16 Letter from Fred Hartley to Bernard Heinze, November 11 1938 (ABC Archives).

17 Mentioned by Hubert Clifford of the BBC in letter to Robert C. McCall (Federal Superintendent of the ABC) who passed it on to the General Manager (Charles Moses) in a memo dated 5 April 1944 when the idea of appointing Hartley was taken up again in 1944 (ABC Archives).

18 Details of the arrangement are in a letter from Robert McCall in a memo to the ABC General Manager, dated 10 January 1945 (ABC Archives).

19 Undated memo entitled Preliminary Note by Fred Hartley (BBC Light Music File 1939–43, R/27/172/1).

20 Memo from F.C., 18 March 1941.

21 Memo from F.C., 18 March 1941.

was re-organised. As before, some of the eighteen players were incorporated into the fourteen-piece Salon Orchestra, playing under the direction of Leslie Bridgewater, who also conducted some smaller ensembles – the Harp Quintet, the Claydon Quintet and the Regency Trio; while a second orchestra, to provide more 'red-blooded light music'[22] than did the Salon Orchestra, was formed from the pool and called the Casino Orchestra. This was under the direction of Rae Jenkins. In addition to the Casino Orchestra, Jenkins also directed smaller 'novelty' groups: the Cuban Caballeros, the Caravan Players, the Boulevard Players and the Casino Players. Reginald Kell, Victor Olof, Sidney Crooke and Tom Jenkins directed small groups with which they had already been associated before the war.

Yet the three-throated appetite for light music – for the Home Service, the Forces and the Overseas Programmes – seemed insatiable, even when to the resources at Evesham were added those of ensembles in London and elsewhere which were regularly engaged by the BBC. And all this was in addition to gramophone records played over the air, although these formed a relatively small part of the overall programming at that time because of a previous arrangement with the Musicians' Union that attempted to safeguard the livelihood of the profession.[23] It was perhaps inevitable that, with so many hours of broadcasting to fill with light music (especially in the Forces programme), standards were seen to be slipping; so much so that an investigation was called for at the beginning of 1942.

First of all, they asked, what was really meant by the term 'light music'? – a question that exercised the bureaucratic mind for some months. One definition was provided in an undated memo, compiled probably in January that year. It was 'music of a predominantly cheerful, fast-moving, melodious character, suitably presented; familiarity in general an important point; suitable classics not excluded if attractively presented; solos governed by above rules, but not frequent, and chiefly justified as a break for the orchestra in a long programme'.[24]

If the BBC was exercised on this matter, so was the military mind of Whitehall, which saw a role for itself in attempting to dictate policy for the Forces programme. It seems that it did not approve of light music with 'pansy' titles. In an outburst of indignation the Overseas Music Director wrote to the Director of Music Arthur Bliss asking if the BBC must deprive the Forces of Bucalossi's *Grasshopper's Dance* and Billy Mayer's *Marigold* because 'some ignorant Blimp of a Brass Hat thinks the titles "unmanly" and "out of keeping with the offensive

---

22 'Reorganisation of Evesham Light Music Pool', memo from Assistant Director of Music (Bedford) to Assistant Director (Programme), 16 September 1941.

23 An agreement had been struck between the BBC and the Union when broadcasting began that only a limited amount of time (called 'needle time') could be given to recordings played over air.

24 Undated memo [1942] (R/27/172/1, Music General, Light Music File I 1939–43).

spirit of the time"?', concluding that 'Never has the Whitehall attempt to dictate Forces programme policy so betrayed its ignorance and half-wittedness.'[25]

Other restrictions to apply to light music programmes generally, and which Kenneth Wright believed may have come from the BBC's own Director of Programme Policy, included having no 'vigorous music' after 10 pm, and no 'contemplative' music in the morning, to which he retorted: 'why should the person who is busy at work and in the garden till late evening, then have to listen only to sleepy and romantic music?', and 'what about the evening workers, who don't hear a normal late period?'.

The exasperation felt by BBC musicians at bureaucratic interference, from both within and outside the Corporation, over light music broadcasts stemmed from a report drawn up after three members of the BBC hierarchy had listened to two weeks of light music broadcast over both the Home Service and Forces programmes starting on 5 April. They heard thirty-three different ensembles, some of which appeared more than once during the two weeks. Some of them were the BBC's own ensembles, but most were from outside.[26]

Having made comments on each of these ensembles, the three listeners sitting in judgement, while approving of the best ensembles, were damning in their criticisms of most of them on the grounds of performance, choice of works, inappropriate time-slots and weak presentation. Julian Herbage (Assistant Director of Music) agreed with most of the findings, claiming that 'no musician can doubt . . . that in the main the items represented are ephemeral, effeminate and decadent to a degree'. Although some of the details and recommendations of the Report did not escape criticism, there was general agreement that there were too many light music programmes resulting in a degree of 'amateurism' that

---

25 Overseas Music Director to Director of Music, 26 May 1942.

26 The list is worth reproducing as it sheds further light on the scene once dominated by Alfredo Campoli: Harold Gee and his Orchestra, Jack Collings' London Novelty Players, Falkman and his Apache Band, BBC Midland Light Orchestra (conductor: Richard Crean), Charles Ernesco and his Sextet, Winter Garden Orchestra (director: Tom Jenkins), Entr'acte Players (director: Sidney Crooks), Geiger and his Orchestra (from Claridges' Hotel in London), BBC Revue Orchestra (conductor: Mansell Thomas – this orchestra replacing the scheduled Bangor Orchestra), Reginald Kell and his Sextet, Reg Leopold and his Players, Victor Fleming and his Orchestra, Leslie Bridgewater Quintet, Sabrina Players, Coventry Hippodrome Orchestra, Louis Voss and his Orchestra, Jack Leonardi and his Orchestra, Cedric Sharpe Sextet, Ernest Leggatt and the Continental Players, Caravan Players, Fred Hartley and his Music, Irish Rhythm Orchestra (director: David Curry), Clifford Quintet, Norman Brooks' Berkeley Sextet, BBC Salon Orchestra (conductor: Leslie Bridgewater), Boulevard Players (director: David Wise), The Little Orchestra (director: Jack Hardy), London Gypsy Orchestra (led by Albert Sandler), London Tango Orchestra, Music for the Balalaika, Norfolk Hotel Orchestra (director: Alfred Jupp), Orchestre Raymonde (conductor: George Walter), and Serge Krish Septet. *Report on Light Music Programmes* (BBC Written Archives).

reflected badly on the BBC.[27] Concern was even expressed about the Salon Orchestra.

It was noticeable that on its re-location to Evesham the morale of the players in the BBC Salon Orchestra had dropped. Many players were bored by the constant repetition of the musical arrangements, brilliant as they were, and which were largely the work of several members of the orchestra. But the repertoire was also limited because of the BBC's prohibition of much European light music. Nor was the situation helped by the deteriorating relationship between conductor and players. Leslie Bridgewater, fine and versatile musician that he was, was not in the same class as many of those he was directing, with the result that there was much 'back-chatting' and poor discipline.[28] And – most unsettling of all – was never knowing when the call-up notice would come, for, although the War Office recognised the value of the BBC Salon Orchestra to military and civilian entertainment, it refused to grant it the status of a 'reserved' occupation. Jean Pougnet was just one of many players who received a call-up notice one week only to have it rescinded the next. It was perhaps not surprising that the BBC decided that the problems of maintaining its Salon Orchestra were too great and on 11 July 1942 it was disbanded.

In practical terms this also meant the disappearance of the Casino Orchestra and fifteen ensembles formed from these two larger groups. Yet there were over thirty programme slots each week to fill with light music. The only solution was to use more ensembles from outside the BBC – providing there could be better supervision of them. In drawing up a list of possible ensembles, Horace Dann excluded 'those trios which, since the broadcasting ban on Alfredo Campoli, have survived but never achieved the excellent standard established by this artist, and which depend largely upon the technical facility and personality of players like Campoli and [Albert] Sandler'.[29]

In the middle of 1942 Fred Hartley was appointed BBC Supervisor of Light Music in Leslie Bridgwater's place. He saw his task as making the best use of the available resources and improving studio conditions, choice of works and their presentation. He recognised that success lay in a much closer contact with those responsible for the overall programme planning of BBC broadcasts, for these highly-placed officers usually had no technical knowledge of music. He also began weeding out the weakest ensembles.[30] However, the vexed question of what actually constitutes 'light music' was a continuing debate in the BBC for the

---

27 'Light Music in Home Transmissions', memo from Fred Hartley to Director of Music, 30 April 1942.

28 Memo from George Willoughby (Manager of the BBC Salon Orchestra at Evesham) to DDM, 25 March 1941.

29 Unsigned memo: 'A Report on the present situation with particular reference to the disbanding of the Salon Orchestra', 5 June 1942. A later memo indicates that it was written by Horace Dann.

30 Memo, Fred Hartley to DDM, 6 August 1942.

next twelve months, culminating in an invitation to the popular composer Eric Coates to draw up a Report.

In a style that appealed to the 'man in the street', the music of Eric Coates (1886-1957), like that of Elgar before him, seemed to catch the spirit of the times in works that, for many people, symbolised all that was most lovable in English life. His march 'Knightsbridge' (from the *London Suite*) was, for example, chosen by the BBC as the signature tune for its regular programme 'In Town Tonight', first heard over the air on 18 November 1933. Trained at the Royal Academy of Music studying viola, piano and composition, Coates was a foundation member of Beecham's Symphony Orchestra, and later became principal viola in the Queen's Hall Orchestra, remaining in it until 1919 after which he devoted himself to composition. His orchestral background and experience is vividly reflected in his most popular works. Colourful and attractive, yet anodyne, his was light music for large orchestras, and, not unnaturally, his eighteen-page Report on Light Music viewed the genre from that perspective. To his mind light music was a branch of 'serious' music, not to be tampered with or 'arranged'. It was not a view likely to appeal to the BBC on economic grounds alone. In commenting on it Arthur Bliss, then Director of Music, wrote to the Controller of Programmes, with a copy to Sir Adrian Boult now conducting the BBC Symphony Orchestra at Bedford

> Eric Coates's remarks shows that there is a wide difference between what he considers light music, and what *we* broadcast as light music. To Coates, light music is Johann Strauss, Massenet, Lehar, Delibes, Bizet, Gounod, Edward German, himself, etc., etc., played exactly as written, and broadcast as part of our serious and important contributions to music. He cannot, for instance, understand why this type of music is not included in the Promenade programmes, and his recent letter to me shows that the playing of his Suite 'Three Men' by section B of the Symphony Orchestra, on Saturday June 26th, gave him the greatest satisfaction he has had for years. As a composer, I can quite understand this, but if we make this exceptional broadcast the rule, and play his light music as Coates wants it played, it means as he says in his report, employing two BBC light orchestras each of 45 players, Can we afford two more orchestras of this size?
>
> Coates is thinking of a public very similar to that which listens to more serious music. Hartley, as Light Music Supervisor under programme guidance, is thinking of a very different public, His listens mainly to dance band music, and has to be entertained by light music that might be of a higher quality and more sophisticated than dance music, but which is not very different in its appeal. His programmes are directed at a public that uses the radio as a background to talk or food or other activities, and not at a public which is first and foremost a listening one . . .
>
> Much of the report is of little practical use, owing to the writer's 'idée fixe' about arrangements, Financial considerations make impossible the

> carrying out of his dictum 'music is written by a composer for performance on certain instruments; once written it cannot be altered except by the composer, and to be performed it should be presented *exactly* as written for the correct complement of instruments.'[31]

Coates had also recommended that articles and discussions of a 'simple, intellectually sound and pictorial nature' about pieces of light music should take place but, as Bliss in his response pointed out, surely the object of light music is to entertain and not be theorised about. Seemingly at odds with what he had written about in connection with arrangements, Coates complimented the Midland Light Orchestra, and programmes in Variety and Revue for their special arrangements! In the end, all that was done with the Report was to put it away and, in a typically institutional way, profusely to thank its writer for his helpful comments.

While BBC brows were knit in debate over light music, Alfredo was no longer overly concerned with its outcome. True, by September 1941 the BBC had relaxed its ban on him to the extent of permitting him to play with the London Studio Players (another 'emergency' ensemble formed in 1941) and other groups in an 'anonymous' capacity – no new thing to him as we have seen in the previous chapter – and a nearly a year later he was being featured as a named soloist once again over the air. But it was a new Alfredo Campoli – or more correctly, a re-incarnated Alfredo Campoli – who was to emerge as a concert artist once again.

---

[31] Memo 'Report by Eric Coates on Light Music', Director of Music to Controller of Programmes, 1 July 1943.

Chapter 4

The War: Crises and Resolutions

On a sunny Saturday afternoon, 9 May 1942, Alfredo married Joy Burbridge in the little Roman Catholic church of St Joseph's at Thame. Special dispensation had been sought from the Pope to enable Alfredo to marry a non-Catholic and, of course, the ceremony had to take place in a Catholic Church. In the midst of war it was an 'austerity' wedding. Friends, who in normal times would have flocked to it, were now scattered all over the world and many of those still in the country were prevented by petrol rationing or the call-up from attending it. Telegrams from well-known musicians with whom Alfredo had worked during the brilliant 1930s – Victor Olof, Victor Sylvester, Reginald King, Fred Hartley, Kenneth Wright, Frederick Grinke, to name just a few – had to make up for their personal absence. Alfredo's best man was a surgeon friend, Dr Basil Kiernander, but because of the difficulties of the times there were no bridesmaids for Joy. She was given away by an uncle.

Although Joy's mother never uttered a word of reproach or disappointment at seeing her daughter, brought up in a strict Methodist family, marry in a Catholic church it must have been painful for her. Even more so when, at the stroke of the priest's pen on the marriage-certificate, by law Joy took on the nationality of her husband, automatically losing her English citizenship and becoming an 'enemy alien'. (She immediately signed an application to become a British citizen again, but unlike Alfredo's request at the beginning of the war, hers was granted a few months later.) It was, indeed, a momentous day for her.

Following her marriage Joy gave up work to devote herself to Alfredo's career as secretary (and sometimes as agent), learning how to play bridge and how to manage as cook and housewife. There must have been many who wondered how this marriage would fare, the two were so different from each other – one wholly Italian in outlook, the other quintessentially English. Moreover, immediately following the short honeymoon they would be sharing the house at Golders Green with Alfredo's mother until her illness made this impossible. Yet, perhaps it was their complementary natures that provided the basis of the affectionate relationship that lasted almost fifty years. And, of course, with her secretarial experience and her ability to handle Alfredo's concert schedules and travel arrangements, Joy brought to their partnership much of the professionalism of a concert agent. He, indeed, owed much to her.

Two months after his marriage, Alfredo was 'on air' again as a named soloist. His first broadcast was the premiere performance in Britain of the *American Concerto*, jointly by the violinist Michel Guiskoff and pianist Benjamin Machen. Reputed to be the violinist's answer to Gershwin's *Rhapsody in Blue*, it is a work that has disappeared, like its composers, into musical oblivion. No doubt Alfredo was grateful enough to be a BBC soloist again not to question the worth of the concerto, which he played with the BBC Theatre Orchestra under Stanford Robinson. It was heard first on the Home Service on the evening of 21 July 1942 and again the next month in the Forces programme. His third and last broadcast for the year was from Torquay on 19 November when he played Rimsky-Korsakoff's *Concert Fantasy on Russian Themes* with the Torquay Municipal Orchestra under Ernest Goss, a work which he had played five years earlier with the BBC Symphony Orchestra under Boyd Neel. Broadcasts were, however, to form only part of Alfredo's return to the role of soloist during the war. Like many other artists he was involved with concert-giving through two of the most important wartime cultural and entertainment organisations: CEMA and ENSA.

At the outbreak of war several groups of people had seen the potential of employing arts and entertainment to raise morale amongst civilians and the armed forces, as well as providing an opportunity for artists to contribute to the war effort through the exercise of their professional skills. To a certain extent this had been the case in the First World War, but entertainment for the troops then had been left largely to enthusiastic, if unco-ordinated, work on the part of individuals and to local effort. Now, however, some concerned public figures envisaged the role of arts and entertainment on a much larger scale and organised in a planned and well-administered way.

A few days after the declaration of war a group of people under the chairmanship of Giles Playfair met informally to discuss this matter and instructed the Honorary Secretary of this self-styled Arts and Entertainment Emergency Council, Mr Thomas Gray, to send a letter to Lord De La Warr, President of the Board of Education, setting out the organisation's aims. These were to preserve and foster all manner of British culture at home; to provide the civilian population with entertainment, cultural education and artistic information, and to institute a wide scheme of National Service in which members of the art and entertainment professions could take their part.[1] An Inaugural Meeting of interested people later took place in the National Gallery at 3.00 pm on 11 December when the speakers included, amongst others, Sir Kenneth Clark.

However, it was a different group of people invited a week later by Lord De La Warr to the Board of Education. These eleven people included Lord Macmillan (then Minister of Information) and the noted musician and broadcaster Sir Walford Davies, as well as Sir Kenneth Clark. It was at this meeting on 18 December 1939 that the idea of the Council for the Encouragement of Music and the Arts (later to be known as CEMA) was born. With remarkable prescience, the President of the Board hoped that, while CEMA's immediate role was to provide morale for people during the war, the organisation might be of more lasting

---

1 Letter from Thomas Gray to The Rt Hon. The Earl De La Warr, 9 November 1939 (Public Records File EL 2/4).

importance than being merely a wartime emergency measure.[2] His hopes were amply fulfilled, for after the war CEMA became the Arts Council of Great Britain.

Its advantage over the Arts and Entertainments Emergency Council, with which, until the early demise of that organisation, it was in competition, lay in its funding. Lord Macmillan was at that time Chairman of the Pilgrim Trust which he believed would be prepared to give £25,000 if a suitable scheme were put to it.

The Pilgrim Trust had been set up in 1930 by the American philanthropist Edward Stephen Harkness (1874–1940), who had inherited enormous wealth from his father, one of the six original shareholders of Standard Oil and a partner of John D. Rockefeller, Sr. The Trust was inspired by Stephen Harkness's admiration for Britain during the 1914–18 war and 'by his ties of affection for the land from which he drew his descent'.[3] CEMA's was, in fact, not the only wartime emergency appeal to have benefited from the Pilgrim Trust. Just before the outbreak of war it responded to an appeal from the Ministry of Labour and National Service to provide funds to employ artists to make water-colours of places and buildings of national importance that might be destroyed by enemy action – as well as by 'the sinister hand of improvers and developers'.[4] The London Philharmonic Orchestra had also just benefited from a grant of £1,000 from the Trust, an amount which, combined with funds from a public appeal, saved the orchestra from bankruptcy.[5] CEMA was, however, by far the larger beneficiary, receiving the requested £25,000, which was matched by the Treasury a few months later.[6]

With its financial base relatively secure, CEMA launched a programme of cultural events covering music, art and drama of such magnitude that specialist panels headed by full-time Directors were soon needed. The post of Director of Music was filled by the conductor Dr Reginald Jacques (who had hitherto acted

---

[2] File EL 2/4.

[3] Preface to the Annual Reports of the Pilgrim Trust.

[4] Introduction (by Lord Macmillan) to the Annual Report of the Pilgrim Trust, 1946. A grant of £6,000 was made to what was to be called 'Recording the Changing Face of Britain', the number of watercolours made by ninety-seven artists reaching a total 1,549 works.

[5] Letter from Thomas Russell, Secretary to the London Philharmonic Orchestra, to *The New Statesman and Nation*, 21 December 1940, pp. 652–3, correcting information in an article by Ivor Brown (see note 16, below).

[6] In 1942 the Pilgrim Trust, having contributed a total of £50,000, withdrew from CEMA, the Treasury by then having taken over most of the funding. In the financial year 1943–44 the Treasury grant reached £115,000 (CEMA Annual Report 1944). Although CEMA had at the beginning also assisted the various national orchestras, that responsibility was soon taken over by the Carnegie Trust which, like the Pilgrim Trust, had been set up by another American philanthropist, the Scottish-born Andrew Carnegie (1835–1919).

as an honorary adviser), and the Panel consisted of Sir Stanley Marchant, pianist Dame Myra Hess, composers Constant Lambert, Arthur Bliss and Dr Thomas Wood, and the Italian-born music critic and composer Ferruccio Bonavia. The three specialist panels were under the general chairmanship of Lord Keynes, who also presided over a Council that included Ralph Vaughan Williams in its membership.

One of its first projects was to arrange for concerts in factories to be given by leading musicians, an idea first conceived by the composer George Dyson early in January 1940 and taken up by Sir Walford Davies who rounded it out and recommended it to the CEMA Music Panel. The first concert took place at midday on 22 February 1940 in a Midlands works canteen. Given by the singer William Pearson, accompanied on the piano by Hugh Fenn, it was a resounding success, and by the end of May twenty-five concerts had been given within a fifty-mile radius of London. The idea of Factory Concerts was as new to workers as it was to performers, and one that was fraught with problems. The concerts usually took place in noisy canteens and to workers who were tired and busy. The programmes, normally half-an-hour in length, were given several times over at different shifts and at any time during the day or night. Audiences might number as many as 7,000. The demand for such concerts grew rapidly, especially once factory managers began to recognise their worth, and by the end of the first year of CEMA's work some 1,500 concerts in factories and other 'emergency' areas had taken place;[7] in the twelve-month period 1942–43 the number reached 4,543.[8] As financial considerations precluded orchestral concerts, the normal concert party consisted of two singers and a pianist, or a singer, instrumentalist and pianist. By 1943 there were on an average ten such groups of 'Music Travellers' per week touring factories in all parts of the country.[9]

Counted amongst its most successful ventures, Factory Concerts were, however, only part of CEMA's overall musical activities. There were air-raid shelter concerts, and the Music Travellers also performed in towns and villages – usually through the local music club, if one existed – boosting local amateur groups, such as choral and orchestral societies, normally offering a guarantee against loss or a subsidy to assist in financing the events, which in the smallest villages might attract only twenty people.[10] In addition to musical events, CEMA, of course, provided theatrical performances and art exhibitions throughout the country.

While CEMA was directing its activities towards the civilian population, another much bigger and more complex organisation, ENSA, was concerned with

---

7 Undated letter from Dr Jones (a Trustee of the Pilgrim Trust) in Public Records File EL 2/4.

8 CEMA Report, 1943, p. 11.

9 CEMA Report, 1943, pp. 25–6.

10 CEMA Report, 1943, p. 11.

entertaining the troops. ENSA (Entertainment National Service Association), the brainchild of stage and film producer Basil Dean, was at first financially supported by and under the control of the Navy, Army and Air Force Institutes (known as NAAFI). Into ENSA were drafted many musicians and other artists who wore uniform and whose job it was to entertain the forces, but it also engaged civilian artists. The different styles of the two organisations, CEMA and ENSA, were reflected in the places of their 'birth', one at the Board of Education, the other at the offices of the Society of West End Managers. ENSA's genesis took place five days after the declaration of war, Basil Dean, without whose bulldozing style little might have been accomplished, becoming its Director.

The position of Public Relations was given to W. McQueen Pope of the Drury Lane Theatre, which, requisitioned by the War Office, became the Headquarters of ENSA. Some idea of both the magnitude of the task confronting ENSA and the talent for organisation of its energetic Director can be gleaned from the fact that, in the space of nine weeks from the beginning of the war, more than 2,000 performances were given to nearly a million service men and women. These included entertainment of all kinds: mobile cinemas, concerts, plays, musicals, revues and variety programmes, community singing and pantomimes for Christmas. In those few weeks entertainment was provided both in England in France.[11] Drury Lane Theatre became the scene of the most intense activity in its long history, every room and space given over to rehearsals of plays, revues and music that would eventually reach camps, military hospitals and factories as well as the ears of the public through broadcasts in association with the BBC. Some of these broadcasts became regular events, such as the 'ENSA Half-Hour' and (for the Overseas Programme) 'London Carries On'.

It was perhaps inevitable that there developed some tension between ENSA and CEMA, and their uneasy relationship was not helped early on by a two-part article in *The New Statesman and Nation* in December 1940. Entitled 'This Entertainment Problem', it was written by a member of the CEMA panel, the drama critic Ivor Brown. Taking a lofty cynical tone, he disparaged the need to 'entertain' the troops with the lightweight offerings of ENSA:

> Other wars have managed to rumble their way to victory without benefit of pierrot-parties. The winning of Waterloo has been attributed to some odd playing fields, but never, I think, to the stage of Drury Lane Theatre. Fighting has always included long, dull vigils. The guardians of the Roman Wall may have eased the weariness of their Northumbrian winters with a home-made song, but a troop of professional comedians was not an inevitable unit of the Roman Expeditionary Force: Wellington sent for foxhounds, not for Mr. Kemble or Mr. Munden to make life tolerable in Spain. But we have altered all that. It is now accepted doctrine (no doubt,

[11] Basil Dean, 'Entertaining the Troops', *The Listener*, 7 December 1939.

justly accepted) that life in modern warfare, whether in shelter, factory, or trench, can only be sustained with liberal doses of music, or more commonly, of music-hall.[12]

Tactless as this may have been, especially from one connected officially with CEMA, the main thrust of the article really was to point out that, as there had been abysmal lack of government support for the arts during peace-time, the state had neither the experience nor the machinery for action during the war. Brown's hope was that the work being done by CEMA (financially supported by the Treasury) in offering cultural activities, rather than 'entertainment', would be maintained by the State after the war.

Remarks such as those quoted above and others threaded through the article were not likely to appeal to the irascible Basil Dean, who, however, replied in a remarkably measured way in a letter to the same periodical a few weeks later. Responding to Brown's suggestions that ENSA had 'butted-in' into the scheme of factory and shelter entertainment initiated by CEMA, he pointed at that, as early as April 1939, he had, on behalf of a group who were working on the idea of ENSA, circulated to the House of Commons and various ministries a pamphlet in which it was stated that ENSA would provide entertainment, not only for the fighting forces, but also for the civilian population concentrated in the munitions areas and in evacuation centres.[13] In the same month that Dean's letter appeared, the short period of co-operation between the two organisations over factory concerts (requested by the Ministry of Labour in June 1940) was discontinued, CEMA reverting to its own scheme, supplying five concert-parties regularly to munitions factories, independently of ENSA.[14]

Heading ENSA's light music entertainment was the bandleader Geraldo. Born Gerald Bright, he had been a student at the Royal Academy of Music, afterwards devoting his energies entirely to light music. For eleven years his band played at London's Savoy Hotel, as well as becoming known to a much wider audience through the BBC. The war years called upon his gifts and his boundless energy as never before. In a short article about him in the *Radio Times* of 27 February 1942, he was said to have completed in that particular week thirteen stage appearances, nine broadcasts, five factory shows and about a thousand miles of travel. The Geraldo Concert Orchestra that he put together for ENSA consisted of his usual dance band together with strings, horns and woodwind from the London Symphony Orchestra, and it featured in many a live show and ENSA broadcast.

However, the overall direction of ENSA's music was in the hands of Walter Legge (1906–79), who since 1927 had been working for HMV before being appointed Beecham's Assistant Artistic Director at Covent Garden. It was

[12] *The New Statesman and Nation*, 7 December 1940, p. 564. The second part of the article appears in the next issue (14 December 1940, p. 619)

[13] Letter to the editor, *The New Statesman and Nation*, 11 January 1941, p. 37.

[14] CEMA Report, 1943, p. 26.

through Legge that music of a more serious kind was also brought to the troops and war-workers, confounding the sceptics who could not imagine that classical music could have any appeal to the ordinary soldier.[15] A Music Advisory Council that included the composers William Walton, Arnold Bax and Constant Lambert and other musical leaders such as Malcolm Sargent was gathered together, and under Legge's leadership and supported by Dean fine music gradually found its way into ENSA programmes.

On 6 November 1942 in the sixth of a series called 'The Stuff We Give the Troops' broadcast in the ENSA Half-Hour (a session regularly heard over the BBC) this new trend was brought to public awareness through a programme designed to 'reflect the more serious side of ENSA's activities'.[16] Although no details of the works are provided in the *Radio Times*, the programme was presented by the singer John McCormack and the violinist Elizabeth Lockhart accompanied by Gerald Moore, and Hedli Anderson accompanied by Benjamin Britten. The following year an ENSA Half-Hour produced by Walter Legge himself, presented singer Joan Hammond in a programme called 'Accent on Opera' (June 30). Later that year was heard the Boyd Neel String Orchestra and the BBC Northern Orchestra. In 1944 ENSA and the BBC jointly presented a 'Music Festival for the Forces' lasting over a fortnight and largely aimed at letting the civilian population know the kind of music that the forces were hearing through ENSA. During that fortnight of concerts were broadcast Elgar's *Enigma Variations* and Second Symphony, Vaughan Williams's *Fantasia on a Theme of Thomas Tallis*, Holst's *The Planets*, Walton's *Scapino Overture*, Ravel's *Daphnis and Chloe*, Debussy's *L'Après-midi d'un faun*, and works by Mussorgsky and Prokofiev, as well as works from those from the major classical repertoire. Walter Legge's description of the enthusiasm with which such concerts were greeted by the forces and war-workers is worth reproducing, as it conveys the tone of that time so clearly. With the allied invasion of Europe the war in Europe had entered it closing stages and morale was high.

> If you could sit among these audiences and talk with them as I have done you would find them freer from prejudice, quicker in their reactions and clearer in their judgements than pre-war concert audiences. They sit and enjoy music as it should be enjoyed – as sound and experience. The rightness of their instinctive perception of greatness puts to shame the majority of practised concert-goers, and their concentration and attention are almost unbearably tense. To watch sixteen hundred sailors and Wrens listening with bated breath to Sibelius's Fifth Symphony – a tough nut for even an experienced listener to crack at first hearing – or four hundred ratings listening rapt to the Philharmonia Quartet playing a programme of Beethoven quartets, or three hundred war-workers in an East End of

[15] Basil Dean, *The Theatre at War* (London, 1956), p. 213.
[16] *Radio Times* programme note.

> London factory canteen spellbound by the Blech Quartet's performances of works by Haydn, Tchaikovsky, Wolf and Schubert – all are experiences which have convinced me beyond doubt that in these five war years we have created in the lives of thousands of people something that is really memorable and worth while – an enjoyment that will remain fresh and vital for the rest of their lives.[17]

Not to be outdone, the following month CEMA provided a description of its audiences for the *Radio Times*.

> . . . There may be twenty evacuees sitting in a remote farmhouse listening to a violinist, whose job it is to travel the countryside making music with and for people. There may be three hundred tired Londoners gathered together in a rest centre for those who have lost their homes by bombing; or a canteen full of factory workers at lunch-time, or perhaps at midnight, listening to a half-hour programme by a trio or a quartet; or a throng of townspeople hearing a string orchestra in a parish church; or a town hall packed for the visit of one of our national symphony orchestras.[18]

Lack of documentation makes it impossible to know how many concerts either for CEMA or ENSA Alfredo actually played. However, a CEMA factory concert involving Alfredo was broadcast on the Home Service on Wednesday, 24 November, 1943, his associate artists being the contralto Doris Cowen, who sang songs by Bridge, Ireland, Gurney and Rachmaninoff, and the pianist and accompanist Dorothy Hogben, who played works by Rachmaninoff and Schubert. Alfredo played Kreisler's *Caprice Viennois* and Bazzini's *La ronde des lutins*. As usual, the location was kept secret, the customary BBC announcement being 'From somewhere in Britain'. A broadcast from the Bedford Corn Exchange (the concert venue for the BBC Symphony Orchestra after it had moved from Bristol) to a 'Forces audience' on 15 October 1944 featured him playing two movements from the Mendelssohn concerto with that orchestra conducted by Adrian Boult. In another concert to a Forces audience, not broadcast, but for which a printed programme has survived, he participated in a 'Celebrity Concert' for members of the British and Allied Forces given in the Sheldonian Theatre at Oxford on 31 August 1944. His fellow artists included the cellist Beatrice Harrison (well-known in her day for championing the cause of Delius's music), accompanied by her sister May. Alfredo played Bach's Chaconne and four works by Paganini. We gain a only tantalising glimpse of him through comments made twenty years later by someone who remembered his courage in playing the Mendelssohn violin concerto during an air-raid.[19] In later

17 Walter Legge, 'Only the Best is Good Enough', *Radio Times*, 18 August 1944.

18 *Radio Times*, 10 September 1944.

19 *Newcastle Evening Chronicle*, 18 May 1962.

years Alfredo recalled a busy life travelling up and down the country for the stipulated fee of 'two guineas and a third-class rail fare',[20] and after the war he received an official certificate thanking him, on behalf of the Army Commander, Southern Command, for his 'invaluable voluntary services rendered during the war years 1939–45 in entertaining all branches of the services in southern England'.

While it is thus not possible to trace Alfredo's (or other artists') complete activities for CEMA and ENSA, he was, however, heard many times over the BBC's Forces programme from April 1943 onwards. The first occasion (7 April) was a broadcast of his recording of Saint-Saëns's *Introduction and Rondo capriccioso*, made with the London Symphony Orchestra, conducted by Walter Goehr and released on Columbia, a recording that was heard a number of times over that transmission, including the 'Request Programme'. When played over the Home Service on 21 February 1944 that particular recording was described in the *Radio Times* as 'the high spot' of the programme. On the evening of the German surrender (7 May 1945) Alfredo had been contracted to appear with the Canadian Band of the Allied Expeditionary Forces in a BBC broadcast, but no details concerning Alfredo's participation – even in the BBC Logbook for that evening – are available. The Forces programme regularly featured bands from the Army, Navy and Air Force, many of them achieving a very high standard. In an interview shortly after taking up his new position as BBC Director of Music in May 1942, Arthur Bliss, in answer to a question about overseas broadcasting, replied that brass bands, regimental bands, choruses and orchestras would be showing what Britain was doing in music, and that the fighting services would be 'treated like princes'.[21]

Outstanding amongst the many bands and orchestras of the fighting services were those of the Royal Air Force. If he had been eligible, Alfredo might well have been drafted into its Symphony Orchestra whose string section included the entire personnel of the Griller, Blech and Hirsch Quartets and the Grinke Trio. Its principal trumpet was Rowland Dyson who had previously been with the London Philharmonic Orchestra; Richard Walthew (clarinet) had been with the Midland Orchestra; Cecil James (bassoon) came from the London Symphony Orchestra, and its principal horn was no less than Dennis Brain. Its pianist was Dennis Matthews. From the time of its formation in 1918, in the closing months of the First World War, the Royal Air Force had prided itself on its music. Its first band came into existence in that year when it was formed by the young Walford Davies, then a major in the new service. At the request of a fellow Welshman, Prime Minister Lloyd George, Walford Davies created the RAF Central Band, of

---

20 A letter dated 20 September 1940 to Ivor Brown of CEMA from Kenneth R. Barnes, General Secretary of ENSA outlines a delicate situation between the two bodies, because CEMA paid their artists more than did ENSA (EL2 2/28 Public Records Office).

21 'Leading Questions put to Arthur Bliss', *Radio Times*, 15 May 1942, p. 5.

which he became Director. In addition to its Symphony Orchestra and Central Band, RAF music during the Second World War (under the general direction of Wing-Commander R.P. O'Donnell, who conducted the orchestra) included the fourteen-piece Royal Air Force Dance Orchestra, which, like its orchestral counterpart, counted amongst its players some from the best pre-war hotel and restaurant orchestras and bands, such as those directed by Ambrose, Eddie Carroll, Lew Stone, Brian Lawrance, Oscar Rabin, Jack Hylton and Jack Harris. Late in 1940 Sir Walford Davies suggested that there could be small dance bands attached to the various RAF stations – not, however, as full-time positions, for the musicians also had to spend time in General Duties. By 1944 there were 109 RAF dance bands playing throughout Britain including the Orkneys, Shetlands and Hebrides, as well as some in East, South and West Africa, Aden, the Azores, Iceland, and Gibraltar. In that year they were playing in the African desert, on the Anzio beach-head and with the troops in Italy.[22] There was even an RAF Male Voice Choir that broadcast over the BBC on 3 November 1944. Such musical activity was not restricted to the Air Force; all the services had similar dance bands in their various regiments.

The part that music played in entertaining, educating and generally lifting the morale of both the forces and the civilians during the war was to have far-reaching effects. Concerts through CEMA, ENSA, the BBC, the National Gallery, through orchestras and individual artists, all created a love of music that long outlived those years. One of the most important developments that enabled musicians like Alfredo to pursue the career of a recitalist after the war in a way that had been impossible before it was the creation of The Arts Council of Great Britain.

During the war, despite the hopes of the founders of CEMA, the post-war future of that organisation was uncertain. However, in the month following the surrender of Germany the Chancellor of the Exchequer announced in the House of Commons that CEMA would function as a permanent organisation under the new name of The Arts Council of Great Britain, receiving its grant-in-aid direct from the Treasury. State aid to the arts on a permanent basis had at last come to Britain. Its Chairman, Lord Keynes, explained that the policy of the Arts Council was still that of CEMA: to encourage the best British national arts, everywhere, and to do it as far as possible by supporting others rather than by setting up state-run enterprises. He added that 'the arts owe no vow of obedience'.[23] Grants, both those ensuring the future growth of established national orchestras, ensembles, opera companies and so on, and those providing support to the hundreds of music clubs and societies throughout Britain wishing to present concerts and recitals in accordance with Council policy, provided a network of opportunities for Alfredo and others to earn as never before a good livelihood as concert artists.

---

22 'R.A.F. Men are Never Music-hungry', *Radio Times*, 30 June 1944, p. 3.

23 *First Annual Report of the Arts Council of Great Britain*, 1945/6.

As it was for countless others – in all walks of life – the war was a watershed for Alfredo. Busy as he was during it, it gave him time and opportunity to reconsider his future, and he resolved to turn his back on light music with its salon ensembles and to follow the more difficult (and less lucrative) path of a concert soloist that had always been so dear to his heart. It was a wise decision in every way for, although he could not have known it at the time, the days of light music of the kind in which he excelled were numbered.

It was not merely that in the grim economic post-war years salon and palm-court orchestras were a luxury that restaurants and hotels could ill afford on the same scale as before the war; tastes were also changing as was society itself.[24] The greater democratisation of British society after the war was accompanied by a surge of new currents in 'popular' music that could not be held back by the once powerful walls of the BBC (which in 1935 had banned some types of popular music[25]), or by educational authorities and other institutions that regarded themselves as the nation's arbiters of good taste. The invasion of American mass culture that accompanied the troops from that country helped open the gates in Britain, bringing with it everything from the racy zest of the new-style American musicals to big bands and to bop. In little more than a decade British popular music itself was to be re-defined in a Liverpool basement. Nothing could be further removed from 'Alfredo Campoli and his Salon Orchestra' than rock-and-roll and the ear-splitting electronics that assisted its birth. Popular music was cultivated in Britain in greater variety than ever before, but the palm-court orchestra, which had sat comfortably in the middle was now on the edge. There was (and still is), of course, a place for rose-tinted nostalgia – filled in those post-war days by music from Mantovani and George Melachrino – but more and more this was giving way to music that reflected the present rather than the past, and which needed the resources of technology to make its full impact. Indeed, the post-war era was to be characterised by music heard through loudspeakers rather than through live performance.

On the other hand, concert life and opera in Britain entered a new and brilliant phase and London became widely recognised as one of the most dynamic musical centres of the world. What was more surprising was the emergence of so many fine British conductors and orchestras, soloists and chamber music players, opera singers and companies – an 'extraordinary reversal of every previous trend' that seems, as Cyril Ehrlich has said, to defy explanation.[26]

---

[24] See Richard Middleton, 'The "Problem' of Popular Music", *The Blackwell History of Music*, Vol. 6, pp. 27–38.

[25] Simon Frith, *Music for Pleasure* (London, 1988), p. 37.

[26] Cyril Ehrlich asks: 'Was it a transmogrification of national temperament, a break in the carapace of phlegm and reticence which had served Blitz survivors and guardians of Empire, but stifled eloquence in the arts? Was it, more simply, the natural justice, at last, to latent talents, providing more cash and better training, with less regard for parental resources and background?' ('The Market Place', *The Blackwell History of Music*, Vol. 6, p. 51).

Whatever the reason, like so many others, Alfredo found in post-war Britain opportunities for a career largely denied him before it. In a sense, Alfredo's new career had already started during the war when from July 1942 the BBC at last permitted Alfredo to appear again on its programmes as a named soloist. Following his decision to resume his career solely as a serious artist, the remaining war years gave him the opportunity to work at his repertoire so that in peace-time he would be fully ready to take up all offers of engagement. From mid-1942 to the end of the war he gave some sixty-three broadcasts spread over the Home Service, the Forces programme and the Overseas Service. Like almost every artist during the war, Alfredo performed a wide repertoire of music, and if some of it veered towards lighter fare (as demanded by BBC programme arrangers), it was now from a 'classical' violinist delighting his audiences with encore-type pieces, rather than a 'light music' violinist playing his stock-in-trade.

In 1945 there was, for example, a series of Richard Tauber programmes in which the famous tenor (with whom Alfredo had been associated before the war) was accompanied by a different instrumental group on each occasion.[27] On at least two of these Alfredo was the guest artist. In the programme on Sunday 5 August the instrumental backing was provided by an orchestra from the Allied Expeditionary Forces (AEF) conducted by Regimental Sergeant George Melachrino (1909–65), whose fifty-piece Melachrino Strings was to become as well known in light music after the war as the Alfredo Campoli Salon Orchestra had been before it. In this programme the orchestra accompanied Tauber in some well-known Italian arias and Ambroise Thomas's *Adieu Mignonne* and Alfredo in Wieniaswki's *Polonaise in D.* (Tauber's performances of some songs by Hugo Wolf were accompanied at the piano by Percy Kahn.) Another singer with whom Alfredo was teamed was Kathleen Ferrier in a programme called 'Violin Music and Songs' (18 April 1944). Alfredo was also featured in various BBC regular features such as The Voice of the Violin, Sunday Rhapsody, Navy Mixture (a programme 'blended to suit the tastes of the Royal Navy') and Melody Time, but there were also programmes of a more serious kind that befitted the new career opening up for him.

These included recitals featuring sonatas by Bach, Tartini, Brahms, Franck and Grieg, mostly played with the pianist John Wills. As a soloist in orchestral concerts he was heard over the BBC in concertos by Saint-Saëns, Bruch, Mendelssohn, Vieuxtemps, Brahms and Tchaikovsky, as well as Lalo's *Symphonie Espagnole*, Saint-Saëns's *Introduction* and Rondo *Capriccio* and Sarasate's *Zigeunerweisen*. His conductors for these performances were Adrian Boult, John Barbirolli, Stanford Robinson, Rae Jenkins, Malcolm Sargent and

[27] In these 'Richard Tauber Half-Hour' programmes, for which 'You are My Heart's Delight' from *Land of Smiles* was the signature-tune, Tauber had to exert great will-power to overcome the violent coughing fits that heralded the lung cancer from which he died three years later (see Diane Napier-Tauber, *Richard Tauber* (London, 1949), pp. 227–8).

Basil Cameron, and they were broadcast from London, Bradford, Liverpool, Sheffield, Hanley, Leeds and Newcastle.

A few weeks before the German surrender Alfredo returned – after twelve years – to the Wigmore Hall to play a recital with Gerald Moore, the programme consisting of Tartini's Sonata in G minor, Bach's unaccompanied Partita in D minor, Franck's Sonata, two Caprices by Paganini and finishing with that composer's *La campanella*.

But it was in the two months leading up to the conclusion of the Second World War on 24 October 1945 that Alfredo's war-time return to the concert-stage reached its climax: two appearances at the Proms in the Royal Albert Hall, playing Lalo's *Symphonie Espagnole* (11 August) and Tchaikovsky's concerto (3 September). Both were conducted by Basil Cameron, and enthusiastically greeted in the review columns of *The Strad*, his performance of the Lalo being described as 'phenomenal'.[28] With the declaration of peace it would seem that his career would take off in full flight. It was, however, to be buffeted by strong winds of prejudice blowing particularly from the BBC, and for the next few years he was faced with a struggle for recognition as a serious concert artist by the very organisation that before the war had helped make the name of Alfredo Campoli one of the best known in the country.

---

28 *The Strad*, September and October issues, 1945.

1 Elvira Celi-Campoli on tour with the Lambardi Opera Company

2 Romeo Campoli

3 Alfredo Campoli as a child in Italy

4 Alfredo Campoli at the time of winning the gold medal in the 'open section' of the London Musical competition aged 13

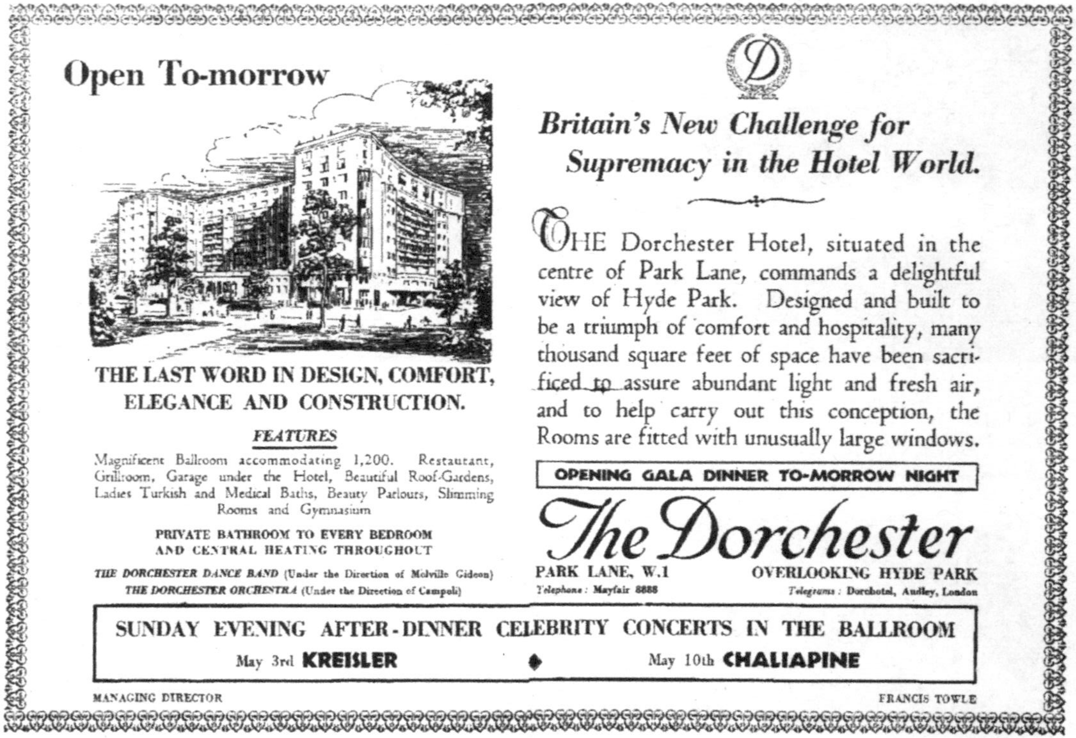

5 Announcement of the opening of The Dorchester Hotel, 1931.
(Courtesy of The Dorchester, Park Lane)

6 Salon orchestra at the Devonshire House Restaurant. Morris Taylor, 2nd violinist, is in front holding the guitar for the sake of the picture

7 The Campoli Trio

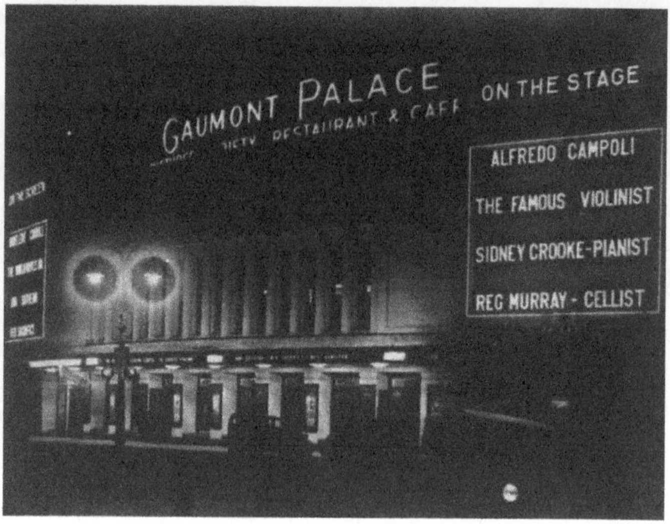

8 Billboard outside the Gaumont Palace, London

9 With the Fred Hartley Sextet

10 Exclusive Decca artist

11 Joy Burbridge and Alfredo Campoli – official engagement photograph

12 Alfredo Campoli, tennis player

13 Alfredo Campoli, broadcasting during the 1930s

14 With Eric Gritton

15 With Daphne Ibbott

16 With Valerie Tryon

17 With Eugène Goossens on Australian tour

18 Recording the Brahms Double Concerto with André Navarra, conducted by John Barbirolli

19 Performing the Bliss violin concerto with the composer conducting during Russian tour

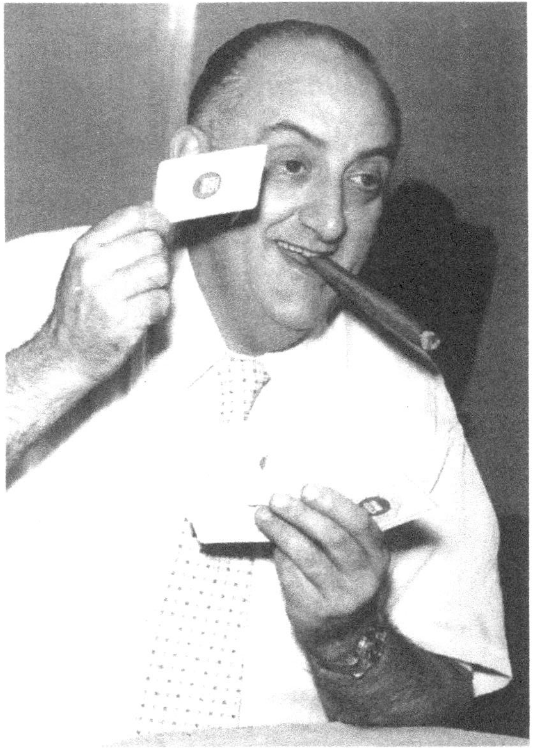

20 A characteristic shot

21 Campoli as musician-in-residence at the University of Western Australia, 1973

22 Campoli at the end of his final appearance. The Huddersfield Senior Youth Orchestra, with conductor Neil Garland, 12 May 1985

23 Campoli before finally laying down his violin, 12 May 1985

Chapter 5

Campoli, Concert Artist 1946–50

Previous chapters have shown that, while for ten years Alfredo's career was largely connected with the light music scene in London, it was by no means exclusively so. During that earlier period he was also heard in concertos by Bruch, Saint-Saëns, Richard Strauss and Paganini (this at the 1937 Proms), as well as in concerto-like works by Lalo, Saint-Saëns and others. Two substantial recitals at the Wigmore Hall were also given by him during his 'light music years'. We cannot trace most of the works he played for ENSA and CEMA during the war, but, as we saw, when the BBC lifted its ban on him in the middle of 1942 his many wartime broadcasts included a substantial cross-section of the classical violin repertoire. Yet to the vast majority of music-lovers the name Alfredo Campoli was for many years still inextricably linked to light music.

Even as late as 1952, by which time Alfredo had returned from an international tour, had performed the Walton Concerto at the Proms (at which he now regularly appeared) and had established himself in the forefront of British violinists, one critic when reviewing his performance of the Elgar Concerto still expressed some surprise at Alfredo's apparent transformation.

> Yes, Campoli is the name. A golden performance of Elgar's Violin Concerto marked the concert at the Royal Festival Hall last night given by the London Symphony Orchestra. And who was the solo violinist? Why, Campoli – yes, the same Alfredo Campoli who before the war specialised in such drawing-room trifles as 'The Teddy Bears' Picnic'. Elgar's masterpiece has technical difficulties which test even a Heifetz. Campoli drove through them to the heart of the music.[1]

When he played in Holland during the winter season of 1947/48 the critics could not conceal their surprise, most Dutch ears having only heard him as a salon orchestra player. His ensembles had performed there before the war, and his many light music recordings had been played frequently over Dutch radio

> In the light music genre the name of Campoli is well-known through many radio broadcasts and records which have spread the popular and light tunes of Alfredo Campoli and his orchestra . . . The people who heard Campoli's recital yesterday evening in the Diligenita (and there were many) now belong to those who know, and they certainly do not regret, this new acquaintance with 'the other Campoli' . . .[2]

---

1 Arthur Jacobs, review in *Daily Express*, 25 February 1952. Arthur Jacobs became a great admirer of Campoli's playing.

2 *Trouw*, 4 October 1947.

Seldom has the transition from popular to classical music been made with such success as by Alfredo Campoli. True, the performances of his light orchestra on the radio and gramophone furnished him with a certain fame, but unless we are very much mistaken, he is becoming a celebrity in Art that is written with a capital A.[3]

Campoli possesses dual fame as violinist . . . He is chiefly known in Holland on account of his gramophone records, where he and his orchestra frequently played pieces of very doubtful worth. His appearance in Amsterdam at the beginning of this season was nothing short of a revelation.[4]

. . . Yesterday Rotterdam had the opportunity of making the acquaintance of another side of this artist, and everyone in the large audience in Boymans Hall will doubtless agree that this pleasant, good-natured Englishman is one of the outstanding figures in the present generation of violinists. It is difficult to know what most to admire: the pure, rich tone, with its many shades, or the fine, masterly style.[5]

One of the critics noted that the name of the violinist was simply billed 'Campoli', without any additional name either on the placard or on the programme. This was part of the 'new look'.

It was one of Alfredo's agents, Harold Holt, who suggested to him that a way of cutting his links with the past would be to be billed (like the pianist Solomon), by his last name only. A letter to this effect was sent from Alfredo to the BBC at the end of September 1946 and, accordingly, all radio announcements from 22 October of that year (when he was to appear with the Theatre Orchestra) carried the new billing.[6] A further break was in pronunciation, the stress coming on the first syllable. '*Cam*poli, like *Na*poli' he used to say, but even some BBC announcers seemed unable to take this last step. The change of name was a wise move, distancing itself as it did from the light music associations and adding a new dignity to his appearances over the radio and on the concert-stage. Yet, fifteen years later he asked to be called Alfredo Campoli once again, retaining only the first-syllable stress of his family name.[7]

The 'new' name was no guarantee, of course, for an easy ride back to a career as a concert artist immediately after the war. There were other impressive violinists of his generation also working in England who were catching the public eye – and that of the BBC. Amongst those who were making their post-war reputations was the Austrian-born Max Rostal (b. 1907), who had studied under

---

3 *Rotterdams Nieuwsblad*, 17 March 1948.
4 *Cost Brabant*, March, 1948.
5 *Het Vrije Volk*, 17 March 1948.
6 Memo to various members of BBC staff, 1 October 1946.
7 Letter from Campoli to BBC, 21 August 1961.

Arnold Rosé in Vienna and Carl Flesch in Berlin and who brought to British audiences for the first time Khatchaturian's Violin Concerto and Bartok's Second Violin Concerto, as well as premiere performances of works dedicated to him. Polish born Ida Haendel (b. 1924) was also a favourite performer in London where she had settled in 1938 after her début there under Sir Henry Wood. Her name was well known during the war through her concerts for the troops and at the National Gallery. In 1952, however, she left England to live in Canada. Yet undoubtedly Campoli's chief rival was Yehudi Menuhin, who after many performances in London as a visiting artist settled there permanently in 1959.

The bright aura that surrounded the thirty-year-old Menuhin's concert appearances in London immediately after the war sprang from many sources. Central to it were, of course, his prodigious musical gifts, which had endearingly revealed themselves to English audiences when, at the age of sixteen, he had played (and recorded) Elgar's Violin Concerto, coached in it and conducted by the composer himself, then aged seventy-five. Now as a young adult Menuhin also offered engaging manners, a mask-like beauty, a command of languages and interest in matters beyond music. To many in England his Russian-American-Jewish background may have also added an exotic touch to an already fascinating personality. Soon to come was his much-publicised interest in Yoga and Indian classical music. And who could forget in those days the hundreds of concerts that he had given to troops in many theatres of war? Against this, what publicity could be hoped for by a forty-year-old portly violinist, who spoke with a London accent and whose real place, in the eyes of musical snobbery, was below stairs in the restaurant. And yet, Alfredo had one advantage over Menuhin: his total reliability as a performer.

Even when Menuhin made his Proms début in the 1946 series playing the very work that had endeared him to English audiences before the war – Elgar's Violin Concerto – his performance drew a devastating criticism from the respected critic Ralph Hill who suggested that if Menuhin wished to retain his reputation he must do something to restore the standard of his playing at once.[8] On the other hand, Alfredo had the uncanny knack of being able to turn out first-rate performances at every appearance.

In the year following the war Alfredo's new career began in earnest. Music-hungry towns and cities were now welcoming visiting artists to their music-clubs and orchestras (soon to be assisted by the Arts Council of Great Britain), and in that year (1946) Alfredo visited fifty places outside London, including in Scotland and Wales. His associates that year included the singers Joan Hammond (with whom he was to enjoy sharing many a future recital), Isobel Baillie, Olive Groves, Dennis Noble, and the veteran pianist Irene Scharrer. It was also at this period that he developed a partnership with the pianist who was to be his main accompanist for the next ten years: Eric Gritton.

---

8 Ralph Hill, *Daily Mail*, 28 August 1946.

Then aged fifty-nine, Eric Gritton was a most experienced and accomplished accompanist who had been engaged by the BBC over many years. Because of the BBC policy of not announcing accompanists' names (which persisted until 1942), it is not possible to trace the many performers with whom he was associated in broadcast recitals. It was through the BBC that he and Alfredo had met, their post-war association as touring artists bringing them together on at least 120 occasions. Following his education at King's College School, Cambridge, where he had been a boy chorister, Gritton studied at the Royal College of Music, gaining the Mendelssohn Scholarship that enabled him to travel abroad. In Rome he studied under the celebrated pianist and teacher Giovanni Sgambati. After six months he moved on to Berlin where he had an introduction to Teresa Carreño, regarded by some as the greatest woman pianist of her day, who inspired him to intensive piano study. After serving in the Army during the First World War, he resumed his career as a pianist, deciding to specialise in accompanying in which capacity he was taken up by the BBC for many engagements. His long association with Alfredo began to taper off in the mid-1950s, the last occasion being 25 February 1957 at Christ Church Hall, Woking, where they performed Tartini's 'Devil's Trill' Sonata, Beethoven's 'Spring' Sonata, and Brahms's Sonata in A, Opus 100.

For the 1946/47 season Alfredo was taken up by the entrepreneur Harold Fielding. Fielding had himself been something of a child wonder as a violinist, and as a youngster had appeared with the singers Tetrazzini and John McCormack, but unlike Alfredo, who suffered no nervousness, Fielding's stage fright was extreme. Although he made an appearance at the Royal Albert Hall during the war he was obviously not cut out for a concert career. He had, however, a flair for organisation, and was engaged as Concert Director for the London Philharmonic Orchestra before setting himself up as an entrepreneur. He opened an office with one assistant and one junior typist, and by 1947 owned the entire building, having created the biggest concert presentation organisation in the country. His list of artists for 1946/47 season included the singers Beniamino Gigli, Lily Pons, Richard Tauber, Frank Titterton, Dennis Noble, Gwen Catley; pianists Moura Lympany, Malcuzynski, Mark Hambourg, Poushnoff and the duo Rawicz and Landauer. Also engaged were the Liverpool Philharmonic Orchestra and London International Orchestra, and conductors Fistoulari, Stanford Robinson, Malcolm Sargent. For those whose tastes were less seriously inclined there was Larry Adler (harmonica), Anne Ziegler, Webster Booth and Jeanette MacDonald (singers), and light music conductors André Kostelanetz and Albert Sandler. For a twenty-seven-year old entrepreneur this was an impressive list. His 'Music for the Millions' earned much money, but, like his profits, his losses were also large scale.

Alfredo took part in eight concerts organised by Fielding during the summer months of 1947 at the popular seaside resorts of Margate, Sandown, Blackpool,

Weymouth, Eastbourne and Shanklin. Inevitably the programmes were relatively lightweight, Alfredo's contributions usually containing Saint-Saëns *Introduction and Rondo capriccioso* (with piano accompaniment). His various associate artists during the Fielding series included Australian singers Peter Dawson and Harold Williams, the popular vocal duo Anne Ziegler and Webster Booth, and the South African pianist Lionel Bowman. The accompanists at these events were Ivor Newton and Adela Kotowska. Alfredo appeared in some more Harold Fielding concerts the next year, but for the most part his provincial tours were organised through direct contact with music clubs and orchestras or through other agents.

It was in her capacity as her husband's full-time secretary and part-time 'agent' that Joy's work also began in earnest from this time onwards. He depended wholly upon her for all his correspondence, both personal and professional, for itineraries, train, ship and plane bookings and for the detailed timetabling of his provincial concert tours. All this in addition to her cooking his favourite Italian meals and attending to their busy social life, as well as looking after Alfredo's mother (now reaching seventy) who was still living with them in their home in Park Drive in Golders Green. In the busy life thrust upon her, the only area that Joy did not organise was his bridge-playing, now becoming more than ever his passionate interest outside music.

It will be recalled that he had met the well-known bridge players the Sharples twins (with whom he also shared a love of music) when he joined the London Duplicate Club in Berkeley Square in 1932, and under their tutelage and his own assiduous practice of the game he was gradually developing those skills that would eventually turn him into a British Master. Another passion was cars, and as petrol rationing gradually eased and his concert career blossomed, so driving to and from his various engagements – often far from London – became his favourite way of travelling, even if it meant hours on the road.

Some idea of the busy schedule that was drawn up for him in that first year after the war can be gained through listing the places that he played at outside London, some of them visited more than once in the twelve months of 1946: Glasgow, Kirkaldy, Liverpool, Worthing, Wakefield, Nottingham, Swansea, Hanley, Birmingham, Manchester, Taunton, Broadstairs, Manchester, Derby, Brighton, Newquay, Brampton, Folkestone, Winchester, Newcastle-on-Tyne, Cardiff, Portsmouth, Weymouth, Mainsforth, Aldershot, Redruth, Wisbech, Belfast, Stirling, Glasgow, Plymouth, Liverpool, Wrexham, Southampton, Eastbourne, Nottingham, Weston-super-Mare, Colne. And, of course, there was London itself and its outlying suburbs. On the basis of surviving printed programmes from that year, Alfredo gave at least forty recitals and made twenty-one concerto appearances (five times at the Royal Albert Hall, including the Brahms under Beecham). The work with which he became most closely associated – Mendelssohn's violin concerto – was heard nine times, once with piano accompaniment, a not unusual situation in those days. Added to these personal appearances must be added twenty-six broadcasts, some of a slight nature, others involving recitals and concertos. His new career seemed to be starting auspiciously.

And the critical response to Alfredo's appearances? It was overwhelmingly enthusiastic, so much so that a parade of reviews would be tiresome. But in a study of his decisive return to the concert stage it would be an injustice if a few were not included here. His extraordinarily brilliant technique was, of course, widely recognised. Indeed, in the previous year, the critic of the *Musical Times* (September 1945) had hoped that the violinist wouldn't mind being called 'The Demon King of Fiddlestickery'. Yet what so impressed his critics and audiences alike was his depth of musical interpretation.

> Injustice would be done to Mr. Campoli by saying that his performance of the Bach Chaconne was a brilliant tour de force. That would imply that one was too conscious of the technical difficulties of this great music, but the celebrated violinist's art is of the character that conceals artifice. In his hands the piece sounded what it was meant to sound, a composition conceived in a perfect understanding of the genius of the violin and therefore to be played without a sense of strained effort.[9]

> Violin playing by Campoli is a joy of exquisite clarity. His unaccompanied Sonata No. 1 in G minor by Bach had the clear texture required of classical style.[10]

During the war Alfredo had worked tirelessly on developing his repertoire in preparation for his career after it. As well as the major 'classical' repertoire – all the sonatas of composers such as Mozart, Beethoven, Brahms (as well as, of course, those of Bach, both accompanied and unaccompanied) – he was now ready to play a number of sonatas by later composers: Arnold Bax, Delius, Dohnányi, Elgar, Fauré, Grieg, Hindemith, John Ireland, Korngold, Milhaud, Pizzetti, Poulenc, Ravel, Respighi and Strauss. For the 1949 Chopin Centenary he joined forces with pianist Franz Reizenstein and cellist James Whitehead for a Wigmore Hall performance of that composer's rarely-played Trio in G Minor. Now with a formidable reputation and a large repertoire of concertos and sonatas it would seem that Alfredo could storm any bastion of prejudice against him. The BBC, however, was not so easily taken.

How different the climate he now found himself in at the BBC from what he had enjoyed before the war! Then, one of their stars; now, one who must prove himself all over again. An idea of the deep-seated prejudice that he now faced in the Music Department can be gained from a BBC memo following his performance of Tchaikovsky's Violin Concerto at the Proms during the last

---

9 *Croydon Advertiser*, 6 September 1946.

10 *Scottish Daily Express*, 13 November 1946.

months of the war. Ralph Hill, writing in the *Daily Mail*, had said of the performance: 'Tchaikovsky's violin concerto is one of those works that sound better than they really are, providing they are superbly played. It sounded extremely well last night when Campoli played it at the Henry Wood Promenade Concert. The music gave every opportunity to show off Mr Campoli's clean and dazzling technique and mellow tone.'[11] In contrast, a BBC memo reporting on that concert stated that 'he nearly brought off the Tchaikovsky, but there is still the uncomfortable feeling of the café player all the time'.[12] Such musical snobbery in the BBC was Alfredo's sad legacy from his success in the 1930s.

To move into the higher reaches of the Music Department was to enter a different world from that which he had enjoyed in the BBC previously. Those who were in charge of 'serious' music were all Oxford or Cambridge graduates: Adrian Boult, Arthur Bliss, Julian Herbage, Herbert Murrill, Victor Hely-Hutchinson, and Steuart Wilson (who, while not a graduate of either, had close musical ties with both). Although Boult and Bliss were to be amongst Alfredo's greatest champions, nevertheless, those with whom Alfredo was now working were very different from Leslie Bridgewater and Fred Hartley. The inauguration of the Third Programme on 29 September 1946 with its vast range of music from medieval times to the contemporary avant-garde reflected the background and tastes of yet another wave of university-trained musicians entering the BBC.[13] It was perhaps only natural that, although he was heard frequently over the air, Alfredo felt that in the eyes of the BBC he was regarded as only on the fringes of serious music. It provoked a letter from him in October that year to Victor Hely-Hutchinson, then Director of Music.

> I hope you will excuse me writing to you about a matter which has been in my mind for some considerable time.
>
> As you probably know, I have been concentrating for the past 7 years on serious music. It has been an uphill battle owing to my previous reputation in light music, but now, for some years, I am glad to say, I have been playing in the finest concerts and with the leading orchestras, and have also given many recitals all over the country with great success. This has been endorsed by the Press. And only last month Edward Sackville West said in the 'New Statesman': 'Surely we should all be glad to hear Alfredo Campoli more often in serious music. His playing in a Mozart Sonata and in that of Poulenc last week, showed him to be among the few really fine violinist in this country.'
>
> Surely an indication of the success achieved can be judged from the fact that I have been chosen to play the Brahms Violin Concerto with the Royal

---

[11] Ralph Hill, *Daily Mail*, 4 September 1945.

[12] Julian Herbage to Sir Adrian Boult, 12 October 1945.

[12] For a detailed study see Humphrey Carpenter, *The Envy of the World: Fifty Years of the BBC Third Programme* (London, 1996).

> Philharmonic Orchestra conducted by Sir Thomas Beecham in an all-Brahms programme at the Albert Hall on Saturday next. In addition, I am to make four other appearances playing concertos at the Albert Hall in the next three months.
>
> It may be of interest to mention that I have refused a great many offers of solo broadcasts in light music and variety programmes in the hope that I might one day be recognised by the Music Department as a serious artist. I am particularly disappointed by the lack of recognition as a concerto player. On the very rare occasion on which I am invited to broadcast a concerto I am asked for either the Paganini, Max Bruch or Saint-Saëns concertos.[14]

As a result of this letter Alfredo was offered a sonata recital in February of the next year. As luck would have it, record-breaking low temperatures that winter caused such a drain on fuel resources in Britain that the Government took action to reduce the demand for electricity. One of the casualties was the Third Programme – and with it Alfredo's recital. Although the Home and Light networks were allowed to transmit for limited periods the Third was shut down for several weeks. Later that year, however, he played Bach's Chaconne in a recital that was broadcast (not, however, over the Third Programme), the quality of his playing softening BBC prejudice against him, as the following memo suggests.

> . . . I would assure you that after having the same misgivings as yours, we were converted on hearing him do the Bach Chaconne, both at his public recital and over the air . . . He has worked tremendously hard to escape from the light music label, and I fear that only a successful tour in America, where they are prepared to receive him without the prejudice we cannot avoid, is likely to commend him whole-heartedly to this country. This is what I am sure will happen. In the meantime, do not hesitate to give him a good recital. He won't let you down.[15]

In the light of Campoli's already overwhelming success with his audiences and critics at that time, it would seem that the BBC Music Department was either blind or deaf to what was going on outside Broadcasting House.

Six months after his letter to the BBC, matters had not markedly changed, although he had been engaged to play Tchaikovsky's Violin Concerto with the BBC Northern Orchestra under Charles Groves on 13 April at Buxton, the performance being broadcast simultaneously. Alfredo's frustration comes through most feelingly in a letter to Kenneth Wright at the BBC written a month after that performance.

---

14 Letter to Victor Hely-Hutchinson from Alfredo Campoli, 31 October 1946.

15 Memo from Kenneth Wright to Mr Lowe, 30 April 1947.

> . . . I am certainly not worrying about the *amount* of work I am doing for the B.B.C.; it is the general attitude of the Music Department, which, to me is most disquieting. The B.B.C. refuses to acknowledge me as a serious artist – a brilliant technician maybe – but *not* a musician. This is quite obvious from the fact that, although the Third Programme has been in operation for over a year, I have, as yet, not had the honour of playing on that programme. I can recall no other fiddler of note in this country of whom this can be said.
>
> I have never been offered a B.B.C. Symphony Concert engagement, nor any Concerto of outstanding musical importance. According to the B.B.C. my musical ability does not go beyond Lalo – Tchaikovsky – Saint-Saëns – Mendelssohn and Paganini! Never am I given a chance to play the concertos of Beethoven, Brahms, Mozart, Elgar, Walton and others; true, something went wrong and I was allowed to play the Brahms Concerto with the B.B.C Scottish Orchestra, following which a letter appeared in the Radio Times which said: 'It was without question, the greatest thing I have ever heard from a violin soloist during my career as a violinist', but to no avail. Week after week performances are given of some of the above concertos, which, to put it mildly, make me smile! And yet, when I perform them throughout the large cities of this country with the leading Orchestras, I am always accorded a great ovation.
>
> Alec Robertson, reviewing my recording of Tartini's' Sonata in 'the Gramophone' writes: 'I cannot imagine any living violinist giving a better performance of the Sonata than Campoli has done on these discs.' These are certainly big words, Ken, but I think I am not exaggerating when I say that this would seem to be the consensus of musical opinion in this country.
>
> I have now been offered a broadcast on the Third Programme to play Viotti's Concerto No. 2 in A Minor – a work which is given to pupils in their fifth year of study![16]

In September Alfredo visited Herbert Murrill, Assistant Music Director in the BBC, leaving with him copies of violin concertos by the Italian composer Ildebrando Pizzetti (1880–1968) and Soviet composer Nikolay Rakov (b. 1908) which he would like to play, but although Murrill recommended the proposal to his colleagues, nothing seems to have eventuated. Nevertheless, from that time onwards Alfredo began to appear more frequently on the Third Programme, including some chamber music recitals with the violist Watson Forbes playing Mozart Duos. Still nothing with the BBC Symphony Orchestra, even though he was playing with the other major orchestras in London and elsewhere.

One of these performances was with the London Symphony Orchestra, under Royalton Kisch, when he played Beethoven's Violin Concerto in the Royal Albert

[16] Letter from Alfredo Campoli to Kenneth Wright, 15 May 1947. The letter in the *Radio Times* referred to by Campoli appeared in the issue of 20 November 1946.

Hall on 18 January of the next year. Herbert Murrill was at the performance and, in view of Alfredo's possible later engagements with the BBC, wrote a report that commended the playing, although with some reservations. At that stage of Alfredo's career, critics invariably spoke of his warm, sweet, but sometimes too small a tone. In fact, it was the instrument he was using, and after the purchase of a fine eighteenth-century violin early in 1948, he was able to project a more powerful sound. The smaller tone may have given the impression that his interpretation of some works (performed in large halls) lacked grandeur, and this is certainly the impression of the Beethoven he gave to Herbert Murrill.

> ... In all technical matters he was completely assured. His tone was warm and acceptable and his intonation true. His conception of the piece is on the small side; one missed the grandeur of the work. It seems that we have to choose between a big musical conception with inadequate technique (as in some recent performances) and a smaller conception with more complete control of technical problems. If this is indeed the case, I for one would prefer Campoli's performance to the recent performances of Busch or Menuhin.[17]

The matter of his small tone – imagined or otherwise – was to dog his footsteps to BBC recognition for another two years. An incident particularly hurtful to him over this occurred in October 1949. Alfredo had been continually asking that he be invited to play with the BBC Symphony Orchestra, and his hopes were raised when he was contacted by the BBC asking if he were free on the 26th of that month when one of the BBC Symphony Orchestra's Wednesday Evening Concerts in the Royal Albert Hall had been scheduled. The violinist Giaconda de Vito had been engaged to play the Brahms Concerto, but had fallen ill. It seemed as if a chance for Alfredo had come. But it was Ida Haendel, not Alfredo, who was eventually engaged to take Giaconda de Vito's place. It was a bitter blow, especially as Ida Haendel had already substituted for Szigeti in the same work at the Proms a few weeks earlier. A letter to Sir Steuart Wilson, now Director of Music at the BBC, expressing his hurt at this treatment, brought the following reply.

> It is fair to be frank with you and to say that, while we regard you as a broadcast soloist at the microphone whose technique and ability are second to none, you must realise that the Albert Hall and the listening public in the Hall do find that your tone is too 'microphonic' for the size of the building. That Hall is a great difficulty – there are many excellent broadcast artists who don't do their best in those circumstances.

---

[17] Memo from Herbert Murrill to BBC Music Booking Manager, 21 January 1948.

> Brahms is a matter of considerable difference from almost any other violin concerto. It was planned specially for de Vita, and we had to consider whether we would change the programme to suit a new artist. As a matter of routine we find out on such occasions what artists are available in order that we may have all facts before us. We decided to stick to the Brahms and, in view of the audience in the Albert Hall, to ask Ida Haendel. Had it been decided to change the concerto, things might have turned out differently.
>
> I appreciate your candour in writing as you do, without rancour, and I hope that you will accept what I say as showing no prejudice towards you personally.[18]

In reply, Alfredo wrote

> Thank you very much for your letter of the 21st October and may I say how grateful I am to you for giving me such a frank explanation of the situation.
>
> Until recently I would have whole-heartedly agreed with you regarding my tone being more suitable to microphone work than the Albert Hall, but I had hoped that since the purchase, about 18 months ago, of my J.B. Guadagnini (1773), this was no longer the case, as people all over the country continually remark and compliment me on the powerful tone of my instrument.[19]

Alfredo's Guadagnini was one of the first of a fine collection of violins (and bows) that he was to acquire in the coming years. Its maker, Giovanni Baptista Guadagnini (*c.* 1711–86) was the most important and prolific of a family of Italian violin craftsmen whose history stretched from the early eighteenth century to the twentieth century. Working at first in Piacenza, then Milan, Cremona and Parma, Guadagnini moved to Turin in 1771 where he created his finest violins, largely modelled on Stradivarius lines, producing instruments with rich and strong tone.[20] The date of Alfredo's Gaudagnini (1773) is thus significant. He had been able to acquire it in England because the aristocratic family (whose name was never revealed to him) in whose vault it had lain unused for some 150 years had been forced, because of death duties, to sell their valuable heirloom. It was valued at what was then the high price of £2,000. Lying unplayed for so many years meant, of course, that the instrument's bloom had faded, and it took him nearly eighteen months before he could get the best out of it, long disuse having taken the resonance from the wood.[21]

18 Sir Steuart Wilson to Alfredo Campoli, 21 October 1949.

19 Alfredo Campoli to Sir Steuart Wilson, 31 October 1949.

20 Entry on Guadagnini in *The New Grove*.

21 Quoted in an interview published in the *Melbourne Herald*, 12 April 1950

Although Alfredo played with the BBC Symphony Orchestra at two Proms (playing Walton's Violin Concerto on 12 August, 1948, and a year later Mendelssohn's, both under Sargent) his engagements as a concerto soloist for the BBC were largely confined to playing with its regional orchestras until his return from his 1950 Australian and New Zealand tour. And yet he had played regularly with such orchestras as the very fine City of Birmingham Orchestra under its conductor George Weldon, the London Symphony Orchestra (always at their Royal Albert Hall concerts), the Scottish Orchestra (under Walter Susskind), the Royal Philharmonic Orchestra (under Beecham) and the Boyd Neel Orchestra (under its founder).[22] Significantly missing from these leading orchestras is the Hallé Orchestra in Manchester. It proved to be another bastion of prejudice against the erstwhile light musician but, like the BBC, eventually overcome.

On 21 February 1949, with the Third Programme in mind, he sent Herbert Murrill a list of works that he would like to play. In the light of his predilection for romantic music the list is interesting, for it included Prokofieff's 2nd Concerto and his D major Concerto, Stravinsky's Suite Italienne for violin and piano, Milhaud's 'Le Boeuf sur le toit' and Suite for violin and piano, and Francaix's 'Musique de cour' for violin, flute and orchestra, as well as the concertos by Pizzetti and Rakov mentioned earlier. Interesting, too, were those in a more romantic style: Suk's Ballade for violin and orchestra, Lekeu's Violin Sonata and Saint-Saëns Fantasy for violin and harp.[23] Despite Herbert Murrill's recommendation to his colleagues in the BBC that Alfredo's suggested repertoire be taken up,[24] nothing seems to have eventuated, or – at least – no performances by Alfredo of any of them can so far be traced. Nevertheless, over the period up to his departure for Australia and New Zealand he played a number of times over the BBC's Third Programme as resistance to him gradually gave way in the face of his superb performances. Indeed, in the twelve months before his departure for his tour to Australia and New Zealand, the BBC engaged him to play concertos by Beethoven, Elgar, Brahms and William Walton. The Brahms, at least, was played with the BBC Symphony Orchestra.

If a survey of the post-war years up to his first international tour taking him to the Antipodes reveals a slow, but eventual acceptance by the BBC of Alfredo's status as a serious performer, it also reveals a busy concert schedule in broadcasts and live performances. Over 400 performances is a conservative estimate of the total number of performances he gave during those four-and-a-half years. Involvement with provincial music clubs and semi-amateur orchestras was part of the normal professional life of the solo performer. Alfredo was no exception, and in fact throughout his career he enjoyed supporting the work of musical

[22] Details of these appearances are: City of Birmingham Orchestra (13), London Symphony Orchestra (11), Scottish Orchestra (8), Royal Philharmonic Orchestra (2), Boyd Neel (4).

[23] Letter from Alfredo Campoli to Herbert Murrill, 21 February 1949.

[24] Memo from Herbert Murrill, 7 April 1949.

enthusiasts, particularly young performers. Histrionics and tantrums were not Alfredo's way. Rather, he inspired others through his unassuming, yet dignified, presence and, of course, through his superbly controlled performances. Thus in 1947 we find him playing Mendelssohn's Violin Concerto at a Schools Festival under Ernest Read, while Bruch's First Concerto with the Huddersfield Senior Youth Orchestra was his last public appearance in May 1985. It was with the Civil Service Orchestra that he played Brahms's Violin Concerto in December 1949, a reminder of the remarkable strength of amateur music-making in Britain at that time. (This was largely attributable to the high standard of school music – principally in the so-called public, or fee-paying schools, but later to be extended into many of the non-fee schools.) Of the eleven performances of Brahms's concerto during those four-and-a-half years, that with the Civil Service Orchestra was the only time with an amateur group. In addition to playing with the well-known orchestras already mentioned, he also played with the Municipal Orchestras of Bournemouth, Torquay, West Ham and Worthing, Liverpool Philharmonic, Yorkshire Symphony Orchestra, Western Philharmonic Orchestra, as well as with smaller groups such as the Capriol String Orchestra, Hendon String Orchestra and others. The works he played with all of these orchestras comprised the well-known concertos, but with the Boyd Neel Orchestra he also played Vaughan Williams's lyrical *The Lark Ascending*.

At this time, his solo recitals, too, were largely made up of the well-known repertoire – classical and romantic sonatas, and modern favourites – as well as those appealing virtuoso works with which he usually concluded his recitals and which were eagerly anticipated by his audiences. Unaccompanied Bach was lovingly played wherever appropriate, but – as was common at the time – most other works from the baroque era were played in arrangements, usually by Fritz Kreisler. In Britain notions of 'authentic' baroque performance practice were still largely confined to where the Dolmetsch Family lived, pioneering the path that has led to the present-day enthusiasm for period-style performance. In any case, as an essentially romantic player, Alfredo never shared this enthusiasm for research-based performance. His love of Bach's music stemmed from his instinctive feel for its lines and gesture. As he was so often to say to accompanists and students: 'Don't think about it; feel it.'

In common with many performers immediately after the war, he took part in many charitable concerts to raise funds for those afflicted by it or other catastrophes: funds for refugees, war aid and 'welcome home' appeals; those for hospitals, sailors, for the rescue of women and children from Europe, for Jewish relief and rehabilitation, and many more. In these charity concerts he was associated with a wide range of performers – from radio comedians like Tommy Handley, to star performers in light and classical fields. On at least one occasion the programme had to be so arranged that he could get from one concert to another on the same evening.

With the opening up of Alfredo's post-war career as soloist came a renewed interest in him as a recording artist. In the years leading up to 1950 he recorded Saint-Saëns's *Introduction and Rondo Capriccioso* (with the London Symphony Orchestra under Walter Goehr), Kreisler's arrangement of Paganini's Concerto No. 1 (with the National Symphony Orchestra under Victor Olof) and Mendelssohn's Concerto (with the London Philharmonic Orchestra under Van Beinum). Shorter works included Bach's unaccompanied Partita in D minor, two sonatas by Tartini, Corelli's La Folia Variations and nearly a dozen shorter pieces – the staple diet of his recital programmes – all accompanied by Eric Gritton. The majority of his recordings at this time were with Decca, marking a new and fruitful post-war association with that company.

Of the many concerts Alfredo gave during this period, one of the most significant was his performance of William Walton's Violin Concerto, composed in 1939 for Jascha Heifetz (who commissioned it). Walton had turned to the Danish-born violinist Henry Holst for constant advice about the solo part in much the same way that Bliss was to turn to Alfredo for help with his concerto, and indeed Holst gave the first British performance of the work. By turns, nostalgic and acerbic, deeply introspective as well as unbridled, it is like an English landscape touched by Italian colour, for Walton's artistic leanings were as much towards the Continent as they were towards his English background. Indeed, through his close friendship with the Sitwells and others inspired by continental culture, he was often regarded as an *enfant terrible* – a kind of British member of that French group known as 'Les Six', who at that time were composing music hilariously irreverent to the romantic past. Yet, despite its modernity, Walton's Violin Concerto is an essentially romantic and lyrical work and as such appealed strongly to Alfredo. But it offered challenges of a kind that are not found in the traditional romantic repertoire, in particular, rhythmic complexity. The fact that Alfredo was able to give performances of this concerto that seemed even to exult in overcoming its enormous technical and musical difficulties must have put an end to any remaining doubts that here was, indeed, a magnificent violinist.[25] He gave several broadcasts of the work with regional orchestras, as well as playing it at the 1948 Proms Season with the BBC Symphony Orchestra conducted by Sir Malcolm Sargent.

Thus, by the time he was ready to embark on his first international tour Alfredo had largely overcome what prejudices there had been in Britain against him. Through his recordings he was also beginning to establish his reputation internationally as one of the finest concert violinists in what he could now truthfully call 'his' country (even if Italy remained his spiritual homeland), for his naturalisation papers had come through in mid-1947. It is not surprising that

[25] Unfortunately there are no commercial recordings of Campoli playing Walton's Violin Concerto, although his widow holds private recordings of his broadcasts.

within this short time he regained that air of success which he had enjoyed a decade earlier.

In the middle of 1949 Elvira suffered a severe stroke. It was now necessary to find a good nursing home for her, and one such place, where she was to live out the few remaining years of her life, was found in Totteridge, a northern suburb of London. To be near her, Alfredo decided that he and Joy should move from Golders Green. And so, from the house where Alfredo had lived with his parents for many years and where he and Joy commenced their married life, they moved to 53 Oakleigh Avenue in nearby Whetstone. He visited his mother daily, his concern for her the only worry when he received an invitation from A.D.M. Longden in Melbourne to make a six-month tour of Australia and New Zealand in 1950. After arranging for friends to visit Elvira regularly during their absence, he and Joy boarded the *Orcades* on 17 March to undertake Alfredo's first international tour.

Chapter 6

First International Tour: Australia and New Zealand

In February 1947 the Harold Fielding agency had written to the Australian Broadcasting Commission wondering if Australia would be interested in a tour by Alfredo Campoli, pointing out that various people were now approaching the violinist about the possibility of tours overseas. In the case of Australia, South Africa and America, Alfredo had expressed the wish that the Harold Fielding agency handle any such arrangements.[1] However, it was to be more than three years before Alfredo embarked on his first overseas tour and, in the event, it was neither Harold Fielding nor the ABC who organised it. It was an Australian impresario A.D.M. (Archie) Longden. Nevertheless, the ABC agreed to broadcast some of Alfredo's recitals and offer concerto engagements to him with four of their orchestras. The tour, which was to last nearly six months, took in both Australia and New Zealand, and on 17 March 1950 Joy and Alfredo boarded the *Orcades* to take them on what was to be the first of a number of visits to both countries over the next quarter of a century.

The voyage took what was then the usual route: through the Suez Canal and down to the island in those days called Ceylon (now Sri Lanka), where the ship berthed long enough for Alfredo, at short notice, to give a recital in the capital city Colombo. Here to a capacity audience in the Savoy Theatre (where he was accompanied by Leon Dudzik) he played to his first Asian audience – in a temperature of 102 degrees. Air-conditioning was still a long way off in Asian, as well as in Australian cities, and also in the ships that plied between Britain and the Antipodes. In his cabin Alfredo practised for five hours each day even in the sweltering heat of the tropics. It was not that he was so much concerned for the effect of the heat upon himself, as upon his Guadagnini violin which he had chosen to take on this long tour.[2] To protect it he had followed the advice of Archie Longden who, having served with the RAAF during the war in New Guinea and Borneo as Squadron Leader in charge of entertainment in the Pacific theatre of war, remembered how aircraft engines to be transported to the tropics had been packed in sodium chloride to absorb the moisture.

[1] Letter from L. E. Corley, Director of the Agency Division of Harold Fielding to Harry Pringle of the Australian Broadcasting Commission, dated 10 February 1947.

[2] This was a very real worry. In his memoirs, the flautist John Lemmoné (Melba's flautist, agent and close friend) recalls, for example, that when the Hungarian violinist Eduard Reményi (1828–98) was playing in Singapore his violin collapsed in the middle of a solo because of the oppressive humidity and heat. (Lemmoné's memoirs have recently been published by Donald Westlake as part of his *Dearest John – the story of John Lemmoné, flute virtuoso and Nellie Melba* (Bowerbird Press, 1997).)

Constantly on the move during this tour, Joy's task as wife and secretary was no easy one. These were the days before drip-dry clothes and before flying had revolutionised the travel wardrobe. An important part of the luggage was, of course, Alfredo's music, for even though many of the programmes were repeated, nearly forty works were to be performed during the tour, including major sonatas and concertos. For the Australian tour alone, Alfredo was averaging a recital or concerto-performance every second day, often travelling long distances to reach each venue. Such a tour demanded careful management of the scores – as well as great physical and emotional resilience.

Both in Australia and New Zealand Alfredo's tour excited much press comment, with interviews, anecdotes and photographs, more usual today with pop stars than classical artists. In the period following the war, however, visits to the antipodes by celebrity artists were widely covered. Inevitably, the items ranged from trivial, but sometimes entertaining, anecdotes (such as in Sydney where some of the locals, confused by his Italian name were said to have addressed him variously as Mr Campanella, Mr Stromboli and Mr Casanova) to relatively in-depth interviews. The press on both sides of the Tasman Sea noted with great approval, Alfredo's love of tennis (he played a number of games on tour), billiards, and table tennis, passing on stories of his prowess in them all to their sports-loving readers. His growing skill in bridge and his newly found interest in photography (resulting in a visual record of that long tour – still in existence), as well as his pleasure in driving powerful cars, all combined to produce the image – and a true one at that – of a fine artist who could also relax with and relate to the 'ordinary' person. That this was largely due to his rubbing shoulders with a wide range of types when he was in the light music field in the 1930s and his participation in sport and games there can be no doubt. Alfredo endeared himself to his public 'down-under' through his gregariousness and balanced life-style as well as his masterly playing. It is not surprising that he was invited back to Australia and New Zealand for a number of later tours.

Australia

Joy and Alfredo arrived in a country very different from what Australia is today – at least in social and cultural terms. Multi-culturalism was neither in the Australian lexicon nor mind in 1950. Instead, the tiny population (less than half the present 19 million) was predominantly Anglo-Celtic, with strong attachment to the 'mother country' England, often called 'home' even by those who had never been there. All public events and performances, including recitals and concerts began with the British national anthem, a local stand-in usually provided for visiting 'foreign' solo pianists who couldn't or wouldn't play it. Only a brave few (budding republicans, communists or militant Catholics of Irish descent) dared sit during the patriotic ritual. Its most superb performances were regularly given by the Sydney Symphony Orchestra in the arrangement made by its conductor Eugène Goossens, who transposed it into the key of G flat major, the unusual key and his unique orchestration lending such silken sheen to the solemn opening that one almost looked forward to it, even though, like all performances of the anthem, it blunted the impact of the first work on the programme.

In material terms, it was a period of great prosperity in Australia, its famed merino fleeces and wheat finding ready markets in Britain and elsewhere. It was a prosperity that beckoned from overseas many who saw the possibilities of a new life in the young country, encouraged by the government in its attempt to build up the population to overcome the serious labour shortage. These post-war migrants were predominantly British and were given 'assisted passages'. But 'displaced persons' from war-torn Europe were also given a chance to make a new life in this distant continent; many of them, however, were helped to get there only on the understanding that a period of manual labour would be required from them. It was through this European migration that the mono-cultural foundation of Australian (white) society was first, and very gradually, chipped away, although at the time of Alfredo's first visit, few would have noticed the dust. Moreover, at that stage, it was only a tiny handful of European migrants who brought with them a love and knowledge of fine music; most of them were from the disadvantaged segments of society. It was their children who would be taking up the various professions, including music, and helping to transform Australian society.[3]

Nevertheless, early on what was to become a permanent fixture in Australian musical life owed its birth to European immigration.[4] This was the organisation devoted to chamber music: Musica Viva. It was founded in Sydney in 1945 by Richard Goldner, inventor and musician who had been a member of an orchestra of the same name in Vienna before the war. At the time of Alfredo's visit Musica Viva was still essentially the name of a String Quartet that included Richard Goldner, but in order to be a viable organisation the group had to perform an enormous number of concerts in Sydney, Melbourne and elsewhere. The strain proved too great, and soon after Alfredo's tour Musica Viva, to Goldner's intense regret, became an entrepreneurial organisation with branches in all Australian cities, bringing to them some of the greatest international ensembles and eventually achieving a reputation as the world's largest chamber music agency. As such, it was, of course, a non-government-funded organisation.

---

[3] See John Rickard, *Australia – a Cultural History* (London, 1988) for a review of the complex nature of these changes.

[4] He was able to invest money in this enterprise through profits accrued from a new type of zip-fastener he had invented and which was taken up by a number of allied forces. All but one other member of the orchestra he left behind in Vienna were gassed by the Nazis at Treblinka. See John Thomson, *Into a New Key* (Wellington, 1985), pp 139–47).

Indeed, despite the prosperity that could have made possible public funding of the arts, successive governments, reflecting what was then the average Australian's indifference towards cultural pursuits, showed no interest in funding them until the 1960s. In any case, it was widely assumed that local practitioners, whether creators or performers, could not possibly measure up to those from overseas. Thus, as in Britain until the transformation of CEMA into the Arts Council of Great Britain in 1947 (see Chapter 4), there was no tradition of government arts funding in Australia. The first move in this direction came four years after Alfredo's first Australian tour when the Elizabethan Theatre Trust was set up, its name commemorating the Royal Tour of Australia that year, the first one by a reigning British monarch. The establishment of The Australian Council for the Arts (later called The Australia Council) was still almost twenty years away (1968). It was not until the 1970s that the infusion of its generous funding encouraged – indeed, seemed to release – a wealth of Australian talent in all fields of the arts, reflecting and expressing the growing sense of Australian identity and gradually overcoming the sense of cultural inferiority. But in 1950 those heady days were a long way off. The only way in which regular finances from the public purse flowed into music was through the Australian Broadcasting Commission.

The history of broadcasting in Australia, though having some parallels with that in Britain (see Chapter 2), evolved somewhat differently. In the same year as the British Broadcasting Company was formed (1922), Amalgamated Wireless of Australia (AWA) applied to the Postmaster-General for permission to broadcast commercially, and over the next four years four other licences were granted (2SB and 2FC in Sydney, 3AR in Melbourne, and 6WF in Perth). The radio receivers (using the so-called 'sealed-set' system) were designed to respond to one signal only and a listening fee was paid directly to the station owner. (In reality, the 'sealed' sets were quite easily modified by the radio ham to pick up a number of signals.) In July 1924 the Postmaster-General divided radio stations into two categories: those funded from listeners' licences (A Class stations) and those funded from advertising (B Class stations). Following a Royal Commission in 1927, appointed to inquire into 'wireless broadcasting within the Commonwealth in all its aspects', the Australian Broadcasting Company applied for and won in 1929 the tender to supply programmes for a national broadcasting service, the technical facilities provided by the Postmaster-General's Department. The Company took over the function of A Class stations (its listeners' licence fees collected, as in Britain, by the PMG), and the following year the Federation of Commercial Broadcasting Stations was formed to look after the interests of the B Class ('commercial') stations. A young man who was making a name for himself in Melbourne was appointed Musical Director of the Australian Broadcasting Company which soon set up studio orchestras in most states. It was Bernard Heinze's vision that one day these would become symphony orchestras.

Bernard Heinze, a violinist, had won various music scholarships that took him to London, Paris and Berlin, and soon after his return to Australia he joined the staff of the Melbourne University Conservatorium (founded in 1885), becoming its Professor and Head in 1926. He founded the Melbourne String Quartet, and conducted the University Conservatorium Symphony Orchestra, also at this time inaugurating children's concerts, an idea which eventually spread to all states in Australia. With his vision, enthusiasm, energy and concern for the musical community he was the ideal man to appoint as Director-General of Music (in a part-time capacity) to the fledgling Australian Broadcasting Company. In 1932 the Australian Broadcasting Commission Act was passed, and the Australian Broadcasting Company became the Australian Broadcasting Commission, funded by the Federal Government and also by revenue from licence fees. Bernard Heinze was appointed Musical Adviser to the new national broadcaster. The provisions of the Act allowed for studio orchestras and by 1936 ABC subscription concerts had begun in all states. Until after the war, however, most of the studio orchestras were small-scale affairs, but in 1946 the ABC's Sydney orchestra was greatly expanded to become the Sydney Symphony Orchestra. It was soon followed by similar developments in other states. It was to the Sydney orchestra that Eugène Goossens came as Resident Conductor the next year, and with his presence swept in a wave of enthusiasm for orchestral music that left a permanent mark on the Australian scene. At the Youth Concert series (one of Heinze's innovations that commenced in 1947) and the annual Concerto and Vocal Competition hundreds of students could be seen camping overnight along the street leading to the Sydney Town Hall in order to secure the best seats at these youthful events. The appointment of Goossens was the catalyst needed at that time, and on the 1950 tour Alfredo was to be one of his soloists in a period of exciting development in those early years of the Sydney Symphony Orchestra

Joy and Alfredo disembarked from the *Orcades* at Adelaide, travelling overland by train to where Alfredo would make his Australian début – Melbourne, capital city of the State of Victoria, which they reached on 12 April. It was here that Longden lived.

Over a period of more than twenty years from 1932 Longden had managed the Australian tours of a number of artists such as John Brownlee, Florence Austral and John Amadio, Marjorie Lawrence, La Meri, Gracie Fields, and Alexander Helman.[5] The British entertainers Flanders and Swann were amongst those whom he brought out to follow Alfredo's tour. Longden was born in the port city of Geelong near Melbourne in 1906 and following his schooling became a qualified accountant. But music had always been his passion, and such was his talent that Edward Goll, Melbourne's finest concert pianist at that time, offered to

[5] I am indebted to Christine Storey, a post-graduate student at the Faculty of Music, Melbourne University, for information about A.D. Longden. She found biographical information in the unpublished 'A Longden Family History' by James N. Longden held by Deakin University, Melbourne.

teach him for no fee. This led to Longden's occasional appearance as a supporting artist for visiting soloists, such as Galli-Curci when she sang in the Melbourne Town Hall. Deeply involved in the Scouting movement, he travelled to Europe towards the end of the 1920s to attend an International Boy Scouts Jamboree. It was the beginning of the 'Europeanisation' of the young colonial who became fluent in French, Italian and Spanish – with a smattering of Russian. Indeed, exuding a European air, he was soon regarded by his fellow Melbournians as something of an exotic. While on that first trip to Europe he was introduced to the singer John Brownlee, also born in Geelong, who had recently made his début at Covent Garden in *La Bohème* in which Melba was making her farewell. Longden and Brownlee became firm friends, and the singer, recognising Longden's unusual combination of business acumen and artistic sensibilities, asked him to manage his 1932/33 tour of Australia and New Zealand. This was the beginning of his career as an entrepreneur, organising lengthy itineraries around Australia and New Zealand, and assuming personal control and responsibility for every stage of them. Alfredo's five-and-a-half month period in Australia and New Zealand was not untypical of a Longden-organised tour.

In Melbourne,which was to be the home-base to which they returned on three occasions, Alfredo also met his pianist for the whole tour, Margaret Schofield. She had studied in London with Solomon and been engaged by the BBC as a staff pianist for two years before returning to Melbourne the year before Alfredo's tour began. Although not apparent to their many audiences, the personal relationship between them was not an easy one – and not helped by the travel arrangements that Archie Longden had put in place. Many of the thousands of miles of touring in Australia were to be covered by car in which travelled Alfredo, Joy, Margaret Schofield, Archie Longden and, of course, the driver. It was taken for granted that the group, including the driver, would have their meals together at each hotel. Such confinement of space and company was bound to breed problems.

It was with the Melbourne orchestra – The Victorian Symphony Orchestra, under its by now veteran conductor Bernard Heinze – that Australian audiences first heard Alfredo in live performance, when he played Beethoven's Violin Concerto in the opening concert of the ABC's 1950 Celebrity Subscription Concerts (Red) Series held on 14 and 15 April in the Melbourne Town Hall. The critics were unanimous in their admiration for his playing (in contrast to their damning reviews of Heinze's performance of Bach's Brandenburg Concerto, No. 3 that opened the concert). To quote just one review

> Campoli revealed a wonderful technique. His flexible tone had an uncommonly fine resonant quality, attributable both to his excellent bowing and to his splendid instrument. In the first movement it was brilliant and fluent; in the larghetto its warmth and singing beauty could compare with that of any violinist heard in this city since Yehudi Menuhin. But his fine performance was more than a technical feat, for there was

> artistry in his sensitive handling of the work and in his concept of the concerto.[6]

Alfredo's next appearance was a few days later, in the so-called 'Blue' Series of the ABC's Celebrity Subscription Concerts, this time playing the Brahms. Subscribers to this series had their appetites whetted not only through the enthusiasm of the critics, but also through a morsel of publicity when newspapers learnt of Alfredo's brush with the Melbourne City Council. The City Fathers had recently decided to charge a £10 fee for practising in the Town Hall and Alfredo's warnings that the Council would face criticism from a long line of visiting artists as a result of this were summarily dismissed by one councillor who was reported as saying that 'If a dozen Campolis came along the charge would be the same. Rehearsal fees are here to stay.' It led to an amusing cartoon in the *Herald* depicting Alfredo practising in the street outside the Town Hall, upturned hat on the pavement, and being accosted by a policeman moving him on unless he paid a busker's fee of a shilling an hour.[7] There was a newspaper photograph of Alfredo, too, practising in the roof-garden of his Collins Street hotel watched by a lucky hotel painter listening to a 'free' recital. His audience must have waited with keen anticipation for his performance of the Brahms Violin Concerto. They were not to be disappointed, and the critics greeted it with the same enthusiasm as they had the Beethoven.

> From a rather dull beginning the concert in the 'blue' series by the Victorian Symphony Orchestra in the Town Hall last night ended in such a burst of artistry as has not been heard here for some time. The artistry came in the second half when Alfredo Campoli was soloist with the orchestra in the Brahms Violin Concerto. On this occasion Campoli had a much surer sense of the capacity of the hall for sound. He was stronger than he was in the Beethoven last Friday, but in his increased strength never for an instant did he sacrifice that beautiful singing tone that is his greatest asset and can even be his weakness.
>
> The first movement was given with a vigorous loveliness that melted into one of the most exquisite adagios ever likely to be heard in this city or anywhere else for that matter.[8]

Two days after appearing with the Victorian Symphony Orchestra Alfredo and Margaret Schofield joined together for the first of the many recitals they would give on this extensive tour. They rehearsed not 'en plein air' in the roof-garden, but in a friend's flat. They began with two recitals in the Town Hall, the major works being sonatas by Brahms and César Franck, Saint-Saëns's *Introduction*

---

6 The *Argus*, 15 April, 1950.
7 The *Herald*, 18 April 1950.
8 The *Age*, 20 April 1950.

and Rondo capriccioso, and Dohnányi's *Ruralia Hungarica*, together with some unaccompanied Bach and concluding with the usual (and expected) showpieces. (Alfredo was quoted as saying: 'After a big dish I like to treat my audience to the sweets and nuts.'[9])

The first country recital was at nearby Geelong, then back to Melbourne for two more before beginning the long drive to Adelaide where Alfredo and Joy had disembarked from the *Orcades* some three weeks earlier. A concert en route to Adelaide was given at Ballarat, seventy-five miles west of Melbourne. Once the centre of the Victorian gold-rush, Ballarat, Bendigo and other areas rich in gold deposits had boosted Victoria's economy to such an extent that for a time in the nineteenth century Melbourne was reckoned to be the wealthiest city in the world. After the gold-rush years Ballarat developed as a marketing centre for the rich agricultural districts around it, and at the time of Alfredo's visit was the second largest city in Victoria. For it he played a programme that was to be repeated many times in country areas: Tartini's 'Devil's Trill' sonata, some unaccompanied Bach, the Mendelssohn Violin Concerto (with piano accompaniment), Mozart's Rondo in G (arranged by Kreisler), finishing with Hubay's *Zephyr*, Elgar's *La capricieuse* and Bazzini's *La ronde des lutins*.

The car in which they were travelling around the countryside was towing a large trailer that contained not only the luggage of the five occupants, but also a grand piano, such instruments being in short supply in rural areas. Ninety miles after leaving Ballarat, they discovered when filling up with petrol at Horsham that the heavy towbar had cracked right through, the trailer being attached only by two metal tie rods about an eighth of an inch thick; by some miracle the trailer had not broken loose. (This was not to be the last hazard encountered on this tour of Australia.) They arrived in Adelaide on 5 May, three days after leaving Melbourne.

Adelaide, laid out in 1836 by a British army officer, Colonel William Light, who had been instructed to make wide streets and reserves for squares, public walks and open spaces, was the most gracious of the Australian capital cities. Proudly untainted by any association with convict transportation, it had been established with permission of the British Government by the South Australian Company who had engaged Colonel Light to plan the new city, and over a period time it developed, in addition to its attractive stone buildings, a cultural life that gained for the city the sobriquet 'Athens of the South'. In retrospect, of all Australian cities Alfredo found Adelaide the most musical. But it also had a reputation for conservatism and respect for convention, so that when Alfredo stepped out on to the platform of the Town Hall for the first of his three recitals, not in tails, but in black velvet jacket, soft shirt and black bow tie, his audience was startled enough to make it a news item in the local paper. As in so many places in Australia in the days before immigration from southern European

[9] The *Melbourne Sun*, 13 April 1950.

cultures changed the way of life, late Saturday nights and Sundays saw most towns and cities virtually die, so that looking around for somewhere to have a suitable meal at 11.00 pm after his first recital on a Saturday in Adelaide was frustratingly unsuccessful. It was not to be the only time when Australian habits (and legislation) confounded the hungry violinist, who made a point of never eating before a performance. In Adelaide he gave what may have been the first performance there of Poulenc's Violin Sonata composed only six years earlier. Back to Melbourne for a 'farewell concert', and then on the road again. It would once more take them to Adelaide, but only after a most circuitous route, taking in recitals in five towns. First down to the coastal resort of Warrnambool (also the centre of a rich dairy and vegetable growing district of Victoria), then up a few miles to the agricultural district of Hamilton, before driving some 300 miles to Mildura where they gave a recital on 18 May. This wine-producing centre is situated on the banks of the Murray River, which, joining the Murrumbidgee to form the longest and most important river system in Australia, also acts as the border between Victoria and New South Wales. This they were to cross and then travel northwards to one of the country's most important industrial centres – the mining town of Broken Hill, where the contrast between the green lushness they had left in Victoria and the semi-desert landscape of this far-western district of New South Wales could not be more striking. Next it was back to the Murray River and westwards along its bank to another wine-producing town, Renmark. Alfredo and Joy returned to Adelaide (by air this time) where he played Tchaikovsky's violin concerto with the ABC's South Australian Symphony Orchestra under Henry Krips.

Alfredo's appearances in Sydney began with five recitals over the period of a fortnight in the Sydney Town Hall. The centre-piece of each was, of course, a major sonata, and he played those by Beethoven ('Spring'), Brahms (D minor and A major), César Franck and Poulenc. Three similar programmes were scheduled for Brisbane, which was reached by air in mid-June, the Campolis and Margaret Schofield being relieved to find clear weather there after the incessant downpours during their stay in Sydney. The blue skies were not to last for long, however, and they soon found themselves in one of the fiercest cyclones experienced by that semi-tropical city. Flooding became the real problem when they took to the car again on their tour of regional Queensland, the itinerary taking in Ipswich, Toowoomba, Maryborough and other northern towns. Returning from Ipswich – a town a few miles from Brisbane – they came to a line of cars held up by floodwaters pouring across the road, but seeing a bus go through safely they decided to make a dash for it. The car stopped in the middle of the torrent. With water starting to come in through the floorboards, Joy held the Guadagnini aloft until a bus soon came to their rescue and towed them out.[10]

---

[10] As reported to the *Auckland Star* of 15 July 1950 when they arrived in New Zealand.

Back in Brisbane a performance of Mendelssohn's Violin Concerto with the ABC's Queensland Symphony Orchestra on 7 and 8 July, under the Italian conductor Alceo Galliera, completed the visit to that state. Only two more appearances remained for Alfredo's first Australian tour; both of them were with Australia's 'star' orchestra and its 'star' conductor Eugène Goossens, and they provided the climax to it.

Eugène Goossens had been enticed from the Cincinnati Symphony Orchestra in mid-1947, at a yearly salary unheard of in Australian musical circles at that time, in the expectation that he would lift the standard of this recently re-formed and enlarged orchestra up to world-class. To achieve this salary, higher than that of the Prime Minister and paid from the public purse, it was necessary also to offer him the Directorship of the Sydney Conservatorium (founded in 1915), a position that had just become vacant through the retirement of Dr Edgar Bainton.[11] By the time Alfredo arrived in Sydney, Goossens had inspired his players to a splendid level of performance and his audiences to a new pitch of enthusiasm. And with Goossens came a repertoire of twentieth-century music hitherto unplayed in Australia, particularly the more brilliant and colourful orchestral works in which he himself revelled. It was not surprising, therefore, that one of the concertos performed by Alfredo with Goossens was Walton's Violin Concerto. The review of that performance by Lindsay Browne, successor to Neville Cardus as music critic of the *Sydney Morning Herald*, himself fearless and knowledgeable, was glowing in admiration for Alfredo's playing, and perceptive also in pointing to some of the work's musical problems.

> Alfredo Campoli gave an astonishing performance of the solo part in Walton's violin concerto at last night's orchestral concert in the Town Hall – an achievement which quite stole the emphasis from the first Australian performance by Eugène Goossens and the Sydney Symphony Orchestra of Bartok's music for strings, celesta and percussion.
>
> Probably no other violinist alive is so richly equipped as Campoli is to throw light into the obscurer places of Walton's score, a large and wide-ranging piece of cosmopolitan music-making which blows like a weathercock in a squall from poignantly forlorn lyricism to demon virtuosity. These elements of desolation and dazzle are beautifully opposed to each other, even though there is a feeling at the finish that Walton has not been able to make choice between them.
>
> Campoli in his violin-playing displays just those points of fine and careful craftsmanship that must have been characteristic, in their different field, of the great fiddle-makers of Cremona. The solitary and wayward lyricism of the opening movement was revealed with enchanting depth of tone and arch of phrase. None of the technical sorcery in the speeding devil-dance of the second movement withheld its secrets from him. Even

[11] For a description of the complex negotations over the salary package, see Charles Buttrose, *Playing for Australia* (Macmillan, 1982), pp. 55–6.

> the last movement – which can seem to waste a good deal of time in hunting about for a logical point of repose and completeness – was held together expertly by the diversity and brilliance of Campoli's resource.
>
> Goossens and the orchestra gave him admirable support. At most times the orchestra, which Walton uses in groups and with sparing weight, provided an ideal environment for the solo line. Such playing, so soon after the baffling and exhausting difficulties of Bartok, was a credit to the orchestra and a rare compliment to Campoli.

It was a gratifying conclusion to the Australian tour. In a few days they would all be crossing the Tasman Sea by air for New Zealand.

New Zealand

On arrival in New Zealand, Alfredo and Joy found a country akin to Australia in many ways, both socially and politically, yet different from the huge continent they had just left. Both countries enjoyed high standards of living and socially advanced conditions, New Zealand, for example, being the first in the world to give the vote to women. Even though drawn together at that time through deep devotion to Britain, from where the majority of their citizens originated and for whom they had both fought in two world wars, the two countries nevertheless prided themselves on being different from the other. To Australian eyes New Zealanders have usually seemed to be of a milder disposition, far more 'English' than their neighbours across the Tasman. Though separated by only 1,200 miles of sea, thriving tourism between the two countries was not yet fashionable, despite the extraordinary scenery that New Zealand had to offer Australians. Packing into its two main islands everything from vast alpine scenery and lakes in the south to lush grasslands, boiling mud and geysers in the north, it was to provide Alfredo's cameras with shots of some of the most beautiful scenery in the world. Its economy, based on agriculture and dairying, was thriving in those post-war days when Britain, years before its entry into the European Common Market, was New Zealand's main customer. As so often happens, New Zealand's thriving economy was accompanied by a cultural life, which, though not as strong in orchestral spread as in Australia, was nevertheless firmly established in chamber and choral music. Margaret Schofield considered that New Zealand audiences at that time were more discriminating than those in Australia.[12]

Alfredo and Joy landed at Auckland airport where a bouquet of flowers greeted them from a friend whom they had known only through correspondence. They were sent from the little town of Te Awamutu where Leslie Haynes, a violin enthusiast and father of six musically-gifted children lived. At the beginning of the war he had written to Alfredo, expressing his admiration for his playing and

12 Personal interview with the author.

requesting a photograph. As usual, it was Joy who, touched that someone so far away should write, replied more fully than usual, and in the years that followed when many commodities were severely rationed in England not only a regular flow of letters passed between them, but also regular food parcels to the Campolis. The two families were to meet eventually on the tour.

As in Australia, things were on the move musically in New Zealand. The National Orchestra of the New Zealand Broadcasting Service, led by the English violinist Vincent Asbey and conducted by Anderson Tyrer, had given its first performance only three years before Alfredo's tour. Based in Wellington, it was, and still is, New Zealand's only full-time professional orchestra, and at the time of Alfredo's first visit its resident conductor was Michael Bowles with whom he was to perform concertos by Tchaikovsky, Mendelssohn, Beethoven and Walton in Dunedin and Christchurch. At that time inexperienced in modern music, the National Orchestra had to work strenuously at the Walton concerto and without Alfredo's help and encouragement it is unlikely that it would have mastered it as it did.[13] If centres outside Auckland had to wait their turn for performances by the National Orchestra, there was, on the other hand, no shortage of chamber music throughout the country. Cultivation of chamber music had its roots in the earliest settlement days, and if its subsequent history up until 1950 was not spectacular this was balanced by a sustained interest in this form of music.[14] The strongest centre for chamber music had been Wellington, and after the war the Wellington Chamber Music Society envisaged a national 'co-operative' that came into being as The Music Federation of New Zealand shortly after Alfredo's tour had finished. Unlike the early days of Musica Viva in Australia there was no single chamber music group touring on behalf of the Federation. A co-ordinating organisation serving the whole country, it was to bring to many centres very fine local and overseas ensembles, many of which were outside the traditional format of trios, quartets and quintets. It was the Federation, for example, who engaged Alfredo for a sonata tour of New Zealand in 1972, which he undertook with the New Zealand pianist Maurice Till.[15]

New Zealand audiences heard much the same repertoire as Alfredo and Margaret Schofield had played in Australia, and during the two and half months they were there they played in Auckland, Wellington and Hamilton in the North

[13] Personal communication with Geoffrey Newson who was Music Administrator of the New Zealand Broadcasting Corporation at the time, and who occasionally played double-bass with its National Orchestra.

[14] John Mansfield Thomson, *Into a New Key. The Origins and History of The Music Federation of New Zealand 1950–1982* (Wellington, 1985), p. 19.

[15] Other performers engaged that year by the Federation were: Amadeus Quartet, Consortium Classicum, Jorg Demus, Simon Estes (with Maurice Till), Michael Houston, The King's Singers, Barry Morgan, Music Players 70, Paillard Chamber Orchestra, Carl Pini Quartet, Sylvia Rosenberg (with Janetta McStay), Bryan Sayer, Farquhar Wilkinson (with Janetta McStay) (Thomson, 1985, p. 181).

Island before moving to the South Island where their first recital was at Dunedin. Then on to the southernmost town in New Zealand – Invercargill – and up to Gore and Christchurch. Returning to the North Island their tour took them again to Wellington, Wanganui, Palmerston North, Hastings, Gisborne, Tauranga, Napier, and finally back to Auckland for their farewell concert in the Town Hall. Looking back to that tour Aflredo found the North Island more appreciative of music than the South, but, philosophical as always, declared that while the audiences at Dunedin may have been small, he at least played some excellent bridge there![16]

They had been away for nearly six months and it was time now to return to London. At the end of September Alfredo and Joy boarded the ship which would bring them home via the Panama Canal, thus ending the first of many international tours which would ultimately take him to almost every major country in the world, including the USA and Russia. The next ten years were, perhaps, the most decisive in his long career, and they were to see him fully emerge as an international artist.

[16] *Auckland Star*, 29 September 1950.

Chapter 7

Campoli, International Artist

The visit to Australia and New Zealand was the beginning of a busy programme of international touring that marked Alfredo's career for a number of years. Following his return from that long and arduous itinerary 'down under' his next concert appearance outside Britain was in July, 1951, when he went to Paris to play with the Orchestra of the Concerts Colonne at the Salle Gaveau. It was his first appearance as a concert artist in the French capital, and he was soloist in a fairly new work by the Spanish conductor and composer Frederico Elizalde (1907–79).

Elizalde's career in some senses mirrored Alfredo's in that it had begun with a serious study of music (at the Madrid Conservatory under Trago and Perez Casas), followed by a début at the age of fourteen – as pianist, conductor and composer. Sent to the USA by his parents to study Law at Stanford University (during which time he had lessons with Ernest Bloch), he then came to England where he entered Cambridge University in 1926 to complete his training as a lawyer. While there he turned to light music in which he made a considerable reputation, especially through his espousal of American jazz. Invited in 1927 to take a band into the Savoy Hotel, Fred Elizalde (as he was then known as) engaged some musicians from New York to play in it, their flair and originality greatly stimulating the jazz scene in London. The band regularly broadcast from the hotel, but their style so aroused the hostility of dancers, who couldn't recognise their favourite tunes in the flamboyant improvisations, that it was taken off the air and eventually replaced by another band at the Savoy.[1]

From 1930 Elizalde shared his activities between orchestral conducting and serious composition, working in Manila, Paris and Spain. As a composer he seems to have enjoyed considerable success. In 1935 he was a delegate for Spanish Music at the Florentine May Musical Festival, and the following year he represented Spain at the International Festival of Contemporary Music at Barcelona. His opera *Paul Gaugin*, to a libretto by Théophile Briant, was chosen and broadcast by French Radio to commemorate the centenary of the birth of the famous painter. After serving in the Spanish Civil War he retired to Bayonne in France for the duration of the Second World War, and it was here, during his most fruitful period as a composer, that he wrote his violin concerto. Its first performance in 1945 was given by Ginette Neveu whose career was cut short by the tragedy of a fatal plane crash four years later.

---

[1] Albert McCarthy, *The Dance-Band Era: The Dancing Decades From Ragtime to Swing* (London, 1971), p. 48. Quoted in D.L. Le Mahieu, *A Culture for Democracy* (Oxford, 1988) and Simon Frith, *Music for Pleasure* (Oxford, 1988).

The composer himself conducted Alfredo's performance at the Salle Gaveau, but in reviewing it the music-critic of *Opéra* was less impressed with him as conductor than as composer. In either role Elizade was eclipsed by Alfredo.

> Frederico Elizalde was already known to us as a conductor, and again showed no great capabilities in this direction. In fact, he is more at home in the sphere of composition such as his Violin Concerto consisting of various Iberian motifs, which a marvellous Italian violinist, Campoli, succeeded in raising to unexpected heights. Marvellous is the word which serves to describe a talent of such outstanding ability, together with great beauty of tone and expression.[2]

Alfredo and Elizalde were to perform the same work three days later at the Royal Festival Hall, this time with the London Symphony Orchestra. On that occasion the music-critic of *The Times*, while complimenting Alfredo on his 'brilliance and suavity' was more impressed by Elizalde as conductor than Elizalde as composer, dismissing the concerto as '. . . a harmless entertainment, with some pleasant sound effects, though it will not survive consideration as other than light music'.[3] Nine years later the BBC wrote to Alfredo asking him if he would ever want to play it again.[4] No reply has survived, but the mute evidence of its absence in his programmes suggests that he did not think very highly of it. It seems to have disappeared entirely from the repertoire.

Alfredo's performance in Paris was his only one outside Britain that year, which was a busy one for him at home, including a number of performances of the Walton concerto, one of which was at the Proms. In another appearance at the Proms that season he played Lalo's *Symphonie espagnole*, the performance of which was made even more memorable by one of Alfredo's strings breaking during the performance, leading to much laughter and applause on the part of the good-natured audience and even making a small headline in *The Times*.[5] Audiences that year also heard Alfredo for the first time in Brahms's Double Concerto with cellist Anthony Pini who, it will be remembered, had often played with Alfredo in salon orchestras and ensembles during the 1930s, and who, like Alfredo, was now devoting himself entirely to concert work. (Later performances of the Double Concerto were to be with Gaspar Cassado and André Navarra.)

Another work he played for the first time was Arthur Bliss's *Theme and Cadenza* for violin and orchestra in a studio broadcast heard on 12 September that year. This piece began as incidental music to a radio play called *Memorial Concert* by Arthur Bliss's wife Trudy, and produced for the BBC by Felix Felton. The play was broadcast on 11 March 1946. For that production the violin solos

---

[2] *Opéra*, 18 July 1951.

[3] *The Times*, 14 July 1951.

[4] Letter from Leonard Isaacs, 26 October 1960.

[5] *The Times*, 13 August 1951.

were played by Max Rostal with the BBC Symphony Orchestra conducted by Lionel Salter. The story concerns a young composer, whose gifts, largely through the encouragement and support of his devoted wife – a concert violinist – are only fully realised in his violin concerto. Their marriage and his creative career are ended when the composer, whose arrogance conceals both insecurity and weakness, is lured to an easy life by a second marriage to the beautiful and rich woman who had attended the première performance of his concerto given by his first wife. After his unexpected death a memorial concert is arranged. On the platform his first wife plays the concerto – the first time she has played it since its première performance; in the audience sits his second wife. It is almost as it was ten years ago. The play concludes with her spoken thoughts: 'I had only to crook my little finger and he came. But that woman playing his music . . . she looks as though she could take anything she wanted and keep it. She is smooth and serene . . . perhaps . . . perhaps I never took Peter from her after all . . .'. Her words are taken over by the last bars of the cadenza and the orchestral chords of the finale.

Arthur Bliss re-cast this music into a short, independent work which he called *Theme and Cadenza*. While the title might suggest that the work ends in solo display, in reality the form is tripartite, opening and closing with the lyrical theme, the middle section (the 'cadenza') being like a free fantasia. Here, the soloist, still accompanied by the orchestra, intensifies the emotional response to the poignant story through exploiting in an expressive way some of the virtuosic resources of the instrument. As might be expected from the nature of the radio play, the music is richly romantic. And as also might be expected from a composer whose output includes a number of memorable film scores, it is wonderfully effective. However, the very shortness of the work (some six or seven minutes) probably precludes it from many live performances, but Alfredo's recording – the only one of this work – made in 1955 with the London Philharmonic Orchestra conducted by the composer (and now re-issued under another label; see Appendix A) offers yet further confirmation of Bliss's consummate craftsmanship as well as Alfredo's superb playing.

Splendidly as it may have started, 1951 ended in great sadness for Alfredo. It will be recalled that Elvira had suffered a severe stroke the year before Alfredo and Joy had embarked upon the tour to Australia and New Zealand. Alfredo's anxiety over her health had, indeed, been the only cloud over that tour. Elvira survived his absence, but a year later she was dying. On 23 December 1951 Alfredo was to broadcast Elgar's Violin Concerto over the Third Programme with the BBC Symphony Orchestra conducted by Charles Groves. Three hours before the broadcast, scheduled for 6.30 that evening, his beloved mother died. He decided he must still play. Afterwards he recalled how his grief seemed to have been transfigured into a vision of his mother beside him, leading to a performance that could truly be called inspired. Some of those who heard it over the air that night were spellbound. Amongst them was the writer and critic Alec Robertson. Unaware of the circumstances, he wrote to Alfredo to say that never before had he heard him play with such depth of feeling. Elvira had meant much to her son. She had relinquished her own career to devote herself to his, and had lived with Joy and Alfredo all their married life until her final illness made that impossible. Her death was the end of an era in Alfredo's life.

The next year, 1952, saw Alfredo in Bombay, Singapore, Kuala Lumpur, Bangkok and Hong Kong, and the following year took him to Spain, the first of his many visits to that part of the world. The highlight at the end of that year and the beginning of the next was, however, his long tour of Canada and the USA which included his début at Carnegie Hall.

With the exception of New York, Alfredo's two-and-a-half-month tour was largely a provincial one, covering many miles on the east coast through countryside, town and city, by coach, train and plane. Unlike his tour in Australia and New Zealand when he was accompanied by the same pianist on every occasion, this time he was partnered by six different pianists, including the well-known John Newmark and Arthur Balsam. The repertoire he chose (or which was chosen for him) was far more limited than for the earlier tour: Tartini's 'Devil's Trill' Sonata, Bach's Chaconne, Beethoven's 'Spring' Sonata, Dohnányi's *Ruralia Hungarica*, and Poulenc's 1944 Sonata. Concerto-type works were Lalo's *Symphonie espagnole* and Saint-Saëns's *Introduction and Rondo capriccioso*, and there was also Bruch's G minor Concerto.

Leaving London by plane on 27 November he arrived next day in Montreal and travelled by coach to the Canadian industrial town of Trois Rivières on the north shore of the Saint Lawrence River where, with Reginald Boardman at the piano, he gave his first recital in North America. As in another Canadian town (Chicoutimi) two weeks later, the critics here placed Alfredo in the same class as Menuhin, Heifetz, Kreisler, Elman and Szigeti, claiming that if he had played in America earlier in his career he would have been as well known as those celebrities. But of course, the big test was his New York début at Carnegie Hall on 5 and 6 December when he played Lalo's *Symphonie espagnole* with the New York Philharmonic Orchestra under George Szell. Audience and critics alike were completely won over, and Alfredo was brought back to the platform four times. The beauty of his tone particularly struck the critics. The review in *Musical America* is typical.

> The precision of his intonation was somewhat relative because he was not above the portamento that is permissible and indeed becoming in the Lalo work, but his huge, heavenly tone quite obviated the usual finicky considerations. His assurance in technical matters was amply manifest in the effortless way that he sailed through the most difficult passages, and he gave to the music a dignity and a compelling loveliness it rarely has, which is measure enough. For sheer loveliness of sound he has few equals today.

Alfredo returned to New York a month later to give a recital with Arthur Balsam in the Town Hall, and once again his playing was glowingly reviewed. Only his performance of Bach's Chaconne was found wanting by the New York critics who felt that it was small-scaled and rather uneven – surely a disappoint-ment to Alfredo who loved the work deeply and who performed it whenever he could. With all the other works Alfredo swept the critics along with him.

Besides those places already mentioned Alfredo gave recitals in Albany and Mount Vernon in New York State; Deland, St Petersburg and Lake Worth in Florida; Augusta and Savannah in Georgia; Roanoke and Rollins in Virginia; Charlotte in North Carolina and Greenville in South Carolina; and Dallas in Texas. At the end of the tour he performed in Montreal before boarding his plane homewards on 21 February, arriving back with the credentials of a successful American tour that, six years earlier, the BBC Music Department had believed to be so essential for his career in England. (See Chapter 5.)

Less than a month later Alfredo was in Paris (the first of two visits that year) to play the Mendelssohn and Brahms concertos at the Concert Lamoureux in the Salle Pleyel, before heading south to Cannes (for a concert with Louis de Froment) en route to Spain to give recitals and concerts in Barcelona, Bilbao, Valencia, Madrid, Santander and San Sebastian. His schedule next took him across to East Africa for recitals in Nairobi, then back home for a few weeks before flying to Durban to take part in the Fifth Civic Centenary Music Festival there with an orchestra conducted by Edward Dunn. 'Not since Menuhin visited many years ago has a violinist received such an ovation' said the *Natal Mercury* of Alfredo's appearance in Durban. On his way back to London Alfredo stopped off once more at Nairobi for what was described as a 'Welcome Back Recital' with the accompanist Egon Weisz who had partnered him there previously.

During the few months that Alfredo was in England during 1954 one of the most notable events was his performance of Moeran's violin concerto at the Royal Festival Hall with the BBC Symphony Orchestra under Adrian Boult. This was the first time he had played this work, one of Moeran's finest and written five years before the composer's death in 1950. This very lyrical work expressing, as did all his music, Moeran's nostalgic love of the English countryside, also contains passages of considerable energy and vitality. It appealed strongly to Alfredo who was to perform it a number of times. Amongst the audience at that concert in the Royal Festival Hall on 13 October was Dr Keith Barry of the Music Department of the Australian Broadcasting Commission. He wrote back to the Director of Music, William G. James in glowing terms about Alfredo's performance, suggesting that the ABC had not 'made the most of him' during his 1950 tour, probably because of the way the tour had been managed. In his letter Keith Barry described how the BBC Music Department had told him that Alfredo was 'far and away the best resident violinist in England'.[6] It is not surprising that the ABC was to engage him for further major tours of Australia in 1960 and 1966.

6 File 1.4.13, ABC Archives, undated, 1954.

During his American tour Alfredo had lunched with Fritz Kreisler (whom he had met once before in London). The possibility of Alfredo making a new recording of Kreisler's arrangement of Paganini's first concerto, replacing the one he had made under Victor Olof released by Decca in 1947, came up in their conversation.[7] In fact, the second recording was eventually to be made with the London Symphony Orchestra under Piero Gamba and released by Decca in 1957. But it was in another recording that Alfredo's life-long admiration of Kreisler found its fullest expression.

On 2 February 1955 Fritz Kreisler turned eighty. To mark the occasion Decca released Alfredo's recording *Homage to Fritz Kreisler* in which he played fifteen works – arrangements and original compositions – by this musician who had become a legend in his own lifetime. Kreisler's own compositions were represented by *Liebeslied*, *Liebesfreud*, *Polichinelle-Serenade*, *Schön Rosmarin*, *Caprice Viennois*, *Tambourin chinois*, *La gitana*, *Rondino on a theme of Beethoven*, as well as *Praeludium and Allegro*, which had been accepted (even by leading writers on music) as the work of the eighteenth-century composer Gaetano Pugnani – until 1935 when Kreisler revealed the hoax. Arrangements of works by other composers were *La chasse* (Cartier), *Minuet in G* (Paderewski), *Danse Espagnole* (Granados), *Variations on a theme of Corelli* (Tartini) and Wieniaswski's *Caprice in E flat* and *Caprice in A minor*. The accompanist, who had played these works over many years with Alfredo, was Eric Gritton, and the recording was greeted with glowing reviews. The opening paragraph from the review in *The Gramophone* says it all.

> Here is something wonderful and unique: a recorded tribute, in music, to a great violinist on his eightieth birthday; a tribute from a violinist who (although Kreisler's junior by about thirty years) is surely one of the very few who has so keen and sympathetic an insight into the master's style. Campoli here has excelled himself. He has chosen fifteen pieces associated in one way or another with the name of Fritz Kreisler, and he plays them for us with that moving merger of subtlety, brilliance and charm that makes this music what it is. His pianist, Eric Gritton, enters into the spirit of the recording with equal enthusiasm and devotion. The result is a disc of rare beauty; one that should on no account be missed by lovers of Kreisler's creative gifts, or admirers of fine fiddle-playing.[8]

A few months after the release of *Homage to Fritz Kreisler* Alfredo gave the first performance of a work in a very different style from that of Kreisler. It was the Violin Concerto by Arthur Bliss written for and dedicated to him.

Shortly after Sir Arthur Bliss had been appointed Master of the Queen's Music in 1953 he had begun work on a BBC commission for a 'violin concerto

---

7 Campoli in recorded conversation with John Allt, May 1985.

8 *The Gramophone*, March, 1955.

for Alfredo Campoli', a project which appealed to him immensely because, as he once said, he liked to have a special performer in mind when starting a composition, which then became a collaboration between performer and composer.[9] Just how much a collaboration it was between Alfredo and Arthur Bliss can be gauged by the composer's description of it in his autobiography.

> I took my time over the Concerto, and found working with Campoli a most rewarding experience . . . I learnt a lot about violin technique from him. As each section of the concerto was sketched I would take it to his house, and we would play it through together. If a passage seemed to him ineffective, he would exaggerate its difficulty, distorting his face in anguish. He would suggest an alteration, and then play it through again, murmuring 'beautiful, beautiful'! I was always amused at his play-acting, but the result of his persuasive cajoling was that, whether the concerto be liked or not, it is certainly apt for the instrument.[10]

Just as Bliss's Piano Concerto owes much to Liszt's, so the Violin Concerto owes much to Paganini's, and Bliss took it as a good omen that on a brief holiday in Genoa shortly after completing the concerto he saw Paganini's violin in the museum, and was told (probably erroneously) that Alfredo had recently given a broadcast from there on the famous instrument.[11] The work is indeed a virtuoso piece in which Alfredo's all-encompassing technique found full play.[12] It was given its première in the Royal Festival Hall on 11 May, 1955 with the BBC Symphony Orchestra under Malcolm Sargent. The critic of *The Times* described Alfredo's performance as 'dazzling and warmly mellifluous', and remarked that the scherzo movement allowed him to 'unfold long stretches of the most prodigious spiccato bowing'.[13]

Bliss recalled that there was only one place in the concerto where he and Alfredo had differing views.

> The argument concerns the joining of the cadenza (in the last movement) to the final coda. After rising to his high notes at the end of this long cadenza Campoli wishes to plunge straight into the *animato* which carries

---

9 Handwritten note by the composer written shortly before his death in 1975 for a BBC recorded concert that year, a copy of which was kindly given to the author by Lady Bliss. The soloist for that broadcast was John Georgidis.

10 Arthur Bliss, *As I Remember* (London, 1970), pp. 193–4.

11 Joy Campoli believes that Arthur Bliss was mistaken about Campoli giving a broadcast on Paganini's violin. She feels that at the most the authorities may have allowed him to handle the instrument for a little while.

12 Campoli's performance under the composer, recorded in Kingsway Hall in 1955, has recently been released on CD by Beulah in the series Campoli Classics (3PD10.)

13 *The Times*, 12 May 1955. Spiccato playing is when the bow is dropped on the string and is lifted again after each note, which in rapid playing produces a very brilliant effect.

> the finale to its quick brilliant close. I quite see the soloist's point of view; he feels he has now said his say, and so wants promptly to say 'good-bye'. But before he can do so I have delayed this with a twenty-four bar passage of mysterious half light, which, as a composer, I find a beautiful bridge passage. Which of us is right? By now, I myself am not sure. So, in future performances, I shall adopt an aleatory attitude, and allow the soloist to decide for himself.[14]

Composer and dedicatee were to perform the work together on a number of occasions, but undoubtedly the most thrilling one was in Russia the year following its première.

During a visit to London in November 1954 the composer/conductor Khatchaturian had come up with the idea of a tour of the Soviet Union by a group of British musicians. Stalin had died the year before, and the first signs of a thaw in relations with the West were beginning to appear under the new leadership of Khrushchev. Khatchaturian's suggestion was taken up a few months later by the British Council and the Soviet authorities, with the result that the Master of the Queen's Musick, Sir Arthur Bliss, was invited to head such a group.[15] It would be the first visit to the Soviet Union by British musicians since the war. At this stage no dates had been settled and it was not until January 1956 that Bliss was contacted to arrange the tour for April and May that year – no easy task to bring together a group of the finest British musicians who would be free for three weeks at such short notice. Nevertheless he gathered seven superb performers: Alfredo, Gerald Moore, Leon Goossens, soprano Jennifer Vyvyan, husband and wife piano duo team Phyllis Sellick and Cyril Smith, and conductor Clarence Raybould. Sir Arthur would also conduct. Lady Bliss, who also came on the tour, affectionately called the group 'The Blissters'. Officially it was called a 'musical delegation', for it was a case of music placed at the service of diplomacy.

An agreement was drawn up whereby the Soviet Ministry of Culture was responsible for all travel costs and artists' fees (paid in sterling) and their living costs (paid in roubles).[16] Generous time was set aside for rehearsals – thirteen hours for each concert, for most of the music to be played by the USSR State Orchestra, and the Symphony Orchestras at Leningrad and Kiev was unfamiliar to them. The chosen repertoire was a shop-window of British orchestral music up to that time, taking into account also what concerto-like works the soloists were prepared to play. It consisted of *Tam O'Shanter* (Malcolm Arnold), Concerto for two pianos (Lennox Berkeley), Piano Concerto, Violin Concerto, Five Dances from *Checkmate* and March from *Things to Come* (these works all by Arthur

[14] Bliss, 1970, p. 194.

[15] Letter from the British Council to the Soviet Ambassador (Y.A. Malik) to Britain, 27 January 1956, in which a brief background to the tour is given (Public Records Office, London).

[16] Letter from Ian Hunter, Managing Director of Harold Holt Ltd, to the Soviet Ministry of Culture, 15 March 1956 (Public Records Office, London).

Bliss), *Young Person's Guide to the Orchestra* (Benjamin Britten), Oboe Concertos (Arnold Cooke and Gordon Jacob), *Cockaigne Overture*, Waltz Song from *Tom Jones* (Edward German), *Street-Corner Overture* (Alan Rawsthorne), *Portsmouth Point Overture* (William Walton) and *London Symphony* (Vaughan Williams). In addition to these British works were *Exultate Jubilate* and *Martern aller Arten* (Mozart) and *Carnival of the Animals* (Saint-Saëns). Solo recitals featured a mix of British music and the classical repertoire.

While most of the delegation were able to leave by plane on 14 April for Moscow Airport, where they were greeted by Kabalevsky and Khatchaturian, together with representatives of the Ministry of Culture and the Philharmonic Society and others, Alfredo and Gerald Moore had to leave London a day later because of previous commitments. (Alfredo was playing the Elgar Concerto in the Royal Festival Hall on 15 April.) While they missed out on the grand welcome at Moscow, and landed unexpectedly in Leningrad because of bad weather, even there – stranded as they were – they were given a cordial welcome.

There were sixteen performances in all, in Moscow, Kiev, Karkhov, and Leningrad, all of which were booked out by the time the British musicians had arrived. Alfredo made five appearances. Three of these were recitals with Gerald Moore in which they performed Handel's Sonata in A, Beethoven's 'Kreutzer' Sonata, and Kreisler's arrangement of Paganini's Concerto in D. Alfredo also played Bach's Chaconne in each of these recitals in the three cities. At a concert given in the Great Hall of the Moscow Conservatory, he played Mendelssohn's Concerto with the USSR Symphony Orchestra under Clarence Raybould. On that occasion the remainder of the programme included some Russian works: Glinka's Overture to *Russlan and Ludmilla* and Theme and Variations from Tchaikovsky's Third Suite featuring a Russian soloist.

At the farewell concert Soviet Premier Bulganin and Communist Party Chief Khrushchev (who wielded the real power) invited Sir William and Lady Hayter to share their box. The tour was not just a triumph for British diplomacy and British music; it was also personal triumph for Alfredo. Gerald Moore recalled that it was not only in the Beethoven and Bach sonatas that the audiences were so enthusiastic, but that it was also Alfredo's dazzling virtuosity and sweetness of tone in his last group of Kreisler pieces that sent them 'wild with delight', adding that nor would this response be different perhaps in any other part of the world.[17] Yet, it was the Bliss Concerto that created the greatest impact – through the presence of the composer on the rostrum, the originality of the work and Alfredo's playing.[18] Looking back to that period he described how string players gathered round Alfredo 'like a swarm of bees' and how in Moscow and Leningrad he was held in just as high esteem as David Oistrakh.[19]

---

17 Moore, 1962, p. 242.

18 Moore, 1962, p. 243.

19 Gerald Moore in an article published in *Music and Musicians*, July, 1956.

Oistrakh had indeed shown great interest in the tour. While Alfredo and Gerald Moore sat in Leningrad airport after their belated arrival in Russia they heard Oistrakh's voice over the radio telling his listeners how much he was looking forward to meeting his old friend Alfredo Campoli and to hearing an artist who was one of the world's greatest violinists.[20] He was present at as many concerts and recitals as he could fit in, despite a heavy teaching load all day, snatching stand-up meals in between lessons, and was particularly impressed by their performance of the 'Kreutzer' Sonata.[21]

In addition to the excitement of the concerts there was the stimulus of social contacts and the rare privilege of seeing behind the Iron Curtain, which at that time was firmly closed to most Westerners. Most surprising of all was that, unlike on his visit to Prague the year before when he played in its Spring Festival and where his camera was confiscated, he was allowed to photograph everything except the Leningrad railway station. Alfredo took advantage of this opportunity and amongst other things produced a movie that caught scenes of all the places they visited, from part of a performance of the Bolshoi Ballet in Moscow to scenes of women labourers working alongside men on the railway lines. One of the most spectacular events he witnessed and captured on film was the May Day celebration at Kiev. Several of the British group were given seats on a dais overlooking the huge new avenue along which the march was to take place and Alfredo was allowed to set his movie camera on a small platform erected specially for him. The event began with the Commander of the Kiev forces and the defender of Stalingrad approaching by cars in opposite directions along the troop-lined thoroughfare, their meeting marked by a salute of guns, and the raising of a huge Ukrainian flag. Following the military march past came a three-hour procession of civilians – over a quarter of a million of them, finishing with a group of young athletes.[22] Much of this Alfredo caught on film. On returning home he edited it and added a sound-track with appropriate music and a commentary spoken by Joy, entering it into a competition organised by the *Amateur Ciné World* which awarded him a special commendation.

On the last Sunday of their visit – three days before they were due to return home – the British Ambassador Sir William Hayter invited the musical delegation to drinks at the Embassy. The Russian guests were the Minister for Culture (Mikailov) and various leading Soviet musicians: the elderly composer Glier (Glière) who died only a month later, Kabalevsky, Khatchaturian, the singers Mark Reyzen, Natal'ya Rozhdestvenskaya and her conductor son Gennady, composer/conductor Alexey Kozlovsky, composer and musicologist Igor Belza, together with some leading violinists.[23] The only members of the British group absent from the reception were Phyllis Sellick and Cyril Smith, the latter having

20 Moore, 1956.

21 Gerald Moore, 1960, p. 242.

22 See Bliss, 1970, p. 198, for a vivid description of the event.

23 Entry dated Sunday 6 May 1956 in Lady Hayter's personal diary.

suffered a severe stroke during the tour and who at that time was in hospital before being allowed to return home some weeks after the others had left. It was the only shadow over what had been a brilliantly successful and highly enjoyable period.[24]

While in Russia the British musicians had received generous fees. There was only one problem. They were not permitted to take roubles out of the country. The only solution was a spending spree. Alfredo spent his roubles on a magnificent 144-piece collection of glassware and gifts for Joy, which the Ambassador arranged (as he did for all the 'souvenirs' brought home by Alfredo's colleagues) to be passed through Heathrow duty-free.

Such was the success of that visit that another was arranged for mid-September that year, this time for an entire orchestra – the London Philharmonic Orchestra under conductors Sir Adrian Boult, George Hurst and Anatole Fistoulari. The two soloists for the occasion were Moura Lympani and Alfredo. Sir Adrian and Lady Boult went by train to Moscow as flying affected Boult's ears badly, but the rest went by air. In all, thirteen concerts were given in Moscow and Leningrad by the LPO in programmes that were predominantly British, including Walton's Violin Concerto in which, of course, Alfredo was the soloist. As before, all the concerts were sold out before the musicians arrived, and everyone was greeted with flowers, speeches and enthusiasm. A memorable event during the visit was the celebration of Shostakovitch's fiftieth birthday on 25 September held in the Great Hall of Moscow University where works of the composer were played by the Moscow Philharmonic Orchestra and the Moscow Radio Orchestra, after which he was presented with the Order of Lenin.[25] As well as performances of the Walton Concerto, Alfredo played a solo recital in the Tchaikovsky Hall in Moscow, accompanied by a Russian pianist Andrei Mytnic. They performed sonatas by Tartini, Brahms and Poulenc, as well as works by Bach and Paganini. On that return trip Alfredo was asked to show the movie made previously to an invited audience at an official banquet. This he did, tactfully omitting the scenes of the women railway workers. It was also on that return visit to Russia that Oistrakh, on hearing that Alfredo would be touring Australia again, produced a coil of his precious Siberian horsehair – stronger that normal horsehair and very difficult to obtain – so that there would be no problems with his bow during that long period away.[26]

The Russian tours alone were taxing, yet in between them Alfredo was away for almost two months in South America, playing in Chile, Argentina and Brazil. When he was in England it was the usual busy round of engagements: four appearances at the Proms, recitals and concerts at the Royal Festival Hall and in

[24] See Cyril Smith, *Duet for Three Hands* (London, 1958), pp. 180–88.

[25] See Adrian Boult, *My Own Trumpet* (London 1973), pp. 159–65, for a description of that tour.

[26] Quoted in the *Richmond River Express*, 20 April 1960, as well as in other Australian newspapers at that time.

the provinces, and performances in Paris. There could be no doubt from the busy schedule alone that Alfredo Campoli had become one of the most celebrated international performers of his day.

Alfredo's ten-year association with the accompanist Eric Gritton came to an end in February of the next year. He had, of course, played with a number of noted accompanists besides Gritton since his re-establishment as a concert violinist after the war. Amongst them were Flora Kent, with whom he appeared many times, and that doyen of the art Ivor Newton, who had first accompanied Alfredo in 1930 and in most of the Harold Fielding seaside concerts in 1949. In January 1953 Alfredo appeared with George Malcolm at the Royal Festival Hall, the first of a number of live and broadcast performances they made together and culminating in one of Alfredo's most welcomed recordings: Six Sonatas by Handel. Following Eric Gritton's retirement, however, it was with three younger pianists that Alfredo was to be most closely associated, two of them for many years. It was the BBC who suggested the rising young pianist Peter Katin as Eric Gritton's replacement as a sonata partner for Alfredo, and at the beginning of February 1956 the partnership was officially announced.

Peter Katin (b. 1930), of Russian extraction, entered the Royal Academy of Music in London at the age of twelve to study with Harold Craxton, making his début at Wigmore Hall six years later. On 30 March 1956 the partnership between Peter Katin, now aged twenty-five and Alfredo Campoli nearly as many years his senior, commenced with a broadcast performance of a work fully testing Katin's musicianship, technical command and rapport with his more experienced partner: Beethoven's 'Kreutzer' Sonata. A measure of the success of this partnership, which lasted until 1964, is that they were to give nearly twenty more recitals, both broadcast and live. Other sonatas included Beethoven's C minor, Mozart's K304 and K526, Brahms's D minor sonata, and those by Fauré and Dvorak (Sonatine).

Yet, especially for his BBC broadcasts, Alfredo had also needed not only a sonata partner but a pianist who would play his wide-ranging repertoire, including the major sonatas and those many pieces that Alfredo's audiences loved as much as he enjoyed playing them – one who would be prepared to tour with him around the country and beyond. It was Alfredo's good fortune to secure the services of Daphne Ibbott.

As a gifted piano student at the Royal Academy of Music during the early 1940s she had played on various occasions for one of the singing students from Roy Henderson's studio there. Asked one day whether she would play for a singer who was coming down from Carlisle to audition for Ibbs and Tillett she found herself playing for Kathleen Ferrier. That rehearsal was the beginning of an association that took them on a number of tours together throughout Britain, the warm-hearted Lancastrian taking it upon herself to look after her 'Little Daf' with motherly care. Invited to fill in for one of Alfredo's accompanists who was unable to play, Daphne Ibbott was soon engaged as his regular pianist, and within less than a week of Eric Gritton retiring she was on her way to Gibraltar with Alfredo for the first of many tours outside and throughout Britain. After Gibraltar it was a whirlwind tour to Spain from east to west, their programmes featuring sonatas by Beethoven and Brahms as well as works by Tartini, Bach and Paganini. On the basis of surviving programmes and Alfredo's engagement diary entries she played at least 165 recitals with him, the last being at the Leeds College of Music on 7 March 1984. It was thus the longest association that Alfredo enjoyed with a regular pianist, lasting as it did for twenty-seven years. Their recitals included appearances in the Sixth International Festival in Spain, at the Royal Festival and Queen Elizabeth Halls, and in the historic Manoel Theatre in Malta. Daphne Ibbot also made Decca recordings with him.

She found him to be a good travelling companion, full of enthusiasm and zest, with an entertaining sense of humour. But above all she recalls the revelation of working with a man of such emotional, indeed passionate, response to the music he played, even in those pieces that he had performed so many times and yet which always sounded so fresh and spontaneous in his hands. In those early days his constant exhortation 'You're too British, loosen up. I don't care if you play some wrong notes, but play with panache!' helped free her from what she describes as her 'English inhibitions' at that time.[27]

When the partnership with Peter Katin came to an end in 1964 the question again arose as to who would be Alfredo's next sonata partner. BBC policy permitted only one such partnership for broadcasting and as Daphne Ibbott was already the sonata partner of the violinist Nona Liddell Alfredo had to find another broadcast pianist. Once again the muses smiled and towards the end of that year a splendid partnership that was to last thirteen years was formed between Alfredo and Valerie Tryon.

As a child Valerie Tryon had given several public performances (including over the BBC's Children's Hour) before winning an Associated Board Scholarship at the age of fifteen to study at the Royal Academy of Music in London where she was a pupil of Eric Grant for five years. A Boise Scholarship took her to Paris for further studies, and a year later saw her in Budapest where she won a prize for her playing. Three years after joining Alfredo she won a Harriet Cohen International Prize, which had been established by the English composer Arnold Bax, and others. Particularly drawn to Liszt's music, she in fact married one of the foremost Lisztian scholars in Britain, Alan Walker.

It was at the suggestion of Peter Gould in the BBC that Alfredo should consider this gifted pianist as a possible partner after Peter Katin. During their first rehearsal at Alfredo's home there was no doubt in his mind that in Valerie Tryon he had an ideal sonata partner. Their successful first meeting was celebrated with red Cinzano, a drink that she had never tasted before, but which became the ritual after rehearsals from that time on.

---

27 Interview with Daphne Ibbott, 13 October 1996.

It had been Alfredo's desire to perform Strauss's Violin Sonata, but the work had never appealed to Peter Katin. Now the conjunction of his new partnership with Valerie Tryon and the centenary of Strauss's birth in 1964 provided the opportunity to prepare this work, first for a BBC recital – their début together – and then for a commercial recording. For the recording, Strauss's Sonata was coupled with Liszt's Duo Sonata and issued on the Pye Virtuoso Label. They performed over thirty major works, including a number of sonatas not often included in violin recitals, such as those by Busoni, Howells, Medtner and Respighi. Unlike his performances with Daphne Ibbott, all those with Valerie Tryon were within the British Isles and Ireland, except in 1973 when they played in Canada.

Both Daphne Ibbott and Valerie Tryon were kept hard at work by Alfredo, for he insisted that even those works that they had played many times together should be meticulously rehearsed the day, or a few days, before any performance. There are many entries in his professional engagement diaries that show in the same week a rehearsal with Valerie on one day and one with Daphne on another. Nothing was left to chance. These rehearsals invariably took place in the beautiful home that Joy and Alfredo had acquired in September 1955.

Standing in a large garden that included a croquet lawn and, of course, a tennis court, 48 Eversley Park Road in the northern suburb of Winchmore Hill was a fine, seventeen-room house that reflected Alfredo's new status as an international artist. It was to be the scene of many a social event – music, bridge, tennis, dinners, rehearsals and private recitals – so that by the end of Alfredo's career the Visitors Book reads like a *Who's Who* of the musical world. The imposing entrance hall was oak-panelled and the floor carpeted in a rich red wine colour. Most striking was Alfredo's studio, a large and well-proportioned room, its high ceiling featuring a dome painted in light blue, with the surrounding ceiling in white, its mouldings picked out in gold. Violins and bows were complemented by the new grand piano chosen for Alfredo by Peter Katin. And it was in this new home that he was able to spread his vast collection of recordings and scores, his films and his trophies. However, Alfredo and Joy were to be in this splendid house for less than ten years, for neighbours who had moved next door made very clear their objections to Alfredo's rehearsals and teaching. Eventually there was no alternative but to look elsewhere. Yet the Campolis loved the area, and when the opportunity came to purchase 50 Eversley Park Road they moved there. It was smaller (and with no tennis court), but it was still a fine home where they were to live until Alfredo retired from the concert platform.

Alfredo continued to tour internationally until 1978 when he and Daphne Ibbott played in Canada, the fifth time he had played there. From the evidence of surviving programmes, his engagement diaries and press reviews, he played in the following countries (in alphabetical, not chronological order: Australia, Canada, Ceylon, Czechoslovakia, East Africa, Egypt, France, Gibraltar, Hong Kong, Iceland, India, Italy, Japan, Las Palmas, Malaysia, Malta, New Zealand, the Philippines, Poland, Portugal, Russia, Scandinavia, Singapore, South Africa,

South America, Spain, the USA). Many of these were very extensive tours, and some places he visited a number of times, Australia and New Zealand being favourites of his, as was Spain where he and Joy also enjoyed summer holidays. In Rome he had the pleasure of performing at the Teatro Argentina where his mother had once sung as an opera star.

Such was his fondness for Australia and New Zealand that in 1972 he toyed with the idea of settling in one or other of those two countries. The main reason for this lay in his increasing arthritis, which he believed might be alleviated in the drier climate. One of his hip joints had already been replaced in July of the previous year and a few years later it was necessary to have the other one done. It was during a tour to New Zealand in the southern summer of 1972 – his sixth to that country – that he began making inquiries about the possibility of living and working in the antipodes. Geoffrey Newson, Music Administrator of NZBC, suggested that he should contact Professor Frank Callaway, Head of the Department of Music at the University of Western Australia in Perth

Never one to turn away interesting possibilities, Frank Callaway suggested that, as Alfredo was to be performing concertos in Sydney and Brisbane after leaving New Zealand, he might call into Perth en route to London to discuss the matter. He also suggested that Alfredo might care to give a recital and a masterclass at the university at that time. Alfredo arrived in Perth in mid-March and plans were worked out, not for a permanent position but – with help from the Lady Lefroy Bequest, the University Music Society and the University Choral Society – for a three-month period as university musician-in-residence in 1973, one the first positions of its kind in Australia.[28] It was the beginning of an unbroken series of residencies that still operates at the university. Alfredo was to be placed on the academic staff at a full-time professorial salary (in those days amongst the top ten per cent of professional incomes in Australia), which, if not providing Alfredo with his normal fee for individual appearances, had the great advantage of considerably reduced taxation. The temporary situation would give both Alfredo and the university the opportunity to consider whether a permanent position would be the wisest way to go. The recital and masterclass that he gave on this stopover suggested that a stimulating time was in store, and indeed one of the results of this preliminary visit was a video recording of that masterclass. It remains one of the few visual records of Alfredo's teaching.

On 26 May 1973, Alfredo and Joy arrived in Perth and were settled into a house along the handsome road opposite the 1,000-acre Kings Park in the centre of the city. The major plan for the residency was a series of subscription recitals under the general title 'Two Hundred Years of the Violin Sonata', and for the

---

[28] Members of the English group The Alberni String Quartet were also appointed musicians-in-residence during 1973, their period being the first term of the academic year and Alfredo's being the second term. It was, however, Alfredo's appointment that initiated the university's musician-in-residence scheme.

occasion a souvenir programme was published that included an essay on the development of the violin and its repertoire. Although Alfredo had on many occasions played on university campuses, it was the first time that he had been appointed to an academic position. He enjoyed the university ambience – a number of academics played excellent bridge – and the opportunity it provided for a series of recitals that he had never performed before in quite the same way. The recitals were held in the university's modern thrust-stage Octagon Theatre designed only a few years before by Sir Tyrone Guthrie, and his pianist for the series was to be the young New Zealander David Bollard, then on the Music Department's teaching staff. They began working immediately on the huge programme that Alfredo had worked out with Frank Callaway:

Recital 1	Sonata in A major	Handel
	Sonata in D minor Op. 108	Brahms
	Sonata	Debussy
	Sonata No. 3 in C minor	Grieg
Recital 2	Sonata No. 3 in E major	Bach
	Sonata in G major, Op. 30, No. 3	Beethoven
	Sonata in A major Op. 100	Brahms
	Sonata in A major	Franck
Recital 3	Sonata in A major K. 526	Mozart
	Sonata in E flat major Op. 12, No. 3	Beethoven
	Sonata	Poulenc
	Ruralia Hungarica Op. 32C	Dohnányi
Recital 4	Sonata in A major ('Kreutzer')	Beethoven
	Chaconne	Bach
	Sonata in B minor	Respighi
Recital 5	Sonata in A major	Vivaldi
	Sonata in G major Op. 78	Brahms
	Sonata in C sharp minor Op. 21	Dohnányi
	Sonata in E flat major Op. 18	Richard Strauss
Recital 6	Sonata No. 2 in A major	Bach
	Sonata No. 2 in E minor	Busoni
	Sonata in C minor Op. 30, No. 2	Beethoven
	Two Caprices and La Campanella	Paganini arr. Kreisler

It was an enormously demanding programme even for a violinist who had played these works before – some on many occasions. For a young solo pianist who had never played the majority of them it was a Herculean task and one which took such toll on David Bollard that he fell ill towards the end of the series. His place was taken by the veteran accompanist Stephen Dornan who had partnered many a celebrity artist in Perth and elsewhere, particularly for the ABC. There were some last-minute modifications to the programme, including the performance of Elgar's Violin Sonata which Stephen Dornan had just prepared and which Alfredo had not played since 1957.

In addition, Alfredo gave a lunch-hour recital at the university, played the Bruch and Mendelssohn concertos with the West Australian Symphony Orchestra, and finally appeared with a chamber orchestra, led by Graham Wood in the university's Winthrop Hall. That Farewell Concert consisted of Bach's Double Concerto (Alfredo with Graham Wood), Mozart's Violin Concerto in A major K. 219, Warlock's 'Capriol' Suite and Philip Cannon's Concertino for piano and strings in the which the soloist was the young Carl Vine, now one of Australia's most prominent composers.

However, Alfredo's idea of living in Perth literally had cold water poured on it, for it was one of the wettest winters experienced there for some years. Clearly, it was not the place to cure arthritis! Perhaps the rain was the answer to Joy's hopes that she would not have to leave her home, family and friends; they departed on 8 August, arriving in London next day.

In between his rehearsals and performances Alfredo had played much bridge in Perth and also did some teaching. Amongst his students was a gifted young violinist, Belinda Bunt, who had flown over from New Zealand to study intensively with Alfredo during his sojourn in Perth. She was to follow him to London where she took up her lessons with him again, living for some time with Joy and Alfredo. Alfredo had done some teaching before this time, but from then onwards it became one of his favourite occupations, as will be described in the next chapter.

Chapter 8

'At Home'

To say that the majority of Alfredo's recitals were made up of 'safe' repertoire is no more than to state the obvious fact that, like most performers, his livelihood largely depended upon the musical goodwill of his audiences. They loved to hear him play the well-known sonatas and the lighter works that he finished up with – as much as he loved playing them. Thus, in the hundreds of recitals he gave in Britain, in cities and towns large and small, there are not many unusual works that call for comment. Those tended to be played in broadcast performances. Over this long period he was associated with many fine pianists in addition to those already mentioned. They included, to mention just the better known, Ernest Lush, Geoffrey Parsons, Ivor Keys, John Pritchard (who laid down the conductor's baton to accompany Alfredo on the piano on several occasions) and Denis Matthews. A notable association was with the seventy-three-year-old Dohnànyi when he played that composer's *Ruralia Hungarica* and Sonata in C sharp and Mozart's A major sonata K526 at the 1956 Edinburgh Festival. Of course, on his overseas tours the number of accompanists he worked with is so extensive as to be impossible to list here.

It was over the air (particularly the BBC's Third Programme) and at the Royal Festival and Wigmore Halls that Alfredo played works that did not usually find a place in the many recitals he gave outside London. His love of the music of Bach and Handel, for example, found many an outlet on the Third Programme in association with George Malcolm at the harpsichord, and also with Edith Peinemann in Bach's Double Concerto at the Royal Festival Hall. It was for the Third Programme that he played Sarasate's *Fantasie on Themes of Bizet's Carmen* and sonatas by Debussy, Turina, Respighi, Busoni, Medtner (Sonata Epica), Howells (Third Sonata), while together with the violinist Derek Collier he performed Malcolm Arnold's Concerto for Two Violins. In a programme at the Wigmore Hall he included Liszt's Grand Duo *Le Marin* and *Epithalam.*

When playing in Britain he was associated with almost all the leading conductors there (as well as many lesser lights). In addition to some already mentioned were John Barbirolli, Harry Blech, Warwick Braithwaite, Alexander Brott, Basil Cameron, Anthony Collins, Meredith Davies, Anatole Fistoulari, Piero Gamba, Alexander Gibson, Charles Groves, George Hurst, Paul Kletzki, Charles Mackerras, Nikolay Malko, Pierre Monteux, John Pritchard, Karl Rankl, Clarence Raybould, Ernest Read, Hugo Rignold, Stanford Robinson, Rudolf Schwarz, Hans Swarowsky, Vilem Tausky and George Weldon, at whose farewell concert he was soloist. His greatest disappointment was that he never had the chance to play under Toscanini. This was as much a personal as a professional disappointment, for it will be recalled from Chapter 1 that Alfredo's father had once played in the same opera orchestra where, as a young man, Toscanini was playing cello.

From 1945 until 1964 Alfredo appeared regularly at the Proms and during those nineteen years he gave twenty-eight performances. His popularity was such that he sometimes appeared more than once in a year's series, as in 1945, 1952 and 1953 when he was the soloist in three different programmes in each of those years. In 1949, 1951, 1954, 1955 and 1956 he appeared twice in each series. There were only four years when he did not play at them, two of them because he was on tour. The works he was asked to play were the concertos by Tchaikovsky, Paganini, Walton, Mendelssohn, Beethoven, Elgar, Bliss, Sibelius and Brahms – both the solo concerto and the double concerto (the latter with André Navarra). The ever-popular *Symphonie Espagnole* by Lalo was featured four times. His final appearance at the Proms was in 1964 when he was invited to perform the violin concerto by the late nineteenth-century Russian composer Glazunov, a work that he had never played before, but which he prepared in a remarkably short time.[1] This was with the BBC Symphony Orchestra under Beecham, the conductor whom Alfredo admired above all others.

The Proms had been given a much-needed revitalisation by William Glock when he was appointed Director of Music at the BBC from 1959 to 1973. A most gifted musician, whose career embraced performance (he studied piano under Schnabel), music criticism, music education and administration, Glock's tastes were unusually wide for the time. English-born, his musical sympathies nevertheless lay firmly with contemporary European music, particularly that of Schoenberg, Webern and Berg, and with forward-looking composers in Britain, who, up until then, had had few opportunities to have their music professionally performed. Glock saw in his appointment the chance to breathe new life into the English musical scene through concerts and broadcasts of contemporary masterpieces and through works by the young British avant-garde, not least at the Proms. Interesting works, including early music that had hitherto been largely neglected, he also championed. While such a policy was bound to meet resistance it was long overdue and was implemented largely through the Proms, the Invitation Concerts, and the BBC Symphony Orchestra programmes.[2] Believing that it was time for Proms audiences to hear Alban Berg's lyrical violin concerto once again (it had been performed in 1955 and 1959), Glock naturally turned (as he put it) to that most lyrical of violinists – Campoli – to play it. Alfredo, who disliked twelve-note music (even though its use in this concerto is fairly loosely adhered to), declined the invitation, subsequently believing that his refusal to play

[1] A bridge-playing friend and violinist, Lionel Monte, was staying with the Campolis when the concerto was being learnt and has described to the author how quickly Alfredo mastered the work.

[2] See Humphrey Carpenter, *The Envy of the World: fifty years of the Third Programme and Radio Three* (London, 1996), p. 206.

this work was the reason why he was never asked back to the Proms. Glock refutes this, saying that it did not influence his attitude towards Alfredo in any way.[3] Yet, the fact remains that Alfredo made no further appearances at those famous concerts after 1964. During the preceding nineteen years he was, however, one of the most familiar figures on the platform and also over the air. How the winds had changed since those early years when he had had to struggle for recognition by the BBC immediately after the war. By the 1960s the BBC was writing to him to ask when he would be in England and whether there were any concertos he would specially like to broadcast.[4]

Alfredo's post-war career as a concert artist was, of course, reflected in the many recordings that he made from this time onwards. Yet echoes of the past still sounded. In 1948/9 HMV had issued five recordings of 'Alfredo Campoli and his Orchestra' which he had made with them in the 1930s, and at the same time Decca released four recordings of 'Alfredo Campoli and his Salon Orchestra' which had originally been released in 1935 and 1936. This was not to his advantage, as he discovered on his tour to Australia and New Zealand in 1950 when his name was still being associated there with *Turkey in the Straw*.[5]

As before the war, he was to record mainly, though not exclusively, with Decca. That company was now on a much firmer financial basis than in the 1930s, thanks partly to its work for the Admiralty during the war. At the outbreak of war an idea for the use of radio to assist air and sea navigation was put to Decca in London by a colleague in Chicago and, after a long period of research and technical development (about which the Admiralty was at first sceptical), Decca's 'Navigator' system was eventually adopted, playing an important part in the Normandy invasion and extensively used for mine-sweeping after the war.[6] There were financial gains to Decca from this, even if they were late in coming. Its other war-time project was to have far-reaching effects for music recording. Decca was requested to produce a record that would help train the ears of those on the look-out for enemy submarines by differentiating between the different sounds of German and English engines; it required the reproduction of a range of frequencies that had not been utilised in recordings before this time. After the war the results of this technological advance were applied by Decca to its commercial recordings of music, the process being known as 'Full Frequency range reproduction' (*FFrr*).[7] The first recordings using this system were released to the public at the end of 1944, but not announced as such until the middle of the

---

[3] Personal communication from Sir William Glock to the author, dated 5 October 1997.

[4] Letter from Leonard Isaacs to Joy Campoli, 3 May 1961.

[5] *The New Zealand Listener*, 4 August 1950 – interview 'With Confidence You Can Do Anything'.

[6] E. R. Lewis, *No C. I. C.* (London, 1956), pp. 82–92.

[7] Roland Gelatt, *The Fabulous Phonograph* (London, 1956), pp 216–17, and Lewis, 1956, p. 89.

following year. Thus, by the time Alfredo's first post-war recordings appeared in 1947 they had the added lustre of the new 'Decca sound'. In that year three Campoli recordings were issued by Decca: Tartini's Sonata in G minor ('Devil's Trill'), Paganini's La Campanella, Bach's Arioso and Kreisler's arrangement of Paganini's Concerto No. 1 (issued on two 78 rpm discs). In his recorded performance of the concerto he was conducted by Victor Olof with a new group called the National Symphony Orchestra. (He was to re-record it ten years later under Piero Gamba with the London Symphony Orchestra.)

Decca's 'Full Frequency range reproduction' was one of the technological developments that helped rescue the recording industry from the malaise it had suffered before and during the war, and was taken up, of course, by all its competitors. Yet the next developments were the most important of all: the long-playing record, developed by Columbia in the USA in 1949 (but not taken up in Britain until 1950), and, in the same year, the tape recorder. As far as producing LPs was concerned, excellent existing master copies of *FFrr* 78 rpm recordings could still be put to the service of the new technology. Thus, a number of Alfredo's performances originally on 78 rpm records found their way on to LPs (such as his Mendelssohn Violin Concerto under Van Beinum, recorded by Decca in May 1949). As far as the tape recorder was concerned, the new-found capacity to record segments of a work on tape, from which could be chosen and spliced the best versions for the master tape, meant that the eventual transfer to the master record or matrix (a most complex and costly electroforming process made even more critical with the introduction of the microgroove) was not going to be spoilt by performance lapses. The previous need to record an entire side – hopefully error-free (both in performance and in the technical process) – was now a thing of the past.[8] The new technology also meant that previously- or newly-recorded works could be re-released over a period of years in different combinations. (The chronological list of Alfredo's recordings that follows as Appendix A gives the serial number of the first English release only.)

Alfredo's career also overlapped the most recent technical revolution: the compact disc. Shortly before his death Alfredo was invited by Pearl (Pavilion Records) to choose a programme of short works from his own collection of pre-war recordings for transfer to compact disc. Appearing in the year of his death *Campoli's Choice* was the first of a number of CDs featuring recordings that had been deleted from the catalogues. Thanks to these 'historical' re-releases we are once more able to enjoy the quality of Alfredo's musicianship from the earliest years of his recording career to some of the last. Two of the concertos now re-released are the Elgar and Max Bruch. It is worth recalling the comparisons

[8] Before 1949 it is not unusual to find that Alfredo (like other artists) had to re-record some works (even those that he had played flawlessly for many years), the matrices having been rejected – perhaps because of flaws in the recording process. (Mozart's 'Haffner' Rondo, for example, was recorded three times before a satisfactory matrix was produced.)

drawn between the original recordings and others made by various distinguished violinists released about the same time. Of the Elgar violin concerto *The Gramophone* wrote: 'Here is a new, thoughtful, original, and eminently valid interpretation of a well-tried classic, though it is only forty-five years old. Campoli has successfully renovated this imposing Edwardian piece without destroying its essential contours; he brings new life to it without seeking to stamp out the old, as I fear Heifetz did in his streamlined performance.'[9] Of the Bruch Concerto No. 1 (comparing Heifetz, Milstein and Campoli): 'I admire Campoli's performance immensely, and find in it a warmth, poetry and lyricism which draw an immediate response . . . This is the performance I would soonest live with.'[10]

Alfredo's final recording was made in 1980 at the age of seventy-four. A programme of virtuoso works by Wieniawski, in which he was accompanied by Daphne Ibbott, reveal that the fire and the power were still there. Thus wrote *The Gramophone*:

> At an astonishing age for the enterprise (it is no secret: he was born in 1906) Campoli turns to Wieniawski to keep his playing in trim. There is not need, however, to make allowances for the ravages of time; if indeed there are any ravages they have not reached the fingers or the bow or the intonation, all of which give the impression that playing Wieniawski is the easiest thing in the world. The lyrical sections of the music go warm-heartedly, the virtuoso sections go elegantly; nowhere are standards less than the very best. The very best, some will think of an older generation of players than to-day's youngest and fittest, and in one respect this is certainly true: a handful of to-day's stars achieve greater brilliance, though seldom greater elegance.[11]

In light of the glowing reviews that invariably greeted Alfredo's post-war recordings, it is surprising that Decca and other companies did not invite him to record more frequently from the standard sonata repertoire that he performed so musically, or those sonatas from the English school – Bax, Delius, Ireland – that deserved a wider audience.[12] In 1977 he made a recording of Sarasate's Eight Spanish Dances, his associate artists being Daphne Ibott and, in the final work *Navarra* (for two violins and pianos), his gifted young violin student Belinda Bunt.

Alfredo's name is not usually associated with teaching, yet from the late 1960s onwards a number of students came to him; some already in their professional careers wanting only a few coaching lessons, others continuing with

9 *The Gramophone*, April 1955, p. 481.

10 *The Gramophone*, December 1954, p. 296.

11 *The Gramophone*, September 1980.

12 A letter to this effect was written to the editor of *The Gramophone* by R.C. MacDonald from Canada, and published in its issue of April 1974. In it Professor Macdonald recalls Szigeti's comment about Alfredo's individuality (see Introduction).

him for some years. His longest and most concentrated work with any student was with Belinda Bunt, whom he had first heard in New Zealand when adjudicating a Festival there in 1972. She was then in her mid-teens and displaying outstanding talent. In the following year she flew to Perth to study intensively with him during the three months when he was Musician-in-Residence there at the University of Western Australia, culminating in a performance with him in Bach's Double Concerto in D minor in the university's Winthrop Hall. Six months later she came to London to continue her studies, for some time living with Joy and Alfredo and having long lessons two or three times a week. As one who had been himself trained this way Alfredo firmly believed in the European tradition of the master–apprentice style of teaching. When he returned to New Zealand in 1975 Belinda came too, both of them appearing together for ensemble sonatas and concertos on a number of occasions. There can be no doubt that her audiences back home felt that the money they had raised on her behalf had been well spent. When the Sarasate recording, in which Belinda shared the performance of *Navarra* appeared, *The Strad* commented: 'The best compliment one can pay to both artists is that it is impossible to tell the difference.' It was keenly disappointing for Alfredo, who had hopes of Belinda becoming a second Ida Haendel, that she decided on an orchestral rather than a solo career.

On the basis of his engagement diaries from 1962 it would seem that Alfredo taught over forty students. These he never sought out, and they included a wide range of talents and experience, some indeed being little more than novices, for his essential motivation was to help violinists of all kinds improve their playing. It was certainly not for financial gain, his fees being extraordinarily modest for one so eminent as a performer.

His first demand was that neck rests and pads be thrown away, believing not only that they inhibited the sound, but robbed one of enjoying the real intimacy of the violin as a projection of the human voice. Next, he would inspect the instrument and demonstrate how it should be looked after and maintained. It must cleaned regularly – varnish, strings, fingerboard and even the peg-box and all nooks and crannies to be dusted. The pegs had to be at the correct angle and the strings wound with meticulous precision on the pegs. It was no mere casual inspection, but one that he took most seriously and carried out regularly. This degree of precision was characteristic of everything to do with Alfredo's approach to the violin and its music. His own copies of music were a model: everything fingered and bowed meticulously, and often transferred into a student's copy – the original not merely crossed out but 'painted' out so that there could be no confusion. His sonata-partner Valerie Tryon recalls that for his own music he even had a little gadget that would cleanly erase anything that he wished to alter.[13]

---

13 Personal communication from Valerie Tryon.

His own stance, which he insisted that his students adopt, was that of Heifetz whom he admired above all other violinists. With the left shoulder somewhat pushed up, the instrument was to be held high, its scroll directly in line with the player's nose. Only in this way, he asserted, can the bow be kept straight (instead of going downwards 'around the Cape of Good Hope' – as he used to say) and fulfil its role as the one of the most important aspects of violin playing. When asked what was the secret of his distinctive tone he was convinced that it was essentially through his bowing rather than the left hand which 'merely found the notes'. It was his fervent belief that the bow to the violin is like the breath to the singer, directing the all-important phrasing that irresistibly recalls the art of bel canto singing. In a broadcast interview he gave over the BBC in 1966 he said

> . . . I feel that the violin is an essential bel canto instrument and I'm afraid I don't quite agree with a school of players who like to play faster and better than anyone else. I like to feel that the violin is the nearest approach of a man-made instrument to the voice. I think that it should be used to bring all the cantabile as from a fine singer, including the intaking of breath, which is controlled in the violin by the bow [and] by sliding, which must be just right – no more, no less, otherwise it becomes banal . . . . And certainly my father was right when I was about nine years of age when he said to me 'Well, you know most of the technical difficulties of this instrument. But what I want you to do now is to learn how to *sing*.' And the way my father went about it was, I feel, most ingenious. He bought me records of all the great singers of the last generation: Fernando de Lucia, Caruso – all the big singers who concentrated on the bel canto style. And that is what I try to emulate today.[14]

Naturally, he endeavoured to pass on this attitude to his own students.

Technique was, of course, also of prime importance, his favourite sets of studies being those of Alard, Dancla (for the left-hand), Casorti (for the bowing arm), Kreutzer, Fiorello, Rode, Gaviniés and Paganini. One of his favourite books of studies was that by Gaviniés some of which he regarded as more difficult that Paganini's Caprices. Yet, Rebecca Shorrock, now a professional orchestral violinist in London who studied with him for five years,[15] remembers that, although a masterful and dogmatic teacher, he would never become bogged down with the extreme technicalities of bowings or shifts, etc., probably because as a child prodigy it had all came so naturally to him. One had only to watch and try

---

[14] 'My Favourite Concertos', Interval talk for BBC broadcast of the violin concertos of Mendelssohn and Brahms, performed with the London Philharmonic Orchestra, conducted by Hugo Rignold, 9 February 1966.

[15] I am indebted to Rebecca Shorrock for much of the information about Campoli's teaching which she conveyed to me both in interview and letter. At the same interview in London I also talked with two other ex-students, Ruth Hudson and her brother Daniel.

to copy. Rigorously vigilant over intonation (he believed that most violinists play too sharp), his incredibly fine ear caught more than that. No eye was needed to catch out a wrong bowing or fingering.

And like the best teachers Alfredo, though demanding, was also encouraging and understanding – and most generous with his time. Those who studied regularly with him became part of the Campoli 'family'. Rebecca Shorrock recalls how, as a shy English teenager she was at first slightly embarrassed by the customary continental kiss on the cheek – which she had never experienced before. After each lesson it was it was never a case of a brief dismissal. Joy would come in with a cup of Bovril and two biscuits (sometimes of the Italian kind sent him by friends, but which he could no longer eat because of diabetes), and then followed enquiries about her family, and sometimes a game of croquet on the lawn at Winchmore Hill.

Teaching filled a greater part of his life as his concert schedules became less taxing. Although in the year he turned seventy he was on a six-month tour of New Zealand, his tours inside and beyond England began to taper off as the effects of age and arthritis began to take their toll. Nevertheless, on his seventieth birthday he was still able to turn in a fine performance of the Beethoven Violin Concerto at a Birthday Concert given at Fairfield Hall, Croydon. Playing with the London Philharmonic Orchestra under George Szell, his anniversary was celebrated with much publicity in the press and over the BBC. On his seventy-fourth birthday another celebratory concert was arranged at the Brighton Dome at which he played the work that he was most closely associated with during his long career – the violin concerto by Mendelssohn. It is worth quoting the review of this concert by Charles Rattray that appeared in *The Strad*, for although it was far from his last appearance, in a real sense it sums up his career as a concert artist.

> Alfredo Campoli, that most distinguished representative of the golden age of violin playing, was seventy-four last month, and to mark the occasion the Brighton Philharmonic Society featured him in their current concert season in a performance of Mendelssohn's Violin Concerto. Leaving aside his beloved Roccas and playing for the first time an instrument by the 19th-century English maker, John Lott, Campoli charmed the packed hall with a reading of the concerto which was at once fresh and mature. Although he has given almost 950 concert performances of this concerto (it is the only one he keeps a count of), to hear him play it again is to hear it as if for the first time; one is taken aback by the delicacy of the interpretation and the sheer exuberance in the finale which reminds one so appropriately of the fresh genius of Mendelssohn's youth. In this performance by the Brighton PO under John Carewe, Campoli's playing was more than that of an assured interpreter, a legendary virtuoso. It was also that of the last great exponent of the *bel canto* style of playing: there was impeccable judgement of rubato, and phrasing so natural that one could almost hear the violin breathe. Nevertheless, the essence of

> Campoli's artistry is in none of these things, but rather in rare and indefinable quality of style. It is this above all else that guarantees his place as one of the most remarkable violinists of our time.

The violin made by the London craftsman John Lott, regarded by many as the finest of all English violin-makers – despite his dubious reputation as a forger of Guarneri instruments – was the last of Alfredo's purchases of fine violins.[16] It will be recalled (see Chapter 5) that the first of these had been his Guadagnini (1773), which he had bought in 1948. Ten years later he owned an Amati and the first of his Stradivarius violins – the 'Baillot Pommerau' instrument of 1694, so called because the Marquis de Pommerau had bought it near the beginning of the nineteenth century from the celebrated French violinist Pierre Baillot. Purchased in Paris in 1902 by W.E. Hill and Sons it passed through various hands before being bought by Arthur Catterell who used it throughout his career until his death in 1943. Although it was in an excellent state of preservation when Alfredo purchased it, when the opportunity arose for him to buy an instrument made in Stradivarius's 'golden period' (1700–20) he sold the Baillot-Pommerau at the end of 1959 replacing it with an instrument now known as the 'Campoli' Stradivarius (1702).[17] It had been acquired by the French violin-maker Jean-Baptiste Vuillaume (1798–1875) who bought a number of fine early instruments after which to model his own. Acquired by a Scottish family in Fifeshire, the instrument lay unused for over 130 years until bought by Alfredo who gradually played back its tone. This was the instrument he used on his 1960 tour of India, New Zealand, Australia and Japan, but as a result of that tour the instrument had to be repaired when Alfredo returned home, tropical heat having caused damage to the wood. He sold it soon afterwards to acquire the finest Stradivarius he ever owned (and one that he certainly did not take on his next tour of Australia, New Zealand and tropical countries in 1966). This instrument was the 'Dragonetti Rivaz' of 1707. Named after the famous eighteenth-century double-bass player Domenico Dragonetti, who refused to sell it in his lifetime, it was one of the few instruments of its maker which still preserved its original neck, and it was in exceptionally fine condition when Alfredo bought it. Nevertheless, it was not the 'Dragonetti' that he favoured playing above all his others. He especially loved those made by the nineteenth-century Italian craftsman Giuseppe Rocca (1807–65), particularly the one known as 'John Dunn', made in 1843 and named after an English violinist. It was the carrying tone of his Roccas that endeared them to Alfredo, the 'John Dunn', in particular, possessing remarkable sonority

---

[16] See Brian W. Harvey, *The Violin Family and its Makers in the British Isles* (Oxford, 1995), pp. 224–7. After Alfredo's death the instrument was bought by Belinda Bunt, but it was subsequently stolen from her home in the USA and has so far not been recovered.

[17] Listed under this name in Herbert K. Goodkind, *Violin Iconography of Antonio Stradivari (1644–1737)* (New York, 1972), p. 727.

on the G string. Other instruments owned by Alfredo were by Gian Francesco Pressenda (1771–1854) whose model was freely based on Stradivarius with low arching and slightly deeper ribs, and who was working in Turin when he made Alfredo's instrument in 1835. Pressenda's instruments have been described as revealing exemplary mastery in all their parts.[18] Giuseppe Domenichino, a follower of Amati, was the maker of another fine Italian instrument owned by Alfredo.[19]

One set of string instruments that Alfredo admired enormously was definitely not for playing. It was a set of miniatures – a string quartet – presented to him in 1961 by Alfred Eaglen of Leeds. The painstaking work that he and his son (who did the mathematical calculations) carried out was a faithful sculpting in wood of instruments by Stradivarius and Guarnerius copied from photographs.

Other works of art in the Campoli home were paintings of Alfredo, by Kenneth Tryon (father of Valerie) in 1977 and by John Bratby in 1980. A fine bust sculpted by T.B. Huxley-Jones in 1949 now stands, sentinel-like, in the Music Library of Cambridge University which houses Alfredo's personal library of violin music and programmes presented to the University by Joy in 1995. The particular value of the music collection lies, of course, in Alfredo's bowing and fingering – part of the key to his unique style.

Time took its toll on Alfredo through increasing arthritis. On his final tour of New Zealand in 1976 his arthritis and general health seemed so poor that the New Zealand Broadcasting Corporation arranged to have someone attending him all the time, even carrying his violin everywhere, the doctors having insisted that there should be no physical strain at any time.[20] In the 1980s Alfredo also began to lose hearing in his left ear, although this did not seem to affect his intonation in any way. However, in his last years, a cruel affliction awaited him. The bones in his ears began to deteriorate at a different rate, leading to one ear hearing music at a different pitch from the other. Not surprisingly, he turned more and more to that other love of his life: bridge. It will be recalled from an earlier chapter that

---

18 Karel Jalovek, *Encyclopedia of Violin-Makers* (London, 1965), 2 vols, ii, p. 173.

19 One of Campoli's instruments was acquired in an extraordinary way. During a tour of India and the Far East in 1952 he was in Bombay to give a recital at St Xavier College. Going upstairs to his room in the Taj Mahal Hotel one evening he heard some remarkably beautiful sounds of a violin coming from the hotel's restaurant. He investigated further, and so bewitched was he by the quality of the instrument that he immediately offered to buy it from the Indian musician entertaining the hotel's patrons. It has not been possible to identify which instrument was bought this way. The story (which I have no reason to doubt) was told me by Mr Addie Meher-Homji (of Perth, Western Australia), who was living at that time in Bombay, and whose father, a collector of musical instruments and a friend of the Indian musician, had often talked about Campoli's extraordinary find. It is possible that it could have been one of his Roccas. Another Rocca he acquired in New Zealand.

20 Personal communication from Geoffrey Newson, at that time Administrator of the New Zealand Broadcasting Commission Symphony Orchestra.

he had been introduced to it about 1928 and for some eight years played – so he confessed – the worst imaginable game. Indeed, he always felt that he was not a 'natural' at bridge and what success he eventually achieved was through assiduous practice and reading. This after being taken in hand by the famous Sharples twins – Bob and Jim – whom he met after joining the London Duplicate Club in Berkeley Square in 1932. Their love of music and skill at bridge led to a warm friendship. From that time onwards the only books that Alfredo read were those on bridge – some 250 of them.[21] By the start of the 1970s he had twice reached the final of the Gold Cup, and in 1973 he became a National Master. Yet, as well as the personal satisfaction from those competitive achievements Alfredo also enjoyed the international network of bridge-playing friends and associates he built up during his many tours. How many times one finds in his diaries that a strenuous rehearsal or performance during the day was followed by bridge in the afternoon or evening. To judge from his diaries, bridge games often seemed to loom as large as his concert appearances. As with Wimbledon, which he would reserve each year in his diary, so too would time annually be set aside for some of the bridge congresses in Croydon, London, Richmond, Eastbourne, Middlesex, Bedford and so on, some lasting almost a week.

In a gesture typical of Alfredo's interest in young musicians his last public appearance was with the Huddersfield Senior Youth Orchestra conducting and giving masterclasses. He was almost eighty. By then both he and Joy were finding the home at Winchmore Hill far too large and tiring, and in the following year, on 4 April 1986, having found a charming Tudor cottage, they moved back to Thame in Oxfordshire, which had already played a large part in their lives and where some of Joy's family were still in the family home in Upper High Street. Attendance at the little Catholic church, where they had been married more than forty years earlier, became part of Alfredo's life.

Wednesdays were bridge evenings at the club in nearby Princes Risborough and on 27 March 1991 Alfredo was as usual looking forward to it. He lit his cigar and waited for his bridge partner to drive them both to the Club. About an hour later his partner was back at the door and Joy knew instinctively from his face what news it was. He had left him at the Club entrance and gone to park the car while Alfredo went to the cloakroom to leave his hat and coat. The players, ready to commence the game, wondered about his delay in coming to the table, and his partner went into the cloakroom and found him lying on the floor. A doctor amongst the bridge players announced that he was dead from a massive heart attack.

After a Requiem Mass at St Joseph's Church at Thame,[22] Alfredo's coffin was carried to the town's inter-denominational churchyard in the grounds of St Mary's

---

21 *Bridge International*, June 1986, p. 219.

22 The original small church in which they were married had been demolished to make way for a fine modern St Joseph's. Near the entrance of the new church are some beautifully etched windows, one of which, depicting an angel with lyre, is dedicated to Alfredo Campoli. The new church was opened in June 1997.

Anglican Church. Here he was laid to rest near the graves of Elvira and Romeo, not far from those of Joy's mother, brother and other members of her family. As the coffin was lowered a muffled peal of bells rang from the tower of St Mary's in tribute to him.

Alfredo Campoli as Man and Musician

An enduring memory of Alfredo is of a portly figure and a beaming face. Impossible to imagine that he was ever slender – and indeed he never was, even as a child – it was as though he needed a large body to contain an expansive personality. Add to this a rare violin, a box of rich cigars and a pack of cards and there are the essential lines of sketch of a consummate artist and a man possessed by an Italian passion to enjoy life to the full.

One of the few personal glimpses we have of Alfredo as a young man comes from one of Romeo's students at the time.[23] The Campolis were then living in the large house near Wandsworth Common and Mary Bond's parents had met Alfredo playing tennis and bridge at their local club. The family struck up a warm friendship with the gifted young man, then in his late twenties. Mary was still at school. Despite the age difference they enjoyed fierce games of table tennis and the occasional swim in the Thames and on one occasion Alfredo joined her family for a holiday in Aldeburgh on the Suffolk coast where they all stayed as paying guests in the Vicarage there. On that holiday Alfredo gave a recital in the Aldeburgh Church to raise funds for repairs to the roof of the building, playing Massenet's 'Meditation' from *Thaïs* and unaccompanied Bach – including the Chaconne. To show his appreciation of the hospitality given him by Mary's family, he took her to the Wimbledon Tennis Championships, buying her a fine pair of shoes at Harrod's to go with her new dress and large-brimmed straw hat for what was, in those days, a very dressed-up occasion. Clearly, his generosity and warm-heartedness that so many remember him by in his later years were just as evident in his earlier ones.

Considering his background – a dislocated education, the centre of attention of his parents (with a mother who undoubtedly gave up her own career to devote herself to her son's), removal from his playmates and the sports field which he loved in order to develop his precocious talent, as well as the inevitable loneliness that accompanies hours of solo practice, in his case under the stern eye (and hand) of his father – it is all the more remarkable that Alfredo's personality was so 'normal', so outgoing.

This was partly because the stresses and strains of a busy concert schedule were balanced by wide recreational interests. Alfredo was as much a 'natural' at

---

23 I am indebted to Mrs Norman-Thomas (née Bond) for this personal communication.

sport as he was at music. As we have seen, he played excellent tennis and table tennis, and perhaps his skill at billiards (which won for him the South London Amateur Cup early in his career) was related to that fine muscular co-ordination which made his 'spiccato' bowing almost legendary. He also loved 'gadgetry' of all sorts, taking photographs and making home movies. With these interests and his passion for playing bridge he was able to relax both at home and on tour, and through them enjoy the company of friends and acquaintances over a wide range of shared enthusiasms. Typically, everything that interested him he pursued with dedication.

With these many interests, his long hours of daily practice and his rehearsal and performance schedule, he had little time for anything else. But nor was there much inclination to go beyond them, for Alfredo's alert and quick mind was not that of an intellectual. His very background almost precluded it. Neither of his parents, despite their artistic involvement, were people of broad culture, and his early departure from school resulted in an imperfect education. Writing remained an irksome task all his life – even for a postcard – and it was a relief to him when he could hand over all his correspondence to Joy.[24] This has sometimes given rise to the idea that he could not write – but nothing could be further from the truth. He was, for example, an excellent speller, as the present author can vouch for, having heard him a number of times spell out with almost pedantic precision 'difficult' names of people and musical works. Despite some fine interviews over the BBC, his was not the kind of musical intelligence that shines when talking about music. He said it all through his instrument. As far as his reading was concerned, we have seen that it was almost exclusively directed towards books on bridge.

In his formative years and early career there were few influences that might have sparked off an interest in a wider culture. During the 1930s his working environment, both day and night, was the restaurant and the musical theatre, hardly conducive to developing the intellectual side of Alfredo's naturally bright mind. It remained highly focused and narrow so that he was often prejudiced and intemperate in his views. Thus, when in Bombay in 1952 he was asked his opinion about Indian Classical Music (a musical form highly regarded by Menuhin), Alfredo was reported as saying that it was 'absolutely without foundation and primitive'. *The Bombay National Standard*, however, had the good grace to defend Alfredo by suggesting that 'foreign artists need to be protected against people seeking their views on Indian music, as they have little or negligible knowledge of Indian classical music, and it is not fair to them to quote their views as final and authoritative judgements'. It is also probably true to say that, Menuhin apart, many professional musicians at that time would have

---

[24] Examples of Alfredo's youthful handwriting (as in Mary Bond's autograph book) display that clear, well-trained style which was the mark of primary school teaching in those days.

felt the same way, although they might have been more discreet in how they said it.

But impulsiveness was characteristic of his nature, and while on the one hand it could lead to rudeness, it was far more likely to lead the other way. He was essentially genial and generous. An Australian singer, for example, remembers how, in 1961 when about to rehearse with the pianist Frederick Stone for a BBC Overseas Service recording, she found Alfredo there taking advantage of the empty studio to do some practice. With good grace and deeply apologetic for being there at all he went out and practised in the corridor.[25]

Various misunderstandings about him arose during his career. There are still those who are under the impression that he was London-born and changed his name from Alfred Campbell to an Italian-sounding one for the sake of a musical career. It is easy to see how this misunderstanding came about, not only because of his Balham background and London accent, but also because, ironically, he did use that name sometimes when playing 'anonymously' during the war with the Victor Sylvester Orchestra and other groups.[26] A further source of confusion lay in the presence of another violinist in the field of light music whose name was also 'Alfredo' and who conducted a gypsy orchestra which often broadcast over the BBC in the 1930s. As late as 1950 when Alfredo made his first tour of Australia and New Zealand he was even then 'haunted' by the ghost of Alfredo the Gypsy Violinist with whom some people still confused him.[27]

The other ghost that still needs to be permanently laid to rest is that Alfredo was a light-music performer who moved to the concert stage after the war. As we have shown, in reality it was a *return* to the concert stage after a mere decade of performing light music, which period was also interspersed with classical recitals and broadcasts.

If ten years in light music provided no intellectual stimulus, on the other hand it was a period that gave Alfredo the experience of rubbing shoulders with a wide cross-section of the musical profession. As far as his fellow light-music performers were concerned Alfredo's only criterion was their musicianship, and although he stood head and shoulders above most of them, he was also 'one of the boys'. It is no wonder that after the war, given his geniality and ability to get on well with the profession, he became a favourite soloist with the members of the many orchestras with whom he played. It was not at all unusual during a rehearsal for him to turn to an orchestral player whose solo entry was beautifully executed to congratulate him or her with a smile or a word. Conductors, too, liked working with him. As early as 1951 the conductor of the BBC Scottish Orchestra

25 Related to the author by the Sydney singer and teacher Paula Clarkstone

26 Conveyed to the author by John Harper-Nelson, who is writing a biography of his sister Margaret Harper-Nelson who was in charge of ENSA's broadcasting section for the whole of the war. She recalls the situation over Alfredo's name.

27 *Brisbane Courrier Mail*, 21 June 1950.

was writing to the Music Department asking for a 'really first-rate violinist' to play the Bruch G minor and giving, in order of preference, a list of prominent performers at the head of which was Alfredo Campoli.[28]

It was, of course, not only his personal warmth and sincerity that endeared him to the profession. It was also his uncanny ability to turn in fine performances whenever he played and his seemingly unflappable temperament – put to its severest test in April 1965 when he was playing with the City of Birmingham Orchestra. It was a time when the orchestra was undertaking a busy schedule that involved not only presenting its concert programmes but also playing for the Welsh National Opera which had no orchestra of its own. Its conductor Hugo Rignold and Alfredo had played the standard concertos so frequently together that sometimes they agreed to forego the rehearsal. On this occasion Alfredo stepped on to the platform ready to play the Bruch G minor Concerto, only to find that in a bar-and-a-half he would have to be playing the solo opening of the Mendelssohn.[29]

Alfredo's reliability as a performer and his emotional poise on stage was the result of his total mastery of his instrument gained through unremitting practice, even of those works which he had played all his life. Six or seven hours a day was the norm when preparing for a concert, the routine usually beginning with a run-through of the Mendelssohn concerto as a warm-up.[30] Nor did it matter if the concert were to take place in the Royal Festival Hall or in some small town; Alfredo was determined to give a first-rate performance wherever he played. Maurice Till, the New Zealand pianist, who accompanied Alfredo on a number of tours both there and in Australia, recalls that Alfredo would put aside the same amount of time for private practice and rehearsal no matter where they played, so that every audience would hear him in top form.[31]

So, too, did his quest for perfection result in magnificent performances not only of the standard repertoire, but also the gems of light music. For example, after hearing Alfredo play Elgar's Violin Concerto with the BBC Scottish Orchestra Lionel Tertis, who revolutionised viola playing in Britain and whose orchestral experience placed in him at a vantage-point to know the worth of a soloist, wrote: 'Among the numerous times I have heard this wonderful work, so full of lyrical moments that stir one to the depths, this performance of Campoli's was certainly the best I have heard.'[32] On the other hand, Fred Hartley's delectable *Twentieth-Century Nocturne* which Alfredo's Welbeck Light String Quartet recorded for Decca in 1940 (unissued at the time but now available on CD), so captivated the French conductor Jean-Pascal Tortellier that he included it

---

28 BBC memo dated 19 October 1951.

29 Beresford King-Smith, *Crescendo! 75 Years of the City of Birmingham Symphony Orchestra* (London, 1995), p. 141.

30 Mentioned in conversation between Campoli and the author.

31 Personal communication from Maurice Till.

32 Lionel Tertis, *My Viola and I* (London, 1974), p. 139.

in his choice of recordings for an hour's interview over the Australian Broadcasting Corporation in 1997.[33] Alfredo's ability to perform outstandingly such disparate works stands in great contrast to the specialisation that marks many of today's performances.

We should not be surprised that classical chamber music was not his scene, for he was essentially a 'star performer'. In recitals he usually wanted to stand out on the stage well in front of the piano and, especially in the lighter pieces, he would often play, like de Groot, bending towards the audience as though he were back in the restaurant, leaving the accompanist – often in the shadows – to cope with the problem of seeing or hearing him.[34] Yet he insisted in all publicity and programmes that Daphne Ibbott, Valerie Tryon, Peter Katin and others were billed as 'duo artists' or 'pianists' and not as 'accompanists'. Nevertheless, it was Alfredo who decided on all points of performance – which is no more than to say that, with all its virtues and vices, he was in the mould of the 'romantic' violinist. He was born to its tradition, nurtured in it and had neither opportunity nor reason to break from it. If part of that tradition was that it was the performer as much as the work that one came to hear, so be it. Fortunately, Alfredo was so much at one with the works he loved to play that his intensely musical personality helped to convey, not to intrude on, the composer's intent. And if sometimes he felt that there was a need to alter a note here or there this was not through capriciousness but through a sincere belief that it was better 'his way'. The result was invariably convincing. His knowledge of the standard repertoire may not have been 'historically informed', as is the fashion nowadays, but it was gained through close familiarity with every note of the score. He loved listening to records, especially of orchestral works, conducting and cueing each important phrase, giving himself up completely to the music in the privacy of his home. Those few opportunities that came his way actually to conduct orchestras revealed a natural gift for it.

The Catholic church meant much to Alfredo. His was a simple and uncomplicated faith that was great source of comfort to him throughout his life. He was not frightened at the thought of death, for he saw it as being re-united with his parents and he was always prepared for it. Valerie Tryon remembers that when flying he would always make the sign of the cross at take-off, and once, on a trip to Ireland when it was very turbulent, he took her hand and said: 'Go *with* it, Valerie, not *against* it', which she felt was a good way of describing his view of life in general.[35]

This view was also reflected in his playing – it never sounded forced or 'going against the music'. So natural was his phrasing that it gave the impression that it could be played in no other way. Nor had he time for violinists whose main

33 Margaret Throsby Programme, ABC Classic FM, 14 October 1997.
34 Recalled by Daphne Ibbott in a personal communication.
35 Personal communication from Valerie Tryon.

concern was speed. Although his own mastery of his instrument was such that he could have made his reputation merely as a virtuoso, it is not his brilliance that one necessarily remembers most of all. Certainly one could be spellbound by it. Yet perhaps what lingers most in the memory is the very tenderness of his playing with its glowingly distinctive tone; a style of playing that perfectly conveyed his fervent belief that the art of bel canto belongs as much to the violin as to the voice.

Bibliography

Anon., *Annual Reports of CEMA.*

Anon., *Annual Reports of the Pigrim Trust.*

Anon., *The BBC Year Books.*

Anon., *Annual Reports of the Arts Council of Great Britain.*

Anon., *History and Development of the ABC* (Sydney: Australian Broadcasting Commission), [n.d.].

Banfield, *The Blackwell History of Music in Britain* (Oxford, 1995).

Barrington, Jonah [Cyril Carr Dalmaine], *And Master of None* (London, *c.* 1948).

Black, Kitty, *Upper Circle: A Theatre Chronicle* (London, 1984).

Bliss, Arthur, *As I Remember* (London, 1970).

Boult, Adrian, *My Own Trumpet* (London, 1973).

Bridges, Doreen, 'Sir Bernard Heinze in Interview', *Australian Journal of Music Education*, No. 12 (1973), April.

Briggs, Asa, *The History of Broadcasting in the United Kingdom* (London) Vol. 1: 'The Birth of Broadcasting' (1961); Vol. 2: 'The Golden Age of Wireless' (1965); Vol. 3: 'The War of Words' (1970).

Brisbane, Katharine (ed.), *Entertaining Australia – An Illustrated History* (Sydney, 1991).

Buttrose, Charles, *Playing for Australia – A Story about ABC Orchestras and Music in Australia* (Sydney, 1982).

Campbell, Margaret, *The Great Violinists* (London, 1980).

Carpenter, Humphrey, *Fifty Years of the BBC Third Programme* (London, 1996).

Castle, C. and Napier, D., *This Was Richard Tauber* (London, 1971).

Covell, Roger, *Australia's Music: Themes of a New Society* (Melbourne, 1967).

Cox, David, *The Henry Wood Proms* (London, 1980).

Culshaw, John, *Putting the Record Straight* (London, 1981).

Dean, Basil, *The Theatre at War* (London 1956).

Doctor, Jennifer, 'The BBC and the Ultra-Modern Problem', doctoral dissertation (Northwestern University, 1993).

Ehrlich, Cyril, *The Music Profession in Britain Since the 18th Century* (Oxford, 1985).

Ehrlich, Cyril, *Harmonious Alliance: History of the Performing Right Society* (Oxford, 1989).

Ehrlich, Cyril, *The Piano: A History* (London, 1976).

Evans, Edwin, 'Music and the Cinema', *Music and Letters* (1929), January.

Frith, Simon, *Music for Pleasure* (London, 1988).

Gelatt, Roland, *The Fabulous Phonograph* (London, 1956).

Giazotto, R., *Quattro Secoli di Storia dell'Accademia Nazionale di S. Cecilia* (Milan, 1970).

Goodkind, Herbert K., *Violin Iconography of Antonio Stradivari 1644–1737* (New York, 1972).

Goossens, Eugene, *Overtures and Beginners* (London, 1950).

Gower, Graham, *Balham – a Brief History* (Wandsworth, 1990, rev. 1996).

Haendel, Ida, *Woman with Violin – an Autobiography* (London, 1970).

Hart, George, *The Violin, Its Famous Makers and Their Imitators* (1885, repr. New York, 1978).

Harvey, Brian W., *The Violin Family and Its Makers in the British Isles: An Illustrated History and Directory* (Oxford, 1995).

Hibberd, Stuart, *This Is London* (London, 1950).

Holmes, John L., *Conductors on Record* (London, 1982).

Jacobs, Arthur, *Henry J. Wood – Maker of the Proms* (London, 1994).

Jalovek, Karel, *Encyclopedia of Violin Makers* (London, 1965).
King-Smith, Beresford, *Crescendo! 75 Years of the City of the Birmingham Symphony Orchestra* (London, 1995).
Lee, Edward, *Music of the People* (London, 1970).
LeMahieu, D.L., *A Culture for Democracy* (Oxford, 1988).
Lewis, E.R., *No C. I. C.* (London, 1956).
Lochner, Louis P., *Fritz Kreisler* (London, 1950).
Longden, James N., 'A Longden Family History', unpublished, held by Deakin University, Australia.
McCarthy, *The Dance-Band Era: The Dancing Decades from Ragtime to Swing* (London, 1971).
McIntyre, Ian, *The Expense of Glory: a Life of John Reith* (London, 1993).
Menuhin, Yehudi, *Unfinished Journey* (London, 1977).
Middleton, Richard, 'The "Problem" of Popular Music', *The Blackwell History of Music*, Vol. 6.
Mike, Celia, 'Dorothy Howell 1898–1982', *British Music*, Vol. 14 (1992).
Miller, Geoffrey, *The Bournemouth Symphony Orchestra* (Sherbourne, 1970).
Moore, Gerald, *Am I Too Loud?* (London, 1962).
Napier-Tauber, Diane, *Richard Taube*r (London, 1949).
Newton, Ivor, *At the Piano: the World of an Accompanist* (London, 1966).
O'Leary, Liam, *The Silent Cinema* (London, 1965).
Palmer, Russell, *British Music* (London, 1947).
Palmer, Tony, *Menuhin, A Family Portrait* (London, 1991).
Payne, Jack, *Signature Tune* (London) [*c*. 1947].
Pearsall, Ronald, *Edwardian Popular Music* (London, 1975).
Philip, Robert, *Early Recordings and Music Style – Changing Tastes in Instrumental Performance 1900–1950* (Cambridge, 1992).
Radic, Thérèse, *Bernard Heinze* (Melbourne, 1986).
Rapée, Erno, *Motion Picture Moods for Pianists and Organists* (New York, 1924).
Rickard, John, *Australia: A Cultural History* (London, 1988).
Scannell, P. and Cardiff, D., *A Social History of British Broadcasting*, Vol. 1: '1922–1939' (Oxford, 1991).
Sinclair, Andrew, *Arts and Culture: The History of the 50 Years of the Arts Council of Great Britain* (London, 1995).
Smith, Cyril and Sellick, Phyllis, *Duet for Three Hands* (London, 1958).
Tertis, Lionel, *My Viola and I* (London, 1974).
Thomson, John M., *Into A New Key: The Origins and History of the Music Federation of New Zealand 1950–1982* (Wellington, 1985).
Thomson, John M., *A Distant Music: The Life and Times of Alfred Hill 1870–1960* (Auckland, 1980).
Tunley, David, 'Australian Composition in the Twentieth Century – a Background', in F. Callaway and D. Tunley (eds), *Australian Composition in the Twentieth Century* (Melbourne, 1980).
Weinreb and Hibbert, *The London Encyclopaedia*.
Westlake, Donald, *Dearest John – The Story of John Lemmoné, flute virtuoso and Nellie Melba* (Terrey Hills, Australia, 1997).
Wetherell, Eric, *Albert Sammons, Violinist – the Life of 'Our Albert'* (London, 1998).
White, Eric Walter, *The Arts Council of Great Britain* (London, 1975).

Appendices

Appendix A

List of Recordings Made by Alfredo Campoli

The release dates given in Appendix A are based upon recording-log archives kindly provided by Decca, EMI and Columbia as well as published catalogues. Because many catalogues were issued from the middle of one year to the middle of the next some dates have been based on serial number chronology.

Year	Title	Accompanist	Serial no.
1931	Selections from 'The Chocolate Soldier' (O. Strauss) and 'The Quaker Girl' (Monckton)	Alfredo Campoli and the Dorchester Hotel Orchestra	Decca: K 598
1931	Caprice Viennois (Kreisler) and La Ronde des Lutins (Bazzini)	accompanist not named	Decca: K 639
1931	Serenade No. 1 (Heykens) and Tales From The Vienna Woods (J. Strauss/Winter)	Alfredo Campoli and the Dorchester Hotel Orchestra	Decca: F 2400
1931	O Cara Mia (Brodsky) and Komm Tzigany from 'Contess Maritza' (Kálmán)	Alfredo Campoli and the Dorchester Hotel Orchestra	Decca: F 2445
1931	Souvenir (Drdla) and Valse Bluette (Drigo)	accompanist not named	Decca: F 2454
1931	Waltzes from Vienna (J.Strauss/Clutsam)	Alfredo Campoli and the Dorchester Hotel Orchestra	Decca: F 2472
1931	Tango (Albeniz/Dushkin) and Tambourin Chinois (Kreisler)	accompanist not named	Decca: F 2512
1931	Blue Danube (Strauss/Winter) and Voices of Spring (Strauss/Wenninger)	Alfredo Campoli and the Dorchester Hotel Orchestra	Decca: F 2521
1931	The Skater's Waltz and España (Waldteufel)	Alfredo Campoli and the Dorchester Hotel Orchestra	Decca: F 2566

1931/2	Selections from 'Bitter Sweet' (Coward) and 'The Student Prince' (Romberg)	Alfredo Campoli and the Dorchester Hotel Orchestra	Decca: F 2715
1931/2	An Old Spanish Tango (Rutter, Jurmann, Eyton) and Speak to Me of Love (Lenoir)	Alfredo Campoli and the Dorchester Hotel Orchestra	Decca: F 2772
1931/2	An Old Violin (Fisher) and By the Waters of Minnetonka (Lieurance)	unnamed pianist; Olive Groves (soprano)	Decca: F 2773
1931/2	Old Vienna Moon (Zadowski, Lebert) and Selection from 'Congress Dances' (Heymann)	Alfredo Campoli and his Salon Orchestra	Decca: F 2809
1931/2	Selection from 'La Belle Hélène' (Offenbach)	Alfredo Campoli and his Salon Orchestra	Decca: F 2890
1931/2	A Nous la Liberté (Auric) and Selection from 'Il est Charmant' (Moretti)	Alfredo Campoli and his Salon Orchestra	Decca: F 2950
1932	English Roses (Dalrymple) and For You Alone (Geehl)	Alfredo Campoli and his Salon Orchestra	Decca: F 2961
1932	Songs of Italy (de Micheli)	Alfredo Campoli and his Salon Orchestra	Decca: F 3049
1932	Kasbell (arr. Campoli) and Andantino in D flat (Lemare, arr. Holst)	Alfredo Campoli and his Salon Orchestra	Decca: F 3100

Year	Title	Accompanist	Serial no.
1932	Happy the Day (Waller, Tonbridge) and Dreams that Don't Grow Old (Ellis)	Alfredo Campoli and his Salon Orchestra	Decca: F 3154
1932	Moonlight, the Danube and You (Mannheimer, arr. Krish) and Mexican Serenade (Tereso)	Alfredo Campoli and his Salon Orchestra	Decca: F 3172
1932	La Capricieuse and Salut d'Amour (Elgar)	unnamed pianist	Decca: F 3174
1932	E flat Nocturne (Chopin/Leon) and Spring Song (Mendelssohn/Towers) and Liebestraum No. 3 (Liszt/Nicholls)	Alfredo Campoli and his Salon Orchestra	Decca: F 3256
1932	Tell Me Tonight (Spoliansky) and Ah! Sweet Mystery of Life (Herbert)	Alfredo Campoli and his Salon Orchestra	Decca: F 3290
1932/3	Selection from 'Wild Violets' (Stolz)	Alfredo Campoli and his Salon Orchestra	Decca: F 3298
1932/3	Selection from 'Words and Music' (Noel Coward)	Alfredo Campoli and his Salon Orchestra	Decca: F 3318
1933	Poème (Fibich) and The Dancing Doll (Poldini)	Alfredo Campoli and his Salon Orchestra	Decca: F 3325

1933	Only My Song (Lehar) and Second Serenade (Heykens)	Alfredo Campoli and his Salon Orchestra	Decca: F 3349
1933	Smilin' Through (Penn) and Rosa Mia (Culzar, Fisher and Potter)	Alfredo Campoli and his Salon Orchestra	Decca: F 3375
1933	Tonight (Lesso-Valero) and Fairies' Gavotte (Kahn)	Alfredo Campoli and his Salon Orchestra	Decca: F 3400
1933	Pale Volga Moon (O'Hagan) and Gypsy Moon (Borganoff)	Alfredo Campoli and his Salon Orchestra	Decca: F 3412
1933	House Beautiful (Laidlaw, Anderson) and Dear Love, My Love (Friml)	Alfredo Campoli and his Salon Orchestra	Decca: F 3431
1933	Where the Woods are Green (Brodsky) and Zigeuner, You have Stolen my Heart (Egen, Groth)	Alfredo Campoli and his Salon Orchestra	Decca: F 3447
1933	Selection from 'La Bohème' (Puccini)	Alfredo Campoli and his Salon Orchestra	Decca: F 3480
1933	Goodnight Waltz (Dobson) and A Broken Rosary (Klein)	Alfredo Campoli and his Salon Orchestra	Decca: F 3532
1933	In Every Nook and Corner You are Missing (Kanal) and My Wishing Song (Kanal, Burke)	Alfredo Campoli and his Salon Orchestra	Decca: F 3554

Year	Title	Accompanist	Serial no.
1933	Friends Once More (Spoliansky) and In the Valley Where the Bluebirds Sing (Salman Rosenfield)	Alfredo Campoli and his Salon Orchestra	Decca: F 3564
1933	In Old Vienna (Jasmyn, Jerome, Hirsch) and The Spinning Wheel (Hill)	Alfredo Campoli and his Salon Orchestra	Decca: F 3580
1933	Fairy Tale (Heykens) and Under Heaven's Blue (Pola, Payon)	Alfredo Campoli and his Salon Orchestra	Decca: F 3607
1933	Serenade (Elgar) and Gypsy Love Song from 'The Fortune Teller' (Herbert)	Alfredo Campoli and his Salon Orchestra	Decca: F 3611
1933	Serenade (Lehar/Kreisler) and Pale Moon (Logan/Kreisler)	Sidney Crooke (piano)	Decca: F 3625
1933	Shadow Waltz (Heykens) and Her First Dance (Heykens)	Alfredo Campoli and his Salon Orchestra	Decca: F 3642
1933	Moths Around the Candle Flame (Dolphe, Gordon, Randal) and Grandma's Birthday (Heykens)	Alfredo Campoli and his Salon Orchestra	Decca: F 3678
1933	Memories of the Ball (medley of pre-war waltzes)	Alfredo Campoli and his Salon Orchestra	Decca: F 3679

1933	Si Petite (Claret) and Mademoiselle (Nesbitt)	Alfredo Campoli and his Salon Orchestra	Decca: F 3707
1933	Aloha Oe (Lieurance/ Kreisler) and Minuet in G (Paderewski/Kreisler)	Sidney Crooke (piano)	Decca: F 3708
1933	Softly Awakes My Heart (Saint-Saëns) and Träumerei (Schumann)	The Alfredo Campoli Trio	Decca: F 3755
1933	Simonetta (Curzon) and Heartless (Mensel)	Alfredo Campoli and his Salon Orchestra	Decca: F 3835
1933	Selection of Viennese Waltzes	Alfredo Campoli and his Salon Orchestra	Decca: K 706
1933	Waltzing to Irving Berlin: All Alone; A Russian Lullaby; Because I Love You; You Forgot to Remember; The Song is Ended; Reaching for the Moon; What'll I Do?; Always; Marie; What Does it Matter?	Alfredo Campoli and his Salon Orchestra	Decca: K 720
1934	Waltz Memories	Alfredo Campoli and his Salon Orchestra, Lew Stone and his Band, Don Rietto and his Accordion Band, dir. by George Scott Wood	Decca: K 726
1934	Operantics (arr. Stodden)	The Alfredo Campoli Grand Orchestra	Decca: K 734

Year	Title	Accompanist	Serial no.
1934	The Mosquito's Parade (Whitney/Mackie) and Hiawatha-Cake Walk (Moret)	Alfredo Campoli and his Novelty Orchestra	Decca: F 3854
1934	Londonderry Air (trad. arr. Morris) and Annie Laurie (trad/Campoli)	unnamed organist	Decca: F 3868
1934	One Life, One Love (May, Kennedy) and Play to Me, Gypsy (Kennedy, Vacek)	Alfredo Campoli and his Salon Orchestra	Decca: F 3888
1934	From the Irish Roads (Hayward)	Alfredo Campoli and his Novelty Orchestra	Decca: F 3893
1934	Over the Waves (Rosas) and Danube Waves (Ivanovici)	Alfredo Campoli and his Novelty Orchestra	Decca: F 3939
1934	Musical Box (Heykens) and Song of Paradise (Reginald King) [both works dedicated to Alfredo Campoli]	Alfredo Campoli and his Novelty Orchestra	Decca: F 3996
1934	Selection from 'Princess Charming' (Kester and Noble)	Alfredo Campoli and his Novelty Orchestra	Decca: F 5074
1934/5	Selection from 'Evergreen' (Woods, Hart, Rogers)	Alfredo Campoli Grand Orchestra	Decca: F 5075

1934/5	King Chanticleer (Ayer) and Whistling Rufus (Mills)	Alfredo Campoli and his Novelty Orchestra	Decca: F 5099
1934/5	Largo (Handel/Campoli) and Abide with Me (Liddle)	unnamed organist	Decca: F 5100
1934/5	Waltz Serenade (Tichy) and Little Valley in the Mountains (Kennedy, Dvoracek)	Alfredo Campoli and his Novelty Orchestra	Decca: F 5144
1935/6	Indian Love Call (from 'Rose Marie') and Violin Song ('Tina')	The Alfredo Campoli Trio	Decca: F 5156
1935/6	Valencia and The Apache Dance (Valse Chaloupée)	Alfredo Campoli and his Salon Orchestra, Lew Stone and his Band, Don Rietto and his Accordion Band, dir. by George Scott Wood	Decca: F 5167
1935/6	Love's Last Word is Spoken (Dixio) and Cuban Serenade (Midgeley)	Alfredo Campoli and his Salon Orchestra	Decca: F 5178
1935/6	Czardas (Monti) and Schön Rosmarin (Kreisler)	Sidney Crooke (piano)	Decca: F 5192
1935/6	Remembrance (Melfi, Allen, Green) and First Flower in the Garden (Heykens)	Alfredo Campoli and his Salon Orchestra	Decca: F 5235
1935/6	Snowman (Archer, Leclesc) and The Dancing Clock (Ewing, Giroud)	Alfredo Campoli and his Salon Orchestra	Decca: F 5372

Year	Title	Accompanist	Serial no.
1935/6	Destiny Waltz (Baynes) and Nights of Gladness (Anclif)	Alfredo Campoli and his Old-Fashioned Waltz Orchestra	Decca: F 5434
1935/6	La Petite Tonkinoise (Scotto, Christine), Poppies (Moret) and Whistling (Gourlay)	Alfredo Campoli and his Salon Orchestra/Alfredo Campoli and his Novelty Orchestra	Decca: F 5450
1935/6	Can I Help It? (Grosz, Kennedy) and You, Me and Love (Connor, Stolz)	Alfredo Campoli and his Salon Orchestra	Decca: F 5461
1935/6	Vienna in Springtime (Leon, Pelosi) and Romanesco Tango (Miller, Gade)	Alfredo Campoli and his Marimba Tango Orchestra	Decca: F 5482
1935/6	Your Heart Called Mine (Edgar, Lewinek-Hayon) and Corcurado-Carioca (Dunn, Rixner)	Alfredo Campoli and his Marimba Tango Orchestra	Decca: F 5496
1935/6	Hejre Kati (Hubay) and Midnight Bells (Heuberger/Kreisler)	Sidney Crooke (piano)	Decca: F 5532
1935/6	Waltzing to Archibald Joyce	Alfredo Campoli and his Novelty Orchestra	Decca: F 5563
1935/6	Si Mes Vers avaient des Aîles (Hahn) and Le Canari (Poliakin)	Sidney Crooke (piano)	Decca: F 5638

1934/5	Operantics	Alfredo Campoli Grand Orchestra	Decca: K 734
1935	'The Eric Coates Parade': Pt. 1: London Bridge, I Pitched My Lonely Caravan, Knightsbridge; Pt. 2: I Heard You Singing, The Three Bears, Sleepy Lagoon, March, Jester at the Wedding, Bird Songs at Eventide	The Alfredo Campoli Grand Orchestra	Decca: K 740
1935	With the Classics: Polonaise (Chopin); Moment Musical and Rosamund (Schubert); March and Waltz of the Flowers, and Dance of the Sugar Plum Fairy (Tchaikovsky); William Tell Overture (Rossini); Minute Waltz (Chopin); Hungarian Rhapsody (Liszt)	Alfredo Campoli and his Concert Orchestra	Decca: K 751
1936	'A Garden of Roses': The Wedding of the Rose (Jessel); Rose in the Bud (Forster); Moonlight and Roses (Lemare); Love's Garden of Roses (Wood); Mighty Like a Rose (Nevin); Roses of Picardy (Wood)	Alfredo Campoli and his Salon Orchestra	Decca: F 5770
1936	Mon Bijou (Stoltz) and San Remo (Hummer)	Alfredo Campoli and his Salon Orchestra	Decca: F 5904

Year	Title	Accompanist	Serial no.
1936	'An Old World Garden': Marigold; Pansy Face; Narcissus; Whispering of Flowers; The Honeysuckle and the Bee	Alfredo Campoli and his Salon Orchestra	Decca: F 6034
1936	The Knave of Diamonds (Steele) and Love in Idleness (Macbeth)	Alfredo Campoli and his Salon Orchestra	Decca: F 6120
1936	Guitarre (Moszkowski/Sarasate) and Sérénade Espagnole (Chaminade)	Sidney Crooke (piano)	Decca: F 6179
1936	Because (Gade) and Why (Gade)	Alfredo Campoli and his Salon Orchestra	Decca: F 6258
1936	Cavatina (Raff) and Canzonetta (Ambrosio) and Canzonetta (d'Ambrosio)	Alfredo Campoli and his Salon Orchestra	Decca: F 6330
1936	Le Cygne (Saint-Saëns) and Narcissus (Nevin)	Alfredo Campoli and his Salon Orchestra	Decca: F 6464
1936	Obstination (Fontenailles/S. Crook) and Tango Habanera (Payan/Hartley)	Alfredo Campoli and his Orchestra	HMV: BD 331
1937	Variations on a Theme of Corelli (Tartini/Kreisler) and Sicilienne and Rigaudon (Francoeur/Kreisler)	Sidney Crooke (piano)	Decca: F 6594

1937	Prelude (Haydn Wood) and Chinese Rhythm (Hellier)	Alfredo Campoli and his Salon Orchestra	Decca: F 6659
1937	Mouse in the Clock (Hunt) and Teddy Bears' Picnic (Bratton/S. Crook)	Alfredo Campoli and his Salon Orchestra	HMV: BD 348
1937	The Fiddlers at the Forge (Ives) and Penny in the Slot (Ashworth-Hope)	Alfredo Campoli and his Orchestra	HMV: BD 360
1937	Under the Balcony (Heykens) and Parade of the Pirates (Bratton)	Alfredo Campoli and his Orchestra	HMV: BD 378
1937	Christmas Fantasy (carols and songs)	Alfredo Campoli and his Orchestra	HMV: BD 381
1937	Manhattan Moonlight (Alter) and Manhattan Serenade (Alter)	Orchestre Raymonde (cond. G. Walter [Walter Goehr], led by Alfredo Campoli)	Columbia: DB1647
1937	Taming the Tiger [Tiger Rag] (La Rocca) and Orient Express (Mohr)	Orchestre Raymonde (cond. G. Walter [Walter Goehr], led by Alfredo Campoli)	Columbia: DB 1669
1938	Voices of Spring (Strauss)	Orchestre Raymonde (cond. G. Walter [Walter Goehr], led by Alfredo Campoli)	Columbia: DB 1737

Year	Title	Accompanist	Serial no.
1938	Toy Symphony (Haydn)	Orchestre Raymonde (cond. G. Walter [Walter Goehr], led by Alfredo Campoli)	Columbia: DB 1739
1938	Moto Perpetuo (Paganini) and Songs my Mother Taught Me (Dvořák/Kreisler)	Sidney Crooke (piano)	Columbia: DB 1772
1938	Hora Staccato (Dinicu/Heifetz) and La Capricciosa (Ries)	Sidney Crooke (piano)	Columbia: DB 1781
1938	Spring Song (Mendelssohn) and Melody in F (Rubinstein)	Alfredo Campoli and his Salon Orchestra	Decca: F 6836
1938	Song of Paradise (King) and Serenata (Moszkowski)	Reginald Foort (organ)	HMV: BD 484
1938	Concerto No. 1 in G minor (Bruch) (Walter Goehr)	Symphony Orchestra	Columbia DX 807–9
1939	Later On (Grimshaw) and Serenade Out of the Night (Spoliansky)	Alfredo Campoli and his Salon Orchestra	Decca: F 7037
1940	Dear Old Home Songs – Medley	Alfredo Campoli and his Orchestra	HMV: BD 696

1940	The Jolly Brothers (Vollstedt) and Phil the Fluter's Ball (French/Hartley)	Alfredo Campoli and his Salon Orchestra	HMV: BD 708
1940	Turkey in the Straw (Hartley) and The Dickey Bird Hop (Gourley)	Alfredo Campoli and his Salon Orchestra	HMV: BD 724
1940	The Butterfly (Bendix) and Neapolitan Serenade (Winkler)	Alfredo Campoli and his Salon Orchestra	HMV: BD 733
1940	The Wedding of the Rose (Jessel) and Killarney (Balfe/Hartley) and The Irish Washerwoman (trad/Hartley)	Alfredo Campoli and his Salon Orchestra	HMV: BD 742
1940	Drink to Me Only (trad.)	Welbeck Light String Quartet	Decca: F 7722
1940	Serenade (Drigo) and Serenade (Toselli)	Alfredo Campoli and his Salon Orchestra	Decca: BD 786
1940	Chinese Street Serenade (Slede/Crooke) and The Grasshoppers' Dance (Bucalossi)	Alfredo Campoli and his Salon Orchestra	HMV: BD 794
1940	Liebesfreud and Liebeslied (Kreisler)	Gerald Moore (piano)	HMV: B 9011
1940	A Prayer at Eventide (Reg King) and Daddy Longlegs (Kenneth Wright)	Alfredo Campoli and his Salon Orchestra	HMV: BD 812

Year	Title	Accompanist	Serial no.
1940	Berceuse de Jocelyn (Godard) and Lieberstraum (Liszt)	Alfredo Campoli and his Salon Orchestra	HMV : BD 846
1940	On Wings of Song (Mendelssohn) and Ave Maria (Schubert/Wilhelmj)	Gerald Moore (piano)	HMV: C 3144
1940	Waltz in A major (Brahms/Hochstein) and Rondino on a Theme by Beethoven (Kreisler)	Gerald Moore (piano)	HMV: B 9023
1946/7	Introduction and Rondo Capriccioso (Saint-Saëns)	LSO (Walter Goehr)	Columbia: DX 902
1947	Danza Española (Falla/Kreisler)	Eric Gritton (piano)	Decca: K 1483
1947	Sonata in G minor (Tartini) and Arioso (Bach)	Eric Gritton (piano)	Decca: K 1531/2
1947	La Campanella (Paganini/Kreisler) and Air on the G String (Bach)	Eric Gritton (piano)	Decca: K 1533
1947	Concerto in One Movement (Paganini/Kreisler)	National Symphony Orchestra (Victor Olof)	Decca: K 1822/3
1948	La Folia Variations (Corelli/Leonard) and La Campanella (Paganini) – on 4th side	Eric Gritton (piano)	Decca: K 1670/1

1948	La Ronde des lutins (Bazzini) and Zéphir (Hubay)	Eric Gritton (piano)	Decca: K 1799
1948	Rondo in E flat (Hummel/Kreisler) and La Fille aux cheveux de lin (Debussy/Hartmann)	Eric Gritton (piano)	Decca: K 2183
1948	Unaccompanied Partita in D minor (Bach)	unaccompanied violin	AK 1955/6/7
1949	Concerto in E minor (Mendelssohn)	LPO (Van Beinum)	Decca: AX 290/2
1949/50	Meditation from 'Thaïs' (Massenet) and Nocturne in E flat (Chopin/Sarasate)	Eric Gritton (piano)	Decca: K 2252
1949/50	Devil's Trill Sonata (Tartini/Campoli) and Presto (Tartini/Bridgewater)	Eric Gritton (piano)	Decca: AK 2366/7
1949/50	Hungarian Dances No. 20 and 7 (Brahms/Joachim)	Eric Gritton (piano)	Decca: F 9396
1951	Presto (Poulenc) and Pièce en forme de Habanera (Ravel/Catherine)	Eric Gritton (piano)	Decca: M 669
1951	Concerto No. 1 in G minor (Bruch)	New Symphony Orchestra (Royalton Kisch)	Decca: AX 558/60
1952	Concerto in D major (Beethoven) – cadenza by Kreisler	LSO (Josef Krips)	Decca: LXT 2674

Year	Title	Accompanist	Serial no.
1952	Sevilla (Albeniz)	Eric Gritton (piano)	Decca: X 971
1952	Cordoba and Sevillañas (Albeniz)	Eric Gritton (piano)	Decca: X 571
1953	Six Sonatas (Handel)	George Malcolm (harpsichord)	Decca: LXT 2751
1953	Symphonie Espagnole (Lalo)	LPO (Van Beinum)	Decca: LXT 2801
1953	Caprices in B flat and D major; La Campanella (Paganini); Ruralia Hungarica (Dohnanyi)	George Malcolm (piano)	Decca: LX 3115
1954	Havanaise and Introduction and Rondo Capriccioso (Saint-Saëns)	LSO (Fistoulari)	Decca: LW 5085
1955	Violin Concerto (Elgar)	LPO (Boult)	Decca: LXT 5014
1955	Poème (Fibich); Estrellita (Ponce); La chasse (Cartier); La capricieuse (Elgar); Souvenir (Drdla); Rondino (Beethoven); Caprice (Wieniawski); Allegro (Fiocco); The Bee (Schubert); Tango (Albeniz); Midnight Bells (Heuberger/Kreisler)	Eric Gritton	Decca: LL 1461
1955	Sonata in G minor ('Devil's Trill') and Sonata in G minor ('Dido Forsaken') (Tartini)	George Malcolm (piano)	Decca: LX 3137

1955	Homage to Fritz Kreisler: Liebesfreud, Liebeslied, Polichinelle, Tambourin Chinois, Caprice Viennois, Schön Rosmarin, Praeludium and Allegro, La Gitana, Rondino on a theme of Beethoven, Variations on a theme of Corelli, La Chasse (Cartier), Minuet in G (Paderewski)	Eric Gritton	Decca: LL 1171 and LXT 5012 Also on two discs LW 5217/8 (Jan 56)
1956	On Wings of Song (Mendelssohn); Valse bluette (Drigo); From the Canebrake (Gardner); Deep River (trad.); Minstrels (Debussy); Old Folks at Home (Foster/?)	Eric Gritton (piano)	Decca: LL 1461 and LW 5242
1956	Concerto Romantique (Godard)	Royal Philharmonic Orchestra (Beecham)	Sir Thomas Beecham Society: WSA 501
1956	Violin Concerto and Theme and Cadenza (Bliss)	Royal Philharmonic Orchestra (Bliss)	Decca: LXT 5166
1956	Zigeunerweisen (Sarasate) and Légende (Wieniawski)	LSO (Gamba)	Decca: LW 5306
Before 1957	Danza española 'Andaluza' (Granados/Kreisler); Etude No. 5 and Etude-Caprice (Wieniawski/Kreisler)	Eric Gritton (piano)	Decca: LK 40110
1957	Violin Concerto No. 3 (Saint-Saëns) and Concerto in One Movement (Paganini/Kreisler)	LSO (Gamba)	Decca: LXT 5302 and LL 1624

Year	Title	Accompanist	Serial no.
1958	Violin Concerto (Tchaikovsky)	LSO (Argenta)	Decca: LXT 5313
1959	Violin Concerto (Mendelssohn) and Fantasia on Scottish Melodies (Bruch)	LPO (Boult)	Decca: CM 9036 and LXT 5453
1962	Concerto in D major (Beethoven)	Royal Philharmonic Orchestra (John Pritchard)	HMV: SXLP 20043
1963	Concerto in A minor for Violin and Violoncello (Brahms)	Hallé Orchestra (Barbirolli) with André Navarra (cello)	Pye: GGC4009 Vanguard: SRV136
1968	Duo Sonata (Liszt) and Sonata in E flat (R. Strauss)	Valerie Tryon (piano)	Pye: TPLS 13017
1971	Campoli Encores: Tango (Albeniz); La Ronde des lutins (Bazzini); Waltz in A flat (Brahms); Akatonbo (Yamada/Campoli); Arioso (Bach); Jogashima No Ame (Yanada/Campoli); La Campanella and Caprices 13 and 20 (Paganini/Kreisler); Rondo (Mozart)	Norihiko Wade	Decca: ECS 639
1977	Eight Spanish Dances, Opp. 21, 22, 23 and 26; Navarra for Two Violins (Sarasate)	Daphne Ibbott (piano), with Belinda Bunt (violin)	Decca: DSL022

1980	Virtuoso Pieces for Violin (Wieniawski): Polonaise de concert; Légende; Obertasse; Dudziarz; Souvenir de Moscou; Scherzo-Tarantella; Romance; Capriccio-Valse; Polonaise Brilliante	Daphne Ibbott (piano)	Decca: DSL045

The following were recorded but not released:

July 1936	Romance in Moonlight - Medley Pts 1 and 2 (Pale Moon; Pagan Love Song; In the Moonlight; Gypsy Moon; Moonlight and Roses; I Love the Moon)	Alfredo Campoli and his Orchestra	HMV Matrices Nos: OEA 3818/9
June 1939	Nuages (Chaumette)	Alfredo Campoli and his Salon Orchestra	HMV Matrix No: OEA 8015
May 1940	The Mill (Raff)	Welbeck Light String Quartet	Decca Matrix No: DR 4779
c. May 1940	Twentieth Century Nocturne (Hartley)	Welbeck Light String Quartet	Decca Matrix No: DR 4766
c. May 1940	Tristesse (Chopin)	Welbeck Light String Quartet	Decca Matrix No: DR 4780
c. May 1940	Tambourin (Gossec)	Welbeck Light String Quartet	Decca Matrix No: DR 4804

Rec. Date	Title	Accompanist	Serial no.
c. June 1940	My Old Kentucky Home (Foster)	Welbeck Light String Quartet	Decca Matrix No: DR 4802
c. June 1940	Traumerei (Schumann)	Welbeck Light String Quartet	Decca Matrix No: DR 4805
c. June 1940	Berceuse (Jarnefelt)	Welbeck Light String Quartet	Decca Matrix No: DR 4801
c. June 1940	Molly on the Shore (Grainger)	Welbeck Light String Quartet	Decca Matrix No: DR 4803
c. June 1940	Barbara Allen (arr. Hartley)	Welbeck Light String Quartet	Decca
May 1947	Rondo in G major ‘Haffner’ (Mozart)	Eric Gritton (piano)	Decca
May 1947	Gavotte in E major (Bach)	unaccompanied violin	Decca Matrix No: AR 11308

Appendix B

List of Recordings Transferred to Compact Disk

Works and Date of Original Recording	Recording Companies/Serial Nos
Bazzini: La ronde des lutins (1931), with unnamed accompanist	'The History of the Violin on Record', Pearl (Pavilion Records) BVA1–111 (on the second of three discs). Sparrows Green, Wadhurst, East Sussex, UK.
Campoli's Choice: Tartini (arr. Kreisler): Variations on a theme of Corelli [1937] Francoeur (arr. Kreisler): Sicilienne and Rigaudon [1937] Hubay: Hejre Kati, Op. 32 [1935] Moszkowski (arr. Sarasate): Guitarre, Op. 45/2 [1936] Chaminade: Sérénade Espagnole [1936] Heykens: Serenade No. 1 [1931] Traditional: Drink to Me Only [1940] Raff: The Mill [rec. 1940, not issued] Gossec: Tambourin [rec. 1940, not issued] La Rocca: Tiger Rag (Taming the Tiger) [1937] Hartley: Turkey in the Straw [1940] Foster: My Old Kentucky Home [rec. 1940, not issued] Schumann: Traumerei [rec. 1940, not issued] Jarnefelt: Berceuse [rec. 1940, not issued] Gourley: The Dicky Bird Hop [1940] Jessel: The Wedding of the Rose [1940] Balfe: Killarney [1940] Traditional: The Irish Washerwoman [1940]	Pearl (Pavilion Records) CD 9744 (1991)

Hartley: Twentieth Century Nocturne [rec. 1940, not issued]
Chopin: Tristesse (Etude Op. 10, No. 3) [rec. 1940, not issued]
Grainger: Molly on the Shore [rec. 1940, not issued]
Traditional: Irish Reels [rec. 1939. not issued]
Traditional: Irish Jig [rec. 1939, not issued]
Siede (arr. Crooke): Chinese Street Serenade [1940]
Bucalossi: The Grasshopper Dance [1940]
Vollstedt: The Jolly Brothers [1940]
French (arr. Hartley): Phil the Fluter's Ball [1940]

Wieniawski: Scherzo-Tarantelle (1980) Sarasate: Zapateado (1977), with Daphne Ibbott (piano)	'The World of the Violin', Decca 433220/2 (1992). Also includes other works played by Nigel Kennedy, Kyung Whachung, Willi Boskovski, Iona Brown, Ruggiero Ricci. (Zapateado also on Decca 4364482/2.)
Sarasate: 8 Danzas Espanolas and Navarra, with Belinda Bunt (violin) and Daphne Ibbott (piano) (1977)	'Musica Espanola', Decca 433938/2 (1992)
Alfredo Campoli: Salon Music of the 'Thirties:	Living Era, Academy of Sound and Vision Ltd, Living Era Series, CD AJA5135 (1994)
Elgar: Violin Concerto, with Adrian Boult and the London Philharmonic Orchestra (1955) Mendelssohn: Violin Concerto, with Adrian Boult and the London Philharmonic Orchestra (1959)	'Campoli Classics', Beulah 1PD10 (1994), 66, Rochester Way, Crowborough, East Sussex, TN6 2HN
Bruch: Scottish Fantasia, with Adrian Boult and the London Philharmonic Orchestra (1959) Beethoven: Violin Concerto, with Josef Krips and the London Symphony Orchestra (1952)	'Campoli Classics 2', Beulah 2PD10 (1994) 66, Rochester Way, Crowborough, East Sussex, TN6 2HN

Saint-Saëns: Violin Concerto No. 3, with Piero Gamba and the London Philharmonic Orchestra (1957)	Decca: 443884/2 (1994). Also includes Ruggiero Ricci playing Lalo's Symphonie Espagnole.
Vivaldi: The Four Seasons, with Boyd Neel and The Boyd Neel Orchestra (broadcast *c.*1939) Bruch: Violin Concerto No. 1 in G minor, with Walter Goehr and Symphony Orchestra (*sic*) (1937) Saint-Saëns: Introduction and Rondo Capriccioso, with Walter Goehr and the London Symphony Orchestra (1938)	Pearl (Pavillion Records) CD 9151 (1995)
Bliss: Violin Concerto, with Arthur Bliss and the London Philharmonic Orchestra (1956) Bliss: Theme and Cadenza, with Arthur Bliss and the London Philharmonic Orchestra (1956) Tchaikovsky: Violin Concerto, with Autaulfo Argenta and the London Symphony Orchestra (1958)	'Campoli Classics 3', Beulah 3PD10 (1995)
Bliss: Violin Concerto, with Arthur Bliss and the London Philharmonic Orchestra (1956)	Carlton Classics (BBC Radio Classics) LC8747 (1996)
Bruch: Scottish Fantasia, with Adrian Boult and the London Symphony Orchestra (1959) Paganini (arr. Kreisler): Violin Concerto No. 1 (first movement), with Piero Gamba and the London Symphony Orchestra (1957)	Karussell International (Polygram) 461142/2 (1996)
Beethoven: Violin Concerto, with Josef Krips and the London Symphony Orchestra (1952) Mendelssohn: Violin Concerto, with Adrian Boult and the London Symphony Orchestra (1959)	'The Boult Historical Collection', Belart (Polygram) 46 13552 (1997)

Elgar: Violin Concerto, with Adrian Boult and the London Philharmonic Orchestra (1955) Bliss: Theme and Cadenza, with Adrian Boult and the London Philharmonic Orchestra (1956)	'The Boult Historical Collection', Belart (Polygram) 4613532 (1997). Also includes Introduction and Allegro for Strings (Elgar).
Alfredo Campoli and his Salon Orchestra Whitney, Mackie: The Mosquitoes Parade [1934] [Heykens]: Shadow Waltz [1933] Elgar: Serenade [1933] [Archer, Leclesc]: Snowman [1935] Monti: Czardas [1935] Chopin (arr. Leon): E flat Nocturne [1932] Mendelssohn (arr. Towers): Spring Song [1932] Liszt (arr. Nichols): Liebestraum [1932] [Hunt]: Mouse in the Clock [1937] Curzon: Simonetta [1933] Dvoracek: Little Valley in the Mountains [1934 or 1935] Heykens: Musical Box [1934] Stolz: Selection from 'Wild Violets' [1932 or 1933] Bratton: Parade of the Pirates [1937] Raff: Cavatina [1937] Dolphe, Gordon Randal: Moths Around the Candle Flame [1933] [Joyce]: Waltzing to Archibald Joyce [1935] Léhar: Serenade from 'Frasquita' [1933] Macbeth: Love in Idleness [1936] Steele: Knave of Diamonds [1936] Heykens: Fairy Tale [1933]	Pavilion Records CD 9707 (n.d.)
Mendelssohn: Violin Concerto, with Adrian Boult and the London Philharmonic Orchestra (1959) Bruch: Scottish Fantasy, with Adrian Boult and the London Philharmonic Orchestra (1959)	Decca (Collectors' Series) IMPX9031 (n.d.)
Tchaikovsky: Violin Concerto with Ataulfo Argenta with the London Symphony Orchestra (1958)	PWK Classics PWK1145 (n.d.)

Saint-Saëns: Violin Concerto No. 3, with Piero Gamba and the London Symphony Orchestra (1957)	Decca 443884–2 (n.d.)
Kreisler: Praeludium and Allegro Kreisler: Liebeslied Kreisler: Liebesfreud Kreisler: Polichinelle-Serenade Kreisler: Schön Rosmarin Kreisler: Caprice Viennois Kreisler: Tambourin Chinois Beethoven/Kreisler: Minuet in G Wieniawski/Kreisler: Caprice in E flat Wieniawski/Kreisler: Caprice in A minor Kreisler: Rondino on a theme by Beethoven Kreisler: La Chasse Kreisler: La Gitana Granados/Kreisler: Danse Espagnole Tartini/Kreisler: Variations on a theme of Corelli Albeniz: Tango Brahms: Waltz in A flat Yamada/Campoli: Akatonbo Bach: Arioso Schubert: Ave Maria Yamada/Campoli: Jogashima No Ame Mozart/Kreisler: Rondo from Divertimento No. 17	'Homage to Fritz Kreisler: Miniatures for Violin & Piano' (1999). Decca ('Eloquence' series) 466 666–2 (available from Universal Music (Australia)) Tracks 1–15 with Eric Gritton (piano) (1955) Tracks 16–22 with Norihko Wada (piano) (1971)

Appendix C
Repertoire Performed by Alfredo Campoli (Excluding Light Music)

In addition to the works listed below there are many others that Campoli marked up for performance, but which have not been included here as they do not figure in programmes or other sources which have been the basis for this study. Campoli's music library is now housed in the Cambridge University Library.

Works with Orchestra

Arnold, Malcolm
Concerto for two violins

Bach, Johann Sebastian
Concerto in E
Concerto for two violins

Bax, Arnold
Concerto

Beethoven, Ludwig Van
Concerto in D

Bliss, Arthur
Concerto
Theme and Cadenza

Brahms, Johannes
Concerto in D
Concerto for violin and cello

Bruch, Max
Concerto No. 1
Scottish Fantasia

Chausson, Ernest
Poème

Delius, Frederick
Concerto

Elgar, Edward
Concerto

Elizalde, Frederico
Concerto

Ernst, Heinrich
Hungarian Dances

Glazunov, Alexander
Violin Concerto in A minor

Godard, Benjamin
Concerto Romantique

Harty, Hamilton
Concerto

Lalo, Edouard
Symphonie Espagnole

Mendelssohn, Felix
Concerto in E minor

Moeran, Ernest
Concerto

Mozart, Wolfgang Amadeus
Concerto in B flat, K207
Concerto in D, K 211
Concerto in A, K216
Concerto in D, K218
Concerto in A, K219
(some of the above with cadenzas by Campoli)

Saint-Saëns, Camille
Concerto No. 3
Introduction and Rondo Capriccioso Havanaise

Paganini, Nicolò
Concerto in D (lst movement arrangement by Kreisler)

Sibelius, Jan
Concerto

Strauss, Richard
Concerto

Tchaikovsky, Peter
Concerto

Vaughan Williams, Ralph
Concerto
The Lark Ascending

Vieuxtemps, Henri
Concerto
Fantaisie Caprice
Ballade and Polonaise

Viotti, Giovanni
Concerto in A minor

Vivaldi, Antonio
Concerto in A
Concerto in G for two violins
Concerto for four violins
Concerto, 'The Four Seasons'

Walton, William
Concerto

Works with Piano or Harpsichord

Albeniz, Isaac
Chants d'Espagne
Malagueña (arr. Kreisler)
Sevilla (arr. Heifetz)
Tango (arr. Duskin)

Achron
Hebrew Melody (arr. Heifetz)

Bach, Johann Sebastian
Sonata No. 1 in B minor
Sonata No. 2 in A
Sonata No. 3 in E
Sonata No. 4 in C minor
Sonata No. 5 in F
Sonata No. 6 in G
Arioso (arr. Kreisler)

Bazzini, Antonio
La ronde des lutins

Beethoven, Ludwig Van
Sonata in E flat, Op. 12 no. 3
Sonata in F, Op. 24 ('Spring')
Sonata in C minor, Op. 30, No. 2
Sonata in G, Op. 30, No. 3
Sonata in A minor, Op. 47 ('Kreutzer')
Romance in F
Romance in G

Bloch, Ernest
Nigun (from Baal Shem)

Brahms, Johannes
Sonata No. 1 in G, Op. 78
Sonata No. 2 in A major, Op. 100

Sonata No. 3 in D minor, Op. 108
Selected Hungarian Dances
Waltz in A (arr. Hochstein)
Weigenlied (arr. Cerne)

Busoni, Ferrucio
Sonata No. 2 in E minor

Chaminade, Cécile
Sérénade Espagnole

Chopin, Frederick
Trio for violin, cello and piano
Nocturne in E flat (arr. Sarasate)

Corelli, Arcangelo
La folia variations

Debussy, Claude
Sonata in G minor
La fille aux cheveux de lin (arr. Hartman)
Minstrels (arr. Hartman)

Dinicu, Grigoras
Hora staccato

Dohnányi, Arnö
Ruralia Hungarica
Violin Sonata in C sharp minor

Dvořàk, Anton
Sonatina in G, Op. 100

Elgar, Edward
Sonata in E minor
La capricieuse

Fauré, Gabriel
Sonata in A

Fibich, Zdenek
Poem

Franck, César
Violin Sonata, Op. 13

Gilardi, Gilardo
Air de Vidala

Granados, Enrique
Danse espagnole (arr. Kreisler)

Grieg, Edvard
Sonata in C minor, Op. 45
Lyrical Pieces

Handel, George Frederic
Sonata No. 1 in A
Sonata No. 2 in G minor
Sonata No. 3 in F
Sonata No. 4 in D
Sonata No. 5 in A
Sonata No. 6 in E

Howells, Herbert
Sonata No. 3

Hubay, Jenö
Zéphyr
Hejre Kati

Hummel, Johann
Rondo in E flat

Kreisler, Fritz
Liebeslied
Liebesfreud
Polichinelle-Serenade
Schön Rosmarin
Caprice viennois
Tambourin chinois
La gitana
Rondino on a theme of Beethoven
Praeludium and Allegro
La chasse (attr. to Cartier)

Liszt, Franz
Duo Sonata
Epithalam
Grand Duo concertant on Lafont's 'Le marin'

Massenet, Jules
Meditation from 'Thaïs'

Medtner, Nikolay
Sonata Epica, Op. 57

Mozart, Wolfgang Amadeus
Sonata in E minor, K 304
Sonata in A, K526
Sonata in D, K306
Rondo 'Haffner' (arr. Kreisler)

Nardini, Pietro
Sonata in D minor

Paderewski, Ignaz
Minuet in E (arr. Kreisler)

Paganini, Nicolò
La campanella (arr. Wilhelmji)
Moto perpetuo

Poulenc, Francis
Violin Sonata 1942–3 (rev. 1949)
Violin Sonata 1944
Presto

Ravel, Maurice
Tzigane
Pièce en forme d'Habanera

Reger, Max
Sonatina No. 1 in D minor

Ries, Franz
Moto perpetuo

Respighi, Ottorino
Sonata in B minor

Sarasate, Pablo de
Zapateado
Malagueña
Zigeunerweisen
Spanish dances
Concert fantasies on Carmen
(Some of the above also played in orchestral versions)

Schubert, Franz
Ave Maria (arr. Wilhelmj)

Smetana, Bedrich
Aus der Heimat

Strauss, Richard
Violin Sonata in E flat

Suk, Josef
Four Pieces, Op. 17

Tartini, Giuseppe
Sonata in G minor ('Devil's Trill') (with Campoli's cadenza)
Sonata in G minor ('Dido Abandoned')
Variations on a theme of Corelli (arr. Kreisler)

Turina, Joaquin
Sonata Espagnole, Op. 82

Vitali, Tomaso
Chaconne (attr. to Vitali)

Vivaldi, Antonio
Sonata in A

Walsworth (?)
Sonata in A (given its lst performance by Campoli with George Malcolm, 27 January 1953, Royal Festival Hall – score not found)

Wieniawski, Henryk
Polonaise de concert, Opus 4
Légende
Polonaise de concert
Obertasse
Dudziarz
Souvenir de Moscou
Scherzo-Tarantella
Romance
Capriccio-Valse
Scherzo-Polonaise Brillante
Caprice in E flat (arr. Kreisler)
Caprice in A minor (arr. Kreisler)

Works for Unaccompanied Violin

Bach, Johann Sebastian
Sonata No. 1 in G minor
Partita No. 1 in B minor
Sonata No. 2 in A minor
Partita No. 2 in D minor
Sonata No. 3 in C
Partita No. 3 in E

Boccherini, Luigi
Duo

Paganini, Nicolò
Six Caprices (some also played by Campoli in arrangements with piano accompaniment by Kreisler)

Viotti, Giovanni
Duo for two violins

Index